Envisioning future academic library services

Initiatives, ideas and challenges

Envisioning future academic library services

Initiatives, ideas and challenges

edited by
Sue McKnight

facet publishing

© This compilation: Sue McKnight 2010
The chapters: the contributors 2010

Published by Facet Publishing,
7 Ridgmount Street, London WC1E 7AE
www.facetpublishing.co.uk

Facet Publishing is wholly owned by CILIP: the Chartered Institute of Library
and Information Professionals.

British Library Cataloguing in Publication Data
A catalogue record for this book is available from the British Library.

ISBN 978-1-85604-691-6
First published 2010
Reprinted digitally thereafter

Text printed on FSC accredited material.

 **Mixed Sources**
Product group from well-managed
forests and other controlled sources
www.fsc.org Cert no. SA-COC-1565
© 1996 Forest Stewardship Council
FSC

Typeset from editor's files by Facet Publishing in 12/14 pt American Garamond
and Nimbus Sans.
Printed and made in Great Britain by MPG Books Group, UK.

Contents

Foreword

Dame Lynne Brindley

I am delighted to have been asked to write a foreword to this important book. I will comment on some of the challenges discussed by the distinguished authors and reflect on the scope and international nature of the debate swirling around the question of 'Whither the academic library?'

It is entirely appropriate that not only are the authors who address this question hugely respected figures in their domains, but also they reflect between them a truly international perspective, or more accurately, a developed world perspective, reminding us all rather painfully of the new kinds of information schisms that divide countries in the digital age.

The future academic library envisioned by our authors recognizes a rapidly changing context – in technology, publishing, user behaviour and expectations, all of which challenge the very nature of academic libraries, their leadership, organizational sustainability and integrity.

I am particularly struck in the debates on the overall theme of the library of the future that we are at a stage in our digital journey which is full of paradoxes, and our library organizations need bold innovation in management now more than ever. Models centred on traditional styles of control and efficiency will not suffice in the world of make-or-break challenges that libraries are facing. Pioneering leadership and radical innovation in management are not generally associated with academic or other libraries: but they really need to be. In this I have been influenced by Gary Hamel[1] and his arguments for a revolution in leadership attributes.

Looking through the contributions, I see commonly agreed challenges, but no common solutions. Everyone refers to the importance, even centrality, of the web and particularly Web 2.0 and Library 2.0. The opportunities of the Web 2.0 and social networking world are clear to all and there is much activity across libraries to embed these technologies in appropriate ways within their services, and more widely within a digital framework of learning and teaching and research processes. This should contribute to the continuing relevance and visibility of librarians and information specialists in supporting enhanced student and academic experiences. It remains, however, a non-trivial challenge to embed this changed approach within libraries, to upskill colleagues, and to try to keep pace with digital-native users.

At the same time, again paradoxically, the contributors are focused on the library as place – for face-to-face and group interactions – no more excitingly so than in academic libraries. We must conclude that, at least for now, both physical and digital experiences are what are needed. Academic libraries have created some stunning examples of successful spaces for student learning, but I believe we all have more to do on what is needed to support 21st-century research activity and its rapidly changing methods and processes, not least because of the centrality of data management and data- and text-mining techniques spreading fast across all disciplines.

Some universities are moving their dominant culture away from an educational model of full-time, on-campus undergraduate education towards a more flexible pattern of learning, with informal and formal pathways to degrees, topped up with work-based and more lifelong (and often open) learning. Embedding a distinctive contribution from the library into virtual and blended learning activity remains a real challenge. The opportunities are enormous: to aggregate born-digital and digitized sources from trusted and varied sources; to embed the learning of information fluency skills into a multimedia setting; to mediate and support group dialogue; to harness citizen and community creativity within this space; these are but a few examples of the valuable roles available to innovative librarians.

But speaking of digital content takes me to the wider potential of libraries to contribute to the wider knowledge management and information-governance challenges that universities face. Issues of information security, data and information repositories, archiving, copyright and intellectual property exploitation, compliance with legal data retention and disclosure responsibilities are complex matters in which our profession should be seeking to play a leading role.

Much of this implies the need for a more critical and challenging approach to business models which we know are already shattered for many traditional players who have not anticipated and adapted fast enough to digital technology transformation. There are lessons here for libraries, and indeed for publishers, as indicated in the book. Whether the looked-for collaboration between authors, publishers and libraries is entirely realistic, I am not sure – I suspect that for some time key players will be vying for as large a space as they can inhabit in the new world order.

What, if anything, do I conclude from these observations? There are no easy, black and white answers. We each have to work with uncertainty and complexity and chart a course into our digital future which is appropriate for our own institution and for the mission it seeks to achieve. It is fundamentally important that the envisioning process is opened up well beyond the library itself and our own professional views, for the real debate is the deeper question about the nature of the academy, the university in the 21st century. From this will flow a clearer and more distinctive purpose for each library, but we can agree, I hope, that our methods need to change rapidly to address the profound impact of information technology on the nature of human connection and the transmission and consumption of knowledge.

I commend this book to library managers, leaders and future leaders. Opportunities exist at all levels for real and vocal leadership in shaping this emerging space, shaping the political economy of higher education, and shaping its interactions with knowledge discovery and creation, knowledge ordering and dissemination, and knowledge interaction. From my personal perspective there has never been a more exciting time to be in libraries: it is both daunting and empowering. I hope that this volume will contribute to an appreciation of the issues and their interconnections, and spur us all to creative and productive action.

Lynne J. Brindley

Note

1. Hamel, Gary with Bill Breen, *The Future of Management*, Harvard Business School Press, 2007.

Contributors

Penny Carnaby is New Zealand's National Librarian and Chief Executive of the National Library of New Zealand, a position she has held since 2003. In 2007 she led the Library's New Generation National Library strategy, aimed at reshaping and redefining services within an increasingly digital environment. In supporting a robust, knowledge-based network for New Zealand, she has also led the organization's contribution to New Zealand's Digital Strategy 2.0 and its Digital Content Strategy.

Penny is Deputy Chair of the ICT Steering Committee for Education, a member of the Library and Information Advisory Commission (LIAC), a member of National State Libraries of Australasia (NSLA), and Adjunct Professor in the School of Information Management at Victoria University of Wellington. In 2008 she was re-appointed to chair the Conference of Directors of National Libraries (CDNL) internationally.

Paul Coyne is Vice-President of Innovation for Emerald Group Publishing Limited, a leading publisher of management research. Over the period of his 20-year career in ICT, learning and research, he has contributed to and led various national and international digital projects and research programmes in the private and public sectors.

Since leaving ICT consultancy in 2004 to join Emerald, Paul has continued to contribute to digital strategy development and original research, exploring social media technologies in learning and research. Now, as VP of Innovation, he provides advice to Emerald on the adoption and application of social technologies, pedagogies and business models in the digital era. He speaks regularly at conferences on the impact of emerging technologies in research, learning communities and scholarly communications.

Helen Hayes has spent 10 years at the senior executive level of two major research universities and 20 years in library management. She was Vice-Principal for Information (1999–2003) at the University of Melbourne, with responsibility for libraries and information management; and Vice-Principal for Knowledge Management at the University of Edinburgh (2003–7). She is currently the inaugural Executive Director, Knowledge Transfer and Partnerships, at the University of Melbourne. This involves developing agreed goals around information and knowledge within a shared services environment, and initiating steps to enhance the business of the University in learning, research and knowledge transfer.

Helen achieved the Australian Quality Council Award for Business Excellence in 1996. She was named the Telstra Australian Business Woman of the Year 1999, and is a Fellow of the Library and Information Association of Australia.

Damon E. Jaggars is Associate University Librarian for Collections and Services at the Columbia University Libraries. Previous positions include Associate Director for User Services, Head Librarian, Undergraduate Library, and Head of Reference, Undergraduate Library, at the University of Texas at Austin Libraries; and Coordinator of Information Technology at Iona College.

Damon holds an MS in Library and Information Science from the University of Illinois at Urbana-Champaign and a BA in Philosophy from the University of California, Davis. Current research interests include service quality assessment and emerging service models for research and teaching support.

Philip G. Kent is the University Librarian at the University of Melbourne. He joined the University in 2009 following a 30-year career in universities and Australia's Commonwealth Scientific and Industrial Research Organization (CSIRO). His previous roles included libraries, information technology, knowledge and information management, risk and audit.

Philip joined the University of Melbourne following the Information Futures Commission and the development of a ten-year information strategy for the University, and the Library is being reinvigorated under his leadership. He intends to maintain its central role as a repository of vital cultural collections and to make it a conduit for the transfer of knowledge through programmes to expose its wealth in collections to the public and scholarly communities.

Derek Law, now a professor at the University of Strathclyde, has worked in several British universities and published and spoken at conferences extensively. Most of his work has related to the development of networked resources in higher education and the creation of national information policy. This has been combined with an active professional life in organizations related to librarianship and computing. A committed internationalist, he has been involved in projects and research in over 40 countries.

Derek was awarded the Barnard Prize for contributions to Medical Informatics in 1993, Fellowship of the Royal Society of Edinburgh in 1999, an honorary degree by the Sorbonne in 2000, the IFLA medal in 2003, and Honorary Fellowship of CILIP in 2004; he became an OCLC Distinguished Scholar in 2006. He is currently Chair of the new JISC Services Management Company and continues to teach and write.

Martin Lewis is Director of Library Services and University Librarian at the University of Sheffield. He is a Board Member of Research Libraries UK and chairs its e-Research Task Force. He also sits on the British Library Advisory Council and is a member of the JISC Committee for the Support of Research and of the Project Management Board for the UK Research Data Service project. His professional interests include the marketing of library services, library staff development, and the design of library buildings and learning spaces. Previous posts have included Deputy Director at the University of Sheffield Library; heading the Health Sciences Library at Sheffield; subject consultant for science at the University of Leeds Library; and a one-year exchange appointment as Visiting Librarian in the MIT Libraries.

Before becoming a librarian, Martin worked as a civil servant in his native Cardiff, with responsibilities in the area of health workforce planning. He was educated at the University of Cambridge, where he read biochemistry; and the University of Wales Aberystwyth, where he took a postgraduate diploma in librarianship. A key strategic focus for the University Library under Martin's leadership has been the envisioning and commissioning of a major new library and learning space, the £23m Information Commons, which opened in 2007.

P. Charles Livermore is an associate professor and eBrarian at St. John's University in New York City. His responsibilities involve working with distance education students as well as service at in-person desks. He has been involved in Second Life on Emgeetee Island for the past two years. He has met with students in Second Life, offering individual appointments and library instruction classes.

Andrew McDonald is Professor and Director of Library and Learning Services at the University of East London. Previously he was Director of Information Services, Professor of Information Management and Strategy at the University of Sunderland, and before that Deputy Librarian at Newcastle University. Nationally he has served on the Executive of the Society of National, College and University Libraries (SCONUL) and has chaired its Space Working Group. A Fellow of the Chartered Institute of Library and Information Professionals, he has sat on the CILIP Council and has chaired both its International Panel and Academic and Research Libraries Committee. At international level, he now chairs the University and Research Libraries Section of the International Federation of Library Associations and Institutions, and was previously a member of its Buildings and Equipment Section.

Conference papers, consultancy and training work have taken Andrew all over the world. He has published widely, and has attracted significant external funding for library projects. His professional interests embrace digital libraries and archives, distance and lifelong learning, information literacy, library planning and design, partnerships for learning, quality management, staff development and strategic planning.

Professor Sue McKnight is an international leader in libraries and eLearning. She is Director of Libraries and Knowledge Resources at Nottingham Trent University in the UK. Sue is a National Teaching Fellow of the Higher Education Academy (UK), recognized for her outstanding support for learning and teaching. She actively contributes to JISC, SCONUL and IFLA and holds fellowships and managerial awards from the Australian Institute of Management, CILIP: the Charterered Institute of Library and Information Professionals, and the Australian Library & Information Association.

James G. Neal is Vice President for Information Services and University Librarian at Columbia University in New York, responsible for academic computing and a system of 22 libraries. He previously served as Dean of University Libraries at Johns Hopkins University and Indiana University, and held administrative positions in the libraries at Penn State, Notre Dame, and the City University of New York.

James has been an active member of, and has held leadership positions in, a wide range of organizations, including the American Library Association, the Association of Research Libraries, the Research Libraries Group, OCLC, the National Information Standards Organization, SPARC, the Freedom to Read Foundation, and IFLA. He is the recipient of ACRL's Academic Librarian of the Year Award (1997), ALA's Hugh Atkinson Memorial Award (2007) and the Melvil Dewey Medal Award (2009).

Frances Pinter is the Publisher at Bloomsbury Academic, a new imprint recently launched by Bloomsbury Publishing, specializing in humanities and social sciences at the tertiary level. She is experimenting with new business models, including using Creative Commons licensing of academic monographs. She is also a Visiting Fellow at the London School of Economics, researching in the area of intellectual property rights.

Frances was previously Publishing Director for the Soros Foundation Network (Open Society Institute), where she established the Centre for Publishing Development in Budapest. There she led a number of initiatives to modernize the book trade infrastructure, introducing ISBN agencies and Books in Print tools. She established the Central European University Press in 1994. In 1998 she founded EIFL (Electronic Information for Libraries), the world's largest consortium of libraries, now covering 50 countries. She has extensive experience in working with international agencies and has advised ministries of education on publishing infrastructure and textbook projects. She founded the Soros translation programme, which is now the independent agency, Next Page.

Prior to this, Frances was the founder of Pinter Publishers Ltd, an academic publishing house that specialized in the social sciences and also owned Leicester University Press. There she also established Belhaven Press, an imprint devoted entirely to environmental issues. She has sat on a number of publishing industry boards, including the UK Publishers Association governing council. She is currently part of the Research

Information Network Research Communications Group. She has a PhD in International Relations.

Michael Robinson is the Institute Librarian at the Hong Kong Institute of Education, as well as the founding Director of the Hong Kong Museum of Education. He has over 25 years' management experience in academic libraries in Australia, Vietnam and Hong Kong. He was formerly Director of Library and Learning Resource Centre projects for RMIT University, Vietnam, an Australian university based in Ho Chi Minh City, and was responsible for a portfolio of philanthropic projects to construct and develop libraries on behalf of four provincial Vietnamese universities.

Michael was also actively involved in a range of national library development programmes in Vietnam, including the management of the authorized Vietnamese translation of the14th Abridged Edition of the Dewey Decimal Classification scheme, and the establishment of the Vietnamese Library Association. He is a recipient of the Award for Culture, Sport and Tourism from the Vietnamese government, and is the immediate Past President of the Hong Kong Library Association, as well as a serving member of the IFLA Regional Standing Committee for Asia and Oceania.

Liz Wright is the founding director of two international leadership development consultancies, The Leadership Cafe and People First International, based in the UK and Melbourne, Australia. Her leadership and coaching programmes have won many awards, and she has gained an international reputation for her design and application of leadership programmes to underpin major organizational change, plus her work in individual performance coaching of leaders at all levels.

Liz is currently working on an interdisciplinary PhD on Boosting Leadership Skills through Literature; she has an MSc in Human Resource Management and an MA in Literature (with Distinction). She is a Chartered Fellow of the UK Chartered Institute of Personnel and Development; a Fellow of the Australian Institute of Human Resources; a Member of the European Council for Coaching and Mentoring; a Member of the Australian Institute of Training and Development; and a Member of the British Association of Psychological Type.

Introduction: We create the future!

Sue McKnight

A stellar cast of international leaders in their disciplines have combined to provide a thought-provoking book on the art of the possible, sharing their extensive experience and visions for a different but exciting future for academic librarianship. Their contributions are aimed at stimulating ideas and identifying challenges that will be faced in the not-too-distant future. Library leaders, managers, would-be managers, library and information science educators and academic library staff will find useful information that can be applied today, as well as issues for envisioning a different academic library future.

Over the years, there have been many articles and books on the future of library services. While some articles have suggested the end of libraries, most offer a thoughtful insight into the need to be constantly monitoring our environment and the needs of our customers. An emerging theme that develops from the literature is the importance of managing change. Sapp and Gilmour (2003, 14) sum this up effectively: 'Change happens. Transformation, however, is planned.' The future will be different, and we can help shape the future if we have models, insights and visions that stimulate innovative management and practice.

Another theme in the literature on future library services is that change keeps happening. So although there have been past predictions, it is important to keep scanning the horizon and developing new visions of what academic library services could be like. Therefore, to help inform future transformations in academic library services, this book brings together a series of essays by international experts to provide a firm basis from where we can envisage a new future.

This book comes at a challenging time. The global financial crisis has focused attention on the need to be more efficient but also to continue to innovate. Lowry et al. (2009, 17) note that financial pressures 'will incentivise some libraries to make profound organizational change rather than incremental adjustments'. Back in 1994, Hawkins wrote an entire article on the need to move beyond incremental adjustments: 'Creating the Library of the Future: incrementalism won't get us there!' (Hawkins, 1994). However, the future is more likely to be a series of incremental changes as well as major new initiatives.

Harle (2009) reported on a recent survey of academic libraries in Commonwealth countries. He found that future priorities were much the same as today (digital library developments, information literacy skills training, online library services, learning commons/changes to library space, institutional repositories and research data management, information systems developments, but with some glimpse of new services, e.g. information-related advice to the institution (knowledge management), engagement with the virtual learning environment (VLE). These findings are consistent with Billings (2003), who asserts that library services will continue to evolve in some natural progression, but will also be punctuated by events that are beyond our control. 'Present trends and transformational forces will continue in the years ahead, but it is likely that wild-card influences will help shape the academic library of 2013' (Billings, 2003, 105). What are these wild cards, and are they already here?

Are the Google Generation scholars a wild card?

According to Sweeney (2005, 165) the millennial generation 'make up the demographic tsunami that will permanently and irreversibly change the library and information landscape'. He goes on to say 'The library lesson is to plan for Millennials by reinventing libraries with different and better services and buildings, not by just incrementally improving existing services and buildings' (Sweeney, 2005, 175). These topics are explored in a number of chapters of this book.

Derek Law provides a compelling chapter on the impacts of digital natives on the entire academic library service, exploring the attributes of the Google Generation scholars/digital natives/Millennials who want instant gratification, with just enough information to get by. Law explores: the need to create and manage information, not just store it; the need for new partnerships in learning, teaching and research; the increasingly important role of developing the information literacy skills of natives; and the skill sets of library staff to enable them to be effective in this new environment.

Penny Carnaby provides an insightful chapter on what she describes as 'the delete generation', which is another take on the Google Generation/digital natives. However, Carnaby's focus is on the urgent need to manage digital content, especially citizen-created digital content, otherwise important information will be lost to future generations. Carnaby challenges the traditional mind-set of librarianship by asking whether we are prepared and willing to boldly engage with this potentially transformative opportunity.

The need for different spaces in libraries, acknowledging the changing study habits of the Google Generation, is discussed by Andrew McDonald. His chapter provides insights into the broad range of issues faced by librarians planning new library spaces: managerial and project management challenges; the importance of leadership and vision; and concrete examples for defining quality spaces. McDonald concludes that the iconic image of the 'library as place', inspiring generations of scholars, will continue, regardless of the impact of technologies on the way academic libraries deliver services and resources.

Will Web 2.0 technologies and virtual realities be wild cards?

James Neal and Damon Jaggars describe Web 2.0 as a fundamental and integral component of an academic library service programme in constant development, and in continuous conversation and interaction with the user. Their challenging chapter emphasizes the importance of personalization, communication and engagement. According to Neal and Jaggars, Web 2.0 represents a fundamental and exciting rethinking of how libraries will interact with their customers.

The Neal and Jaggars chapter is complemented by a specific case study by P. Charles Livermore on using Second Life, a multi-user virtual environment, to support reference services and information literacy skills development amongst distance education students. This informative chapter explains the development of Second Life as a tool in educational institutions and demonstrates the proactivity of an 'e-brarian' to enhance services to students who are geographically remote from a physical campus. He asserts that virtual realities will be seen in the future very much as we regard library web pages today: a key tool for providing access to a range of library services and resources.

Are changes to scholarly publishing wild cards?

Frances Pinter provides an insider's perspective on the challenges facing traditional publishers as they try to adapt to a new digital environment. In her chapter she explores different publishing models, including open access models, focusing on the book, and explains how the supply and demand sides to publishing are not working in harmony. Pinter asks librarians to help educate authors along the pathway to digital publishing; to work with publishers to develop policies and to experiment with different models that will bring a global benefit.

Paul Coyne's chapter also brings a publisher's perspective, but focusing more on the technologies associated with search and retrieval of digital content. He highlights how libraries have always been at the forefront of technological innovation and clearly outlines the challenges of managing 'information abundance'. Coyne also explores the impact of Web 2.0 and the characteristics of digital natives, highlighting the need to adopt mobile-ready technologies to fit in to the life-style of the digital native. Future challenges associated with federated searching of multiple information environments and the issues of sustainability and preservation of digital content are discussed.

Is the global financial crisis a wild card, encouraging exploration of new organizational responsibilities and structures?

Lowry et al. (2009, 18) said of academic libraries that 'future success, in part, will be fostered by the adaptability of staff; the recruitment of differently skilled staff; the reorganization of library work and services around emerging academic, research, and learning practices; and a commitment to experiment, innovate, and take risk'. A number of chapters emphasize new or strengthened responsibilities, new skills sets and new organizational structures to be addressed by academic libraries in the future.

Helen Hayes and Philip Kent provide an informative case study of the library's role in leading and supporting a university's knowledge management strategy. They provide a holistic definition of knowledge management and clearly articulate a role for library professionals as knowledge managers within the university. Importantly, this chapter articulates why it is necessary to embrace knowledge management, stating impacts, benefits and values that are derived from active knowledge management.

Martin Lewis provides a compelling argument for academic libraries to assume a far greater role in managing research data. He provides a research data management pyramid for academic libraries, from providing advice to an individual researcher to influencing national government data policies. Importantly, Lewis raises the issue of developing 'library workforce data confidence', highlighting that new skills and professional training will be required if academic librarians are to be successful in this new endeavour.

Liz Wright also supports the need for new skills, and her chapter provides a consultant's insight into leadership and management challenges of the future. Predictions about the workplace of the future and future leadership style are offered, as is a new model for considering 21st-century leadership capabilities, the Star Cluster Model. Wright challenges library leaders and managers to consider new ways of working that will be more appropriate in the predicted fast pace of change of the next 5–10 years.

Sue McKnight explores new partnerships and services that will evolve in response to the online learning revolution, advocating new organizational structures that reflect how information is used rather than how information is stored and managed. Taking the library to students, whether they are in virtual learning rooms or on personal mobile devices, will be the focus of services to enhance learning and teaching in the future. She advocates leadership across boundaries, influencing other parts of the academy and the administration and professional services so as to provide an enhanced student experience.

Michael Robinson outlines the rapid rate of change in the provision of academic library services in China. His chapter serves as an important reminder that the Western world does not have the monopoly on good and great academic library services. Since the 1990s, investment in China's universities and libraries has rapidly increased, with a concentration of funds into elite universities that rank in the world's top 100. Robinson reminds readers about the power of political will and a determination to achieve excellence; we need to be aware of and work with our colleagues in China, and indeed other countries, if we are to learn from each other to improve global academic library services into the future.

This book provides a window on what is possible so that we can plan a transformative agenda and manage change effectively. Hopefully, we can create a future that builds on traditional values, services and skills of academic librarianship while increasing the value adding we make to universities, staff and students.

References

Billings, H. (2003) The Wild-Card Academic Library in 2013, *College & Research Libraries* (March), 105–9,
   www.ala.org/ala/mgrps/divs/acrl/publications/crljournal/2003/mar/billings.PDF.

Harle, J. (2009) *Unlocking the Potential: new opportunities for Commonwealth libraries*, Association of Commonwealth Universities, London.

Hawkins, B. L. (1994) Creating the Library of the Future: incrementalism won't get us there!, *Serials Librarian*, 24 (3/4), 17–47.

Lowry, C. B., Adler, P., Hahn, K. and Stuart, C. (2009) *Transformational Times: an environmental scan prepared for the ARL Strategic Plan Review Task Force*, Association of Research Libraries,
   www.arl.org/bm~doc/transformational-times.pdf.

Sapp, G. and Gilmour, R. (2003) A Brief History of the Future of Academic Libraries: predictions and speculations from the literature of the profession, 1975 to 2000 – Part two, 1990 to 2000, *portal: Libraries and the Academy*, 13 (1), 13–34.

Sweeney, R. T. (2005) Reinventing Library Buildings and Services for the Millennial Generation, *Library Administration and Management*, 19 (4), 165–75.

1

Waiting for the barbarians: seeking solutions or awaiting answers?

Derek Law

Introduction

Cavafy's (1961) famous poem describes the paralysis induced when waiting for an event that never happens, finding distraction in other things while expecting imminent cataclysm. Libraries have perhaps been guilty of this in recent years, joining the chorus bemoaning the imminent arrival of the digital barbarians and undertaking a whole series of avoidance tactics which make libraries ever more efficient but ever less relevant. Like Cavafy's senators, libraries have prepared themselves, decked themselves in finery but have waited for the future to come to them rather than gone out to engage with it.

The arrival of aliteracy

Recently, a well known national chain of bookshops stocked perhaps the ultimate symbol of what a post-war baby-boomer and wholly literate generation would see as the final, conclusive evidence of dumbing down – a Leonardo Da Vinci action figure. Leonardo Da Vinci, the advertising blurb noted, was the original Renaissance man. He was a master of painting, science, language and (most importantly of all!) the inspiration for Leonardo Di Caprio's name. The website proudly noted that an Einstein action figure would follow. Presumably he would conquer evil with equations. While it is very easy to make the case for this as dumbing down, it is also a marker for the seismic shift which is taking place. There is always inter-generational tension, but we are on the cusp of an era when all the certainties of literacy may well disappear. We are close to a world of aliteracy, where reading and writing as generations have known them become optional, life-style choices rather than the fundamental attributes of a civilized person. Coupled with this is a move from a text-based society to an image-based society. A whole range of shared cultural reference points relied on words:

- Doctor Livingstone, I presume
- The Charge of the Light Brigade
- Never in the field of human conflict . . .
- $e = mc^2$
- I have a dream.

These vaguely remembered phrases, and dozens like them, carry a raft of meaning and shared values known to everyone, or rather, everyone above a certain age. But consider the shared cultural reference points of recent years. Everyone can conjure the images of the fall of the Berlin Wall, of the lone protester in front of the tanks in Tiananmen Square, or of the little girl running naked and screaming down the road in Vietnam. One does not have to be of an age to remember these images at the time when they were created. They are now used repeatedly on film, television and in magazines to represent these cultural points. When the tube bombs exploded in the London Underground in July 2007, the most common reaction was to reach for a cellphone – not just to call home, but to take pictures, recording one's part in events. Images rather than words define the new millennium.

Probably the first to note that what we faced was a fundamental discontinuity and not simply the ratcheting up of technology, coupled with generational conflict, was Marc Prensky (2001, 2001a). It has been almost a decade since he launched the concept of digital natives (the post-www generations) and digital immigrants (everyone else) on the world. His definitions and terms have come in for scrutiny and debate since then, but they are an undeniably powerful metaphor for the change which all too evidently surrounds us. Rather like the debate on climate change, the sheer growing weight of evidence points firmly to the conclusion that Prensky is right. The most important point in his argument is that we are not witnessing a simple speeding up of incremental change, but have reached a point of discontinuity marked by fundamental change.

Digital natives are, quite simply, different people.

Prensky's concept can be combined with that of aliteracy. Much less noticed in his writing is the notion that content may itself be in the process of change. A short quotation from his seminal articles shows just how chilling a concept this is:

> It seems to me that after the digital singularity there are now two kinds of content: Legacy content (to borrow the computer term for old systems) and Future content. Legacy content includes reading, writing, arithmetic, logical thinking, understanding the writings and ideas of the past, etc – all of our 'traditional' curriculum. It is of course still important, but it is from a different era. Some of it (such as logical thinking) will continue to be important, but some (perhaps like Euclidean geometry) will become less so, as did Latin and Greek. 'Future' content is to a large extent, not surprisingly, digital and technological. But while it includes software, hardware, robotics, nanotechnology, genomics, etc, it also includes the ethics, politics, sociology, languages and other things that go with them.

Quite different from illiteracy, aliteracy applies to those who can read and write, but for whom literacy in the classic sense is an optional extra. On a regular basis newspapers are full of stories of what is seen as dumbing down. Their dyspeptic columnists and correspondents bemoan students who can neither spell nor punctuate, nor construct a sentence – far less parse one; students wholly reliant on calculators and unable to manage the most basic mental arithmetic, and who use strange abbreviations when txtng frnds. And yet those students communicate perfectly. This could be construed as simple inter-generational grumpiness, but in reality it forms part of the larger discontinuity. Prensky quotes some figures:

> Today's average college grads have spent less than 5,000 hours of their lives reading, but over 10,000 hours playing video games (not to mention 20,000 hours watching TV). Computer games, email, the Internet, cell phones and instant messaging are integral parts of their lives.

To perceive and regret a drop in standards is quite fundamentally to misunderstand the nature of the change which is taking place.

Instant results, instant gratification and just enough

This new breed of information user doesn't just require that everything be made simple. They have a quite different value structure. On the one hand they want choice, being much less clear that there is right information and wrong information, but at the same time they want selectivity. From creationism to climate change, to the (mis-)use of information to justify political expedience in everything from political expenses to invading Iraq, it is much less clear that they do not inhabit a black and white world of right and wrong, but rather, one of shades of grey. They want instant results and instant gratification because a fundamental tenet is that convenience trumps quality. They want just enough to complete the task in hand – not complete or perfect. So it has to be cheap, fast and good. Both information and technology have to be mobile and available anytime, anyplace, anywhere. Such users are not generally inclined to seek advice and help. Quite apart from a working assumption that a Google search will display all known human knowledge, to work through an intermediary requires an input of time and effort which is not seen as commensurate with any benefit.

And yet the work by CIBER (2007) clearly shows that such users wildly overestimate their ability to manage information. Students will often give up after their initial searches, assuming they have completed the research process. If it's not on the web, it doesn't exist. Access to full-text articles also seems to have changed students' cognitive behaviour, although rather depressingly this easier access is accompanied by very short spells of time spent reading the material. Students no longer have to take notes or read through them to develop themes and ideas, an activity central to a focused research project. Electronic articles enable cutting and pasting, almost certainly leading to increased plagiarism, although it may be more than a suspicion that this is usually done from ignorance rather than malice. Research by the CIBER group is unequivocal in its findings, based on huge volumes of log analysis (Nicholas, 2009). The shorter an item is, the more likely it is to be read online. If it is long, users will either read the abstract or squirrel it away for a day when it *might not* be read (digital osmosis). Users seem to prefer abstracts much of the time, even when given the choice of full text. In short, they go online to *avoid* reading (Nicholas, 2009).

Adapting to the natives

If this view of an emerging breed of digital natives is correct, it should quite fundamentally affect how librarians approach the changing environment. Social networking tools can then be seen not as yet more technology to which we must respond, with institutional Facebook accounts and local Twitter managers, but as a manifestation of how digital natives manage their world. The dangers and opportunities lie not in new systems or in social networking, but in understanding what has happened as students and scholars move rapidly into the virtual scholarly space. Above all, they want speed and simplicity. Advanced search tools are largely ignored (Nicholas, 2009). The Gartner Group's hype cycle tool for analysing new technologies clearly demonstrates the need to address underlying issues, not current fads, and shows how the hype cycle is at present reflected in the virtual learning and Web 2.0 area (Gartner, 2009).

More and more we must expect to inhabit a world shorn of its certainties and in which even information is very often ephemeral. We already have a situation in which 44% of websites disappear within a year – and sadly this applies just as much to long-standing national institutions and libraries as it does to the transitory interests of those in student halls of residence. The 404 Error Message is an all too familiar one. It is a world in which much content is both user created and image based and where Wikipedia, not Britannica, will be the normal entry point to information. There is a curious paradox in hackles rising at the thought of the expert's being replaced by the wisdom of crowds, thereby making information democratic rather than authoritative. The foundation of science is that any experiment can be replicated, thus validating it, making science at least nominally consensual and democratic.

Managing, not just storing information

Perhaps the most effective response for libraries is to work with the grain. For example, the Bodleian Library at Oxford University recently found an entry on Wikipedia describing one of its South American manuscript treasures, the Codex Mendoza. The entry was wrong. Rather than complain or have the entry withdrawn, the Library simply had its staff correct it. That is much the most effective response (Thomas, 2008). The

British Library has done the same to correct an urban myth concerning version control of the Bible (Ainsley, 2009). These small examples point perhaps to a more aggressive attitude to considering how we can manage information and access to it, and not simply store it. There is no point in bemoaning the failure to use 'proper' resources. The market has decided.

A recognized gap in a web-based information world is trust metrics. A curious by-product of our professional past is that librarians are trusted as impartial, even handed and good at getting appropriate information. This provides an obvious building block where resources validated by librarians or 'kite-marked'[1] on websites will become preferred sources. The very Ranganathan (1931)-like concept of the right information to the right user at the right time becomes a perfect response to this discontinuity.

Born-digital content

It is a curiosity of the library profession in the last ten years or so that it has significantly failed to engage with the e-resources produced by its institutions. Rather than manage this burgeoning and difficult-to-organize material, we have, as a profession, been obsessed with negotiating licences for commercial material and with digitizing the collections we already possess, creating cabinets of curiosities rather than setting out our skills to deal with and take responsibility for managing corporate assets. It has been calculated that the worldwide annual growth in digital data will rise from 161 exabytes[2] in 2006 to 988 exabytes in 2010, in other words, a sixfold growth in five years. Yet no one appears to be dealing with this coherently at corporate level (Ganz, 2008). Universities are part of this trend, and yet it is doubtful if any university has any idea of what its annual digital outputs are, far less has a collection and curation policy for them. It is probable that all e-outputs are managed by someone, but typically in a wholly unco-ordinated way, with no single point of knowledge, standards, advice and monitoring, which is the minimum one might expect. Librarians do not seem to be asserting their central role in this task. Nor is it evident that any university library has a collection policy for the e-archives of poets, politicians or physicists that are already at risk. A wonderful example of what we could be doing is the University of

Texas Human Rights Initiative (Heath, 2009). It has a clear set of priorities:

- bulk harvesting of human rights sites from the world wide web
- custom harvesting of human rights themes from the internet
- preservation and disclosure of born-digital documentation.

It applies archival principles ranging from selection to dark archiving – i.e. formally archived but not available to the public, generally for copyright reasons – of material relevant to outstanding trials, e.g. in Rwanda, and it relates the collection quite explicitly to the mission of the institution.

It is, of course, true that there have been a number of initiatives both locally and nationally to address specific issues, varying from the IRI-Scotland project on institutional repositories (Institutional Repository Infrastructure for Scotland, which links academic repositories) to the UK Research Reserve, which set out to develop and maintain a national shared digital research data service for the UK Higher Education sector, but these are fragmented and problem specific, rather than offering any generic or philosophical approach to the future management of born-digital collections.

Aggregation of resources

Libraries are at their best when they collaborate and aggregate. Librarianship has a proud record of international standards setting, from Dewey to Dublin Core, of co-operation through such groups as OCLC and through international services such as inter-lending. Each of these has required a degree of willingness to work together which is neither self-evidently natural nor without significant collective work being required on standards. The same kind of activity will be needed in the development of e-collections – the electronic equivalent of rare books and special collections. Once all commercial material is available through Google, our unique selling point in terms of our collections will lie in the non-commercial born-digital material that we acquire or that our organizations create. We then need to aggregate and add value to these electronic resources, to provide bibliographic security as well as metadata and to add value by linking to the collections of other libraries.

Good if historic examples of this adding value can be seen in the bringing together of the various scattered parts of the Codex Siniaticus (British Library, 2009), or in the Emory University Slave Records project, which links the records of the Atlantic slave trade from many archives (Emory University, 2009).

Academic partners, not servants

Throughout this author's career many graduation ceremonies have been attended, and always on principle. Two beliefs lie behind that principle. The first and most straightforward belief is that the graduates are as much the library's as the departments'; they represent the fruits of our labours too. Our value may be minor compared with that of a tutor, but it is none the less real and should be celebrated. The second belief is that it does no harm to remind academic colleagues who process through graduation halls that we too are part of the academic enterprise. Sadly, the number of library colleagues in any institution who seem to share these beliefs can be counted on the metaphorical fingers of one hand. To detach us from the outcomes of teaching is to diminish us in what we do.

Related to this, and perhaps more important, is the perception of a change which rests on the way in which libraries and librarians have shifted from being academic partners to academic servants (Law, 2009). Historically the librarian was one of the three named officers of the university and seen as a participant in the academic process, albeit a minor one. Then libraries grew in size, staffing and budget and the librarian became much more managerial and much less academic. We slowly elided into that amorphous group of service providers ranging from human resources to estates. Libraries have never been better managed but we are increasingly servants, not partners in the academic process. That is ground which needs to be reclaimed.

Teaching and learning

Some depressing statistics come from a recent OCLC (2006) survey which showed that:

*   89% of students use search engines to begin a search

- 2% use a library website
- 93% are satisfied or very satisfied with this approach to searching
- 84% are satisfied if librarian assisted.

One explanation for this reduction in satisfaction when librarians try to help is the so-called 'eat spinach syndrome'. Thus, when a student wants a quick fact or a short cut or the answer, library staff insist on showing them how to undertake the task properly. Do it properly or not at all; eat your spinach, it's good for you. Worthy as such an approach is, it is clearly not what the market wants, and we have to devote much more effort to meeting user needs, not handing on traditions of competence – or indeed hanging on to traditions of competence. We have huge potential to be real partners in the teaching and learning process, but this will require a fundamental rethinking and refashioning of the concept of user support. For example: managing the collections of learning objects; managing and preserving the wiki and blog spaces; managing the content links and licensing. These are all well within existing library competences.

Information literacy

Libraries have a good record in dealing with information literacy for students and this should be built on. The ineptitude of students in this area is clearly understood and recorded (CIBER, 2007). Information literacies – including searching, retrieving, critically evaluating information from a range of appropriate sources and also attributing it – represent a significant and growing deficit area (Hughes, 2009). This student ineptitude is matched by two less well understood areas. The first is making the technology work effectively. The need to train and enthuse academic staff is understood but all too rarely addressed, and even where pockets of excellence exist, translating best practice across disciplines within an institution is a Sisyphean task. Even where the issue is addressed it tends to be seen in terms of supporting academic staff in the use of teaching applications. And yet the information literacy skills of academic staff are just as much in need of upgrading. There is a huge area of exploration and innovation to be undertaken in everything from reference management to social networking for research; in the use of tools and applications ranging from Delicious to Openwetware. The second area is making the technology work. New technology for teaching and learning is a major investment for an institution, and there is a tendency to manage acquisition but not maintenance. Under-resourcing everything from technicians to projector bulbs is an understandable but misguided option. The library often has a clearly understood role as the leader in developing information literacy for students and it is then a realistic aspiration to broaden and extend this role to engage much more with developing the information literacy of academic staff and ensuring that the library at least has reliable and well provided teaching spaces where information literacy skills can be developed.

Staffing

But it is not enough to identify the issues which we are neglecting and the issues to be addressed. The ability of library staff to deal with these has to be considered. Thus library staff skills are key. Corrall (2009) rightly argues that professional boundaries are continually evolving and that our professional competency needs continue to be multifaceted, with demand for both breadth and depth of expertise. She suggests that library and information science (LIS) organizations can build capacity through recruitment, development and/or partnership; that job design, project working and systematic reflection can contribute significantly to workplace learning; and that academics and practitioners can both benefit from collaborative partnerships in education and research. There is a need to address the underlying implications of the seismic shift to social networking and beyond. There is little point in encouraging individual members of staff to invest in specific but transient technologies, whether Second Life or Moodle, without a clearer philosophical view of what the library is trying to achieve. Yet all of this is happening at a time when LIS education is in steady decline. The number of library schools, certainly in the United Kingdom and the United States, is diminishing and a recent study (King, 2009) has shown that insufficient numbers of graduates are being produced in the United States to meet the needs of libraries.

Quite apart from the reduction in the number of graduates, there are questions about the relevance of the curricula. To be fair, this is a hoary old area of controversy rather than a new development. In the UK the

Chartered Institute of Library and Information Professionals (CILIP) has attempted to address the issue by considering making continuing professional development (CPD) a requirement for CILIP members. Some institutions require, or at least encourage staff to undertake post-appointment training, ranging from professional qualifications to qualifications in teaching and learning. There is a real need for a much wider professional debate on how skill sets achieved at the start of one's career are to be refreshed, extended and developed as a routine part of professional life.

Conclusion

It is all too easy to see the prospect of an aliterate world in apocalyptic professional terms. Much better to recognize that repurposing our skills, particularly in the areas of building collections of born-digital materials, providing trust metrics and kitemarking, teaching information literacy skills and acting as partners in the academic enterprise will be more prized than ever. The trick will be to ensure that our profession responds to this, rather than abandoning the field to others while we guard the gates of our paper-based storehouses of knowledge. The French politician Alexandre Auguste Ledru-Rollin's perceptive comment on leadership that 'Ah well! I am their leader, I really ought to follow them!' is absolutely pertinent. In the developing world the market will decide what is useful, valid and relevant. However, it would be fatal to follow Cavafy's senators and assume that we know what the market wants. Determining what the market wants and then providing it will be a key component of building relevant and appropriate services. Good practice exists in pockets in this (McKnight and Berrington, 2008) as in everything described above. We must discover what our customers want and then build on that, rather than attempting to lead them towards a future which they find irrelevant.

Notes

1   A symbol similar in shape to a kite, granted for use on products approved by the British Standards Institution.

2   Formally an exabyte is a unit of information or computer storage equal to one quintillion bytes. Another way of describing it is that a single exabyte is equivelent to 50,000 years of DVD recordings.

References

Ainsley, R. (2009) Great Arse. Letter in the *London Review of Books*, 31 (15), 6 August, British Library,

British Library (2009) http://publishing.bl.uk/book/codex-sinaiticus.

Cavafy, E. (1961) *The Complete Poems of Cavafy*, translated by Rae Dalven, Harcourt, Brace & World.

CIBER (2007) *Information Behaviour of the Researcher of the Future*, CIBER, www.bl.uk/news/pdf/googlegen.pdf.

Corrall, S. (2009) *Hybrid Roles and Blended Professionals. What competencies are needed? How can they be acquired?* Unpublished paper given at the SCONUL 2009 Conference, Bournemouth.

Emory University (2009) The Trans-Atlantic Slave Trade Database Project, http://metascholar.org/TASTD-Voyages/.

Ganz, J. (2008) *The Diverse and Exploding Digital Universe*, www.emc.com/collateral/analyst-reports/diverse-exploding-digital-universe. pdf.

Gartner (2009) *Gartner's Hype Cycle Special Report for 2009*, www.gartner.com/DisplayDocument?ref=g_search&id=1108412&subref= simplesearch [this important report is usefully analysed in Jane Hart's blog, Social Media in Learning, http://janeknight.typepad.com/socialmedia/2009/08/the-gartner-hype-cycle-2009.html].

Heath, F. (2009) *Human Rights: the challenge of documentation in the digital age*, 11th Fiesole Collection Development Retreat, www.digital.casalini.it/retreat/retreat_2009.html.

Hughes, A. (2009) *Higher Education in a Web 2.0 World*, www.jisc.ac.uk/publications/documents/heweb2.aspx.

King, D. (2009) *Facing up to the Economic Realities: placing a bet on the future*, unpublished paper from the 2009 SCONUL Conference, Bournemouth.

Law, D. (2009) The Changing Roles and Identities of Library and Information Services Staff. In Whitchurch, C. and Gordon, G., *Academic and Professional Identities in Higher Education: the challenges of a diversifying workforce*, Routledge.

McKnight, S. and Berrington, M. (2008) Improving Customer Satisfaction: changes as a result of customer value discovery, *Evidence Based Library and Information Practice,* 3 (1), 33–52.

Nicholas, D. (2009) *What Is Beyond Books and Journals? Pointers from CIBER's Virtual Scholar programme,* Third Bloomsbury Conference on e-publishing and e-publications, 25 and 26 June 2009. Beyond Books and Journals, www.ucl.ac.uk/infostudies/e-publishing/e-publishing2009/.

OCLC (2006) *College Students' Perceptions of Libraries and Information Resources: a report to the OCLC membership,* OCLC.

Prensky, M. (2001) Digital Natives, Digital Immigrants, *On the Horizon,* 9 (5), 1–6.

Prensky, M. (2001a) Digital Natives, Digital Immigrants Part 2: do they really think differently?, *On the Horizon,* 9 (6), 1–6.

Ranganathan, S. R. (1931) *The Five Laws of Library Science,* Madras Library Association (Madras, India) and Edward Goldston (London, UK).

Thomas, S. (2008) *I've looked at Life From Both Sides Now.* Paper given at the 10th Fiesole Collection Development Retreat, Fiesole, http://digital.casalini.it/retreat/2008_docs/thomas.pdf.

2

The delete generation: how citizen-created content is transforming libraries

Penny Carnaby

Our world is changing

There is a grass-roots-led revolution happening in communities right around the world and it's about to get a whole lot noisier. It is a revolution challenging established knowledge systems and practices. Above all, it is shaking the very foundations of information management and professional practice in libraries throughout the world. It is a citizen-created revolution, one that puts the content creator at centre stage. Established professional practices are expanding to new horizons and opportunities. And the once sacrosanct and established body of knowledge is now much more blurred, with educators, information and communications technology (ICT) specialists and, increasingly, individuals shaping the world of librarians and libraries in an unprecedented way. Alongside this people-led revolution we have a further challenge, in that every second of every minute of the day people are deleting their history, their thoughts and arguments, which these days are invariably presented in digital form.

Given the seismic changes for the profession, this is not a time for professional complacency, nor is it a time to feel anything but excited. With the new knowledge wave sweeping the globe, it would be natural for the library profession to ask: 'Are we prepared and engaged boldly enough to effectively capitalize on this potentially transformative opportunity?'

How well is the library profession really responding?

If we had to rate our response to these changes, a tough but fair assessment would be that the profession 'has done quite well' internationally. Certainly, we have responded to the Web 2.0 world, with its emphasis on social networking and citizen-created content. We know and talk about 'widgets' at www.en.wikipedia.org/wiki/Widget and 'mashups' at www.en.wikipedia.org/wiki/Mashup and we understand the value of reusing and repurposing content. While we may not all be ecstatic about the burgeoning use of Wikipedia at www.wikipedia.org as a key reference source, rather than a more traditional and authoritative source such as Britannica at www.britannica.com, we can say with some confidence that the profession generally 'gets' it.

There are some excellent examples of libraries engaging with Web 2.0 in innovative and effective ways. First, in Australia, where in 2008 the National Library of Australia released an innovative beta version of its Australian Newspapers service that saw several thousand members of the public become active searchers, taggers and text correctors. By February 2009, 2.2 million lines and 104,000 articles had been corrected and 46,230 tags had been added (Holley, 2009, 14).

In New Zealand we are creating effective and simple ways of enabling content to be explored, such as Digital New Zealand at www.digitalnz.org. Digital New Zealand is an open source, open standards one-stop shop that has delivered hundreds of thousands of digital objects in just a few months across multiple content feeds, enabling access to New Zealand content that has never been accessible to the wider public before. Because it is inexpensive to develop, every school, every New Zealander, every museum could put a Digital New Zealand widget on their screen and bring it into their own creative space.

Educators are increasingly using Web 2.0 e-learning tools to transform the way students are learning in a virtual environment. Traditional learning management systems are being challenged as the benefits of e-learning tools come into play. Students are now at the centre of the learning experience, with the result that it is sometimes difficult to determine who is designing and leading the learning experience – the educator or the student?

Open source virtual learning environments such as the Moodle at www.moodle.org community have become very popular among educators around the world, providing tools for creating online dynamic websites for their students. The online experience for students at Macquarie University at www.mq.edu.au in Australia demonstrates how librarians in tertiary education are liberating content into these learning environments. Gone are the days of multiple sign-ons and barriers to access; instead we have free and open access to a plethora of technologies, tools and information, and all at our fingertips (Carnaby, 2005, 346–54).

Given the speed of transformation, it would be reasonable to suggest that we should feel satisfied that we are indeed ahead of the game as a profession. But is the library profession really ahead? While clearly there is evidence of some strong engagement with the changing environment, particularly in relation to the opportunities presented by Web 2.0, there are few examples of truly transformative thinking internationally. One of the key problems is that there are very few maps to follow. It is all so new and different that at times we may not even know the right questions to ask!

What we do know is that we are experiencing a once-in-a-generation paradigm shift. According to well known internet commentator Clay Shirky (n.d.), it may be of the magnitude of some of the past major technology shifts, like the introduction of the printing press, of sound and film and, more recently, the computer age. Shirky argues that emerging technologies are enabling loose collaboration, and so fundamentally changing the way our society works. In his very topical and informative broadcast 'How Social Media Can Make History' at www.ted.com/talks, Shirky talks about the next revolution, which is leading to the 'largest increase in expressive capability', with web and mobile phone technology enabling individuals to generate and broadcast news before traditional media agencies. Shirky cites the example of the Sichuan County earthquake in China in 2008, when the British Broadcasting Corporation at www.bbc.co.uk accessed Twitter, the social network, to get its first update on the earthquake.

Not only does this indicate a shift in the way society is reporting news; more importantly, it highlights the valid and emerging role of individual citizens in generating content. So where is the evidence that real integration of this new knowledge wave is occurring at a professional sector level? While we may recognize the contribution of individuals in the Web 2.0 environment as adding value and understanding to existing knowledge, how seriously are we taking it? Do we understand the long-term benefit of content created in a Web 2.0 environment? We may pay lip service and say it is valuable, but in reality we seem to be willing to tolerate unacceptable loss in the digital environment.

The delete generation

Loss of content in the digital environment is quickly defining this generation as the 'delete generation'. Our understanding of the impact of this kind of loss has not really matured. It may take a generation to actually understand what this means for the transmission of ideas and information over time. Do we yet understand what we are losing, and does it matter? What is the economic, social and cultural impact of this loss of data?

We have terms such as the 'digital dark ages' (introduced in 1998 at the *Time and Bits* conference[1]) or 'digital amnesia' (Carnaby, 2005, 353) or more recently 'digital landfill' (Summerfield, 2008, 1) to jolt our consciousness into appreciating the urgency of the situation. So what do we do about it? All of us will have deleted valued information, often unintentionally. How uncomplicated and predictable the analogue, print and tangible world now seems!

To an extent, we have thought about some issues around long-term preservation, of web harvesting born-digital publications or material produced through established systems on the web. However, not a lot has been developed to protect and preserve citizen-created content over time. There is very little professional debate about the implications of the newly emerging knowledge system. Typically, librarians know a great deal about knowledge systems that are formal and authoritative, and where we trust or know the author or originator of an idea in a published or unpublished work, whatever the format or medium in which it is delivered. For centuries we have catalogued, indexed, described and managed information in an ordered and predictable way so that it is protected and preserved for future generations to explore and enjoy. We also do this so that it may be accessed and used to build new knowledge and understanding, as well as help us to understand our past or better understand the present.

What we are much less certain about is the new knowledge and content created by an individual or community that has no apparent authority of legitimacy. Yet isn't citizen-created content potentially just as important and worthy of attention as information created in more known, legitimate, authoritative circumstances? These are extraordinarily uncomfortable professional questions that need to be answered, and answered quickly. They are causing librarians to rethink what is authoritative, trustworthy information, and we need to engage professionally with this seismic shift in the way new knowledge is created.

There is an emerging equity that needs to be understood and which enables each of us to potentially be a writer, creator or film-maker. While the literature on community/citizen-created content is clear regarding the worth of this content and the need to readily access and share it (Salz, 2005), there is a deafening silence about the need to protect and preserve citizen-created content. This protection and preservation are necessary so that we can harness the ideas of 21st-century creativity and inspiration for future generations to understand, and to draw new learnings.

In this anarchic web of social networking and citizen-created content there are challenging ethical questions to ask, as well. For example, who owns the content? What are the rights issues which underpin this content? What do we collect? Are 'hate' sites (Brown-Sica and Beall, 2008) such as pornographic websites, which may be politically uncomfortable, part of our social history of the web? By failing to capture these accounts, are we effectively sanitizing our social history? Will we be able to look back on society in 50 or 100 years to understand what was so important at the beginning of the 21st century?

Once again, these are hugely challenging professional issues for the library sector, and in many ways it is not the difficult technology solutions that are now challenging our professional boundaries, but rather the softer, ethical, cultural and political issues. These issues are around censorship rights, management, cultural property rights and perhaps something as simple as personal prejudice. The point that underpins these questions is that much of the professional transformation needed is as much about cultural, political, policy and ethical issues as it is around interoperability standards, long-term digital curation and technical convergence. These are indeed complex times.

Reimagining a 21st-century knowledge organization

As a response to the Web 2.0 environment and the changing contribution that individuals are making to the creation of new knowledge, we are seeing organizations rethink and reimagine what a 21st-century knowledge organization should be. It is no accident that some organizations are adapting very quickly to the rapidly changing digital environment, which involves significant cultural change. In this context, it may be better to see the change process as a whole system and look holistically at the information environment.

As in all systems, there is an interdependence whereby if you change one thing, it will impact on something else. Importantly, it is difficult to change an organization without first understanding the environment or community in which it operates. Changing an organization can sometimes seem the easy part. However, as we know, fundamental organizational and cultural change is never straightforward. All too often organizations change one aspect of their operations rather than executing a fundamental rethink of the whole system. For example, as part of the change process we need to think as much about organizational culture, such as the people and the new-generation workplace, as we do about the architecture of an organization.

To embrace and understand the full impact of the changing information landscape takes courageous leadership. It also takes enormous organizational courage to change a whole system and essentially deconstruct what we know in order to really embrace and understand the 'ecology of change' (Carnaby, 2004).

'The ecology of change' best describes the various systems, connections and interdependencies that need to be recognized and understood within an organization. We are all part of, and relate to, a much larger social system, and our internal cultures need to be congruent with the various communities to whom we relate. In seeing and understanding those communities and connections we need to move from the traditional 'silo' thinking to more joined-up, collaborative thinking, on both local and global scales. We are starting to see the culture of our organizations adapting rapidly as hierarchies and departmental silos are being replaced by more integrated, joined up organizations. As a result, the professional boundaries of librarian, educator, ICT specialist and researcher are now more blurred than ever before. We have much more cultural, as well as technical, interoperability in our workplaces. The once impenetrable organizational membrane is perforated more often, through greater collaboration and interoperability between professions and organizations and across sectors.

Global collaboration

As an example, the galleries, libraries, archives, museums (GLAM) sector is much more joined up and collaborative these days, developing and delivering some inspirational online partnerships. The initiative Europeana at www.europeana.eu is a very good example of collaboration amongst the GLAMs in Europe, while the World Digital Library at www.wdl.org, which 'makes available on the Internet, free of charge and in multilingual format, significant primary materials from countries and cultures around the world', is an excellent example of cross-border collaboration. At a local New Zealand level, over 120 GLAM organizations collaborate in the online environment through initiatives such as the National Digital Forum at http://ndf.natlib.govt.nz to share expertise, and through Matapihi at www.matapihi.org.nz to provide access to joined-up digital collections. Across the wider Australasian region, the National and State Libraries of Australasia (NSLA) at www.nsla.org.au are pooling resources collaboratively on several leading-edge projects. One of these, the Rethinking Libraries Project, has aimed to transform these organizations over the period 2009 to 2012, delivering innovative 'One Library' solutions that could not be achieved by the organizations acting individually.

A new-generation workplace

As outlined earlier, if we are to truly understand and capitalize on the knowledge revolution that we are experiencing, most of us will need to entertain a fundamental rethink of our professional capabilities, workplaces, organizational cultures and new-generation skills, which will be needed to engage with the deluge of digital information. Best-practice employers are already thinking differently about how to attract and, more importantly, keep new-generation professionals, even in these recessionary times.

Let's face it, we need to adapt, and to adapt quickly, because the new-generation school student, researcher and individual citizen will demand it of us as millennials/Generation Y'ers (Pitt-Catsouphes et al., 2009) who 'are tech savvy, with every gadget imaginable almost becoming an extension of their bodies. They multitask, talk, walk, listen and type, and text. And their priorities are simple: they come first' (Safer, 2007).

We live in a world of convergence and a blurring of traditional certainties, so we need to be transforming our workplaces and professional practices to reflect the changed environment. As Wan Wee Pin (2008, 245), manager of the Strategic Planning Office of the National Library of Singapore, succinctly argues, 'libraries must stop trying to change the [content creation] behaviour of their users. Libraries must give up control and allow engagement and sharing of information, rather than just being the providers of information.' This transformation is to some extent happening already, particularly in those libraries close to the citizen-created knowledge revolution. Public and community libraries may well be the first to really embrace new ways of working in different collaborations and partnerships in this environment.

Typically, more traditional organizations, where authoritative knowledge sources tend to be predominant, may be slower to adapt. Yet even here we are gradually seeing a change to established systems. For example, scholarly communication has traditionally rested heavily on peer review through publishing outlets, such as scholarly journals. Today, it is becoming more commonplace to see scholarship and research communicated in open access repositories, with peer assessment opened up to much greater international review and comment, through social networking and Web 2.0 tools. David Lewis (2007, 418) observes that a new equity is emerging in terms of knowledge. What is undeniable is that 'the wide application of digital technologies to scholarly communications has disrupted the model of academic library service that has been in place for the past century', creating opportunities 'for new forms of research and scholarship', which will require new forms of infrastructure to ensure the availability of digital content (Larsen, 2008).

The 'publish or perish' imperative for scholars in the print world, to a degree, still underpins the focus of scholarly communication. However, where we publish and how we publish are very different indeed. Here in New Zealand, the National Library offers a metadata harvesting service through the Kiwi Research Information Service (KRIS) at www.nzresearch.org.nz, which will harvest metadata across research repositories in all New Zealand's universities and Crown entities and some polytechnics.

Taking citizen-created content seriously – New Zealand case studies

In this environment we need to learn from each other and exchange the lessons, successes and failures. Internationally, the library and information community has a wonderful track record of collaboration over many decades. The digital revolution has sped up this collaboration enormously. It has been a great democratizer as well. For example, a small country or community can easily access the global and local networks that were once the sole domain of the very large and very wealthy.

In this context, case studies from a very small nation, New Zealand, are used. While each country will have its own story, the following New Zealand case studies will have resonance for those wanting to embrace change on personal, organizational, national and global scales.

CASE STUDY 2.1: NEW ZEALAND'S DIGITAL LANDSCAPE

Two landmark policy and legislative pieces of work have defined New Zealand's digital landscape. To summarize, in 2003 the National Library of New Zealand Act (www.natlib.govt.nz) made New Zealand one of the first countries to legislate so as to bring legal deposit into the electronic or digital domain. It gave the National Library the mandate to collect and preserve New Zealand born-digital publications and all digital activity in New Zealand – blogs, wikis, anything publicly accessible on the web.

At a policy level, New Zealand was a significant contributor to the World Summit on the Information Society (WSIS), and was successful in getting the principles of freedom of access to information enshrined in the WSIS principles of 2003.[2]

Subsequently, the New Zealand government launched the New Zealand Digital Content Strategy (NZDCS) in 2007.[3] The NZDCS is significant in that it does not discriminate between digital content created in the authoritative formal space and content which is community generated by an individual or by a group of citizens. Additionally, it provides a whole-of-government and strategic view of digital content that 'is about making New Zealand visible and relevant in a connected digital world, ensuring we are innovative, informed and capable as a nation in creating our digital future and telling our stories to each other and the world' (National Library of New Zealand, 2007, 7). Another noteworthy aspect of the strategy is the end-to-end view it takes of a digital object, from creation through to discovery and access, through to protection and preservation of that asset.

The Digital Content Strategy traverses new ground in that it gives an equal weighting to all processes, from creation (of the idea) through to protection and preservation (looking after the idea), as outlined in the Strategy's Five-element Framework (see Figure 2.1). The strategy implies that new investment is needed, not only in the generation of new content, but also in the preservation of the digital asset. This is done for social, economic and cultural reasons so that we can look back on New Zealand society in 50 or 100 years' time and understand more about New Zealand intellectual and social activity on the web in 2009. Additionally, given the current global economic crisis, it simply does not make sense to invest in content creation and yet fail to protect or preserve that content so it can be reused, repurposed for new research, thought generation or business opportunities.

It is important to realize that the economic argument for protection and preservation of digital assets is just as compelling as the better-understood social and cultural reasons for doing so. After all, if New Zealand is to build economic growth, we have an obligation to ensure that our innovators, entrepreneurs and creatives have access to premium New Zealand content.

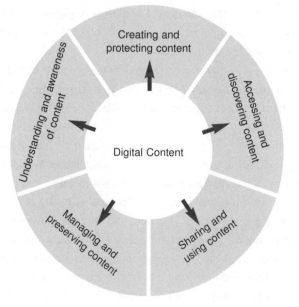

Figure 2.1 *The Digital Content Strategy's Five-element Framework*

CASE STUDY 2.2: DIGITAL CURATION – THE NATIONAL DIGITAL HERITAGE ARCHIVE

With the mandate to bring legal deposit into the digital domain, the next step was to build a trusted, curated digital repository for the long-term preservation and protection of New Zealand's digital assets through the National Digital Heritage Archive (NDHA), a NZ$24 million project undertaken by the National Library of New Zealand. In February 2009 the National Digital Heritage Archive at www.ndha-wiki.natlib.govt.nz was launched as the first fully contained commercial answer for the protection and preservation of digital heritage.

The NDHA was developed in partnership with Ex Libris and Sun Microsystems, working as software and hardware partners. Sun Microsystems has recently published a white paper/case study on preservation at the National Library of New Zealand (Sun Microsystems, 2009) on the information architecture reference site using the NDHA. The digital preservation system is marketed as Rosetta by Ex Libris.

It was very important from the outset to involve both international and New Zealand stakeholders in how we ultimately shaped the NDHA. They included the Peer Review Group, whose mandate was to guide the partnership and the resultant creation of a commercially viable solution; and highly respected institutions such as the British Library, Cornell University Library, the Getty Research Institute, the National Library of China and Yale University, to name a few.

The NDHA is highly intuitive in that when technology changes, for example a CD becomes obsolete, the archive is notified and ensures that the CD is migrated from one generation to the next. This guarantees that a digital object created in 2008 – perhaps a born-digital cartoon from one of our eminent cartoonists – will be exactly the same in 50 years time. This is a real breakthrough.

Of course there are still unanswered questions and ongoing challenges. For example, new policy is needed to guide decisions on what is added and kept and what is deleted. The less resolved, and arguably equally, important aspect is how to manage citizen-created content in terms of long-term curation and protection. While the Web 2.0 explosion of citizen-created content has unleashed human creativity at new levels, what should and could be collected over time? What should we add to New Zealand's heritage archive and what are the technical issues that need to be resolved?

However, good progress has been made in addressing community-created content and some of the issues that have already been raised. The next case study highlights how New Zealand is starting to connect its knowledge systems across the country.

CASE STUDY 2.3: CONNECTING KNOWLEDGE

In New Zealand, the term *kete* is Maori for basket, and we use this term as a metaphor for connecting New Zealand knowledge. It refers to the growing institutional, research and community repositories that are emerging across New Zealand, and how these will impact on new-generation learning environments.

Kete Horowhenua

A great example of a community repository is Kete Horowhenua, a rich story of grass-roots, spontaneous content, collected by communities within the Horowhenua, a lower North Island region of New Zealand. Kete Horowhenua has had an extraordinary journey – and is a strong example not only of how community and marae-based repositories can work together and connect in the digital world, but also of how they can be capitalized on, and be applicable to, every community around the country.

Aotearoa People's Network

In 2006 public funds were made available to develop a joined-up framework for open source community repositories in New Zealand. The first intervention was the need to raise the ability of communities to create content to contribute to community memory projects. The Aotearoa People's Network Kaharoa (APN),[4] launched in 2007, is a strategy for getting broadband and internet into communities, particularly in rural and provincial New Zealand. Based on the United Kingdom's People's Network initiative, the APN is run through local public libraries and has been an extremely rewarding experience whereby minimal improvement to broadband capability has seen an extraordinary outpouring of community creativity.

Drawing on the very successful *kete* community repository project led by the Horowhenua Library Trust[5] and the Aoteroa People's Network initiative, open-source, open-standard community repositories are emerging all around the country. With the originators' permission, through Creative Commons licences[6] the National Library continues to harvest metadata and to add digital objects to the Heritage Archive, thus ensuring some protection from loss of this precious and unique story of New Zealand, as told from a community perspective. In bringing it all together the strategy is to cluster content feeds from all of these repositories in a huge metadata-harvesting strategy channelled through the discovery environment of Digital New Zealand.

Conclusion

The case studies give a taste of what one country, albeit small, is doing in response to the enormous potential of the digital world. They also demonstrate that the 21st-century library profession is shaping up to be something quite different to what has been experienced in the past, while still retaining and practising its essential values and skills.

The challenge for the profession is to ensure that our future library and information professionals are prepared for the knowledge-led world of the 21st century. Are we preparing professionals to address the issues surrounding unacceptable loss of data, memory, ideas and creativity? Are we preparing the new generation of professionals to understand the information management issues of the delete generation of which they are themselves a part? Some of the issues we need to think about are strangely comforting for those of us who have spent our whole professional lives ensuring the free flow of information in our society. Structuring and understanding the digital is conceptually similar to the analogue and print world in which most of us have grown up.

As outlined earlier, these are not primarily technical problems, but rather one of how we re-engineer our current processes to accommodate the complexities of citizen-created content. There are no quick fixes or immediate answers, and the challenges may seem insurmountable. But in this new and exciting world the potential to take the library profession to new heights and new horizons is well worth the turmoil that always accompanies a revolution.

Notes

1   www.longnow.org/projects/conferences/time-and-bits/.

2 www.itu.int/wsis/docs/geneva/official/dop.html.
3 www.digitalstrategy.govt.nz.
4 www.aotearoapeoplesnetwork.org.
5 www.horowhenua.kete.net.nz.
6 www.creativecommons.org.

References

Brown-Sica, M. and Beall, Jeffrey (2008) Library 2.0 and the Problem of Hate Speech, *E-JASL: The Electronic Journal of Academic and Special Librarianship*, 9 (2), Summer, http://southernlibrarianship.icaap.org/content/v09n02/brown-sica_m01.html.

Carnaby, P. (2004) *The Ecology of Change: looking back on my first year in the job*, an open letter to the staff of the National Library of New Zealand Te Puna Matauranga o Aotearoa, (February).

Carnaby, P. (2005) E-Learning and Digital Library Futures in New Zealand, *Library Review*, 54 (6), 346–54.

Holley, R. (2009) *Many Hands Make Light Work: public collaborative OCR text correction in Australian historic newspapers*, National Library of Australia, www.nla.gov.au/ndp/project_details/documents/ANDP_ManyHands.pdf.

Larsen, R. L. (2008) On the Threshold of Cyberscholarship, *JEP: The Journal of Electronic Publishing*, 11 (1), http://quod.lib.umich.edu/cgi/t/text/text-idx?c=jep;view=text;rgn=main;idno=3336451.0011.102.

Lewis, D. W. (2007) A Strategy for Academic Libraries in the First Quarter of the 21st Century, *College & Research Libraries*, 68 (5), 418–34.

National Library of New Zealand (2007) *Creating A Digital New Zealand: New Zealand's digital content strategy*, National Library of New Zealand, (August).

Pin, Wan Wee (2008) Library 2.0: the new e-world order, *Public Library Quarterly*, 27 (3), 244–6.

Pitt-Catsouphes, M., Matz-Costa, C. and Besen, E. (2009) *Age and Generations: understanding experiences at the workplace*, Sloan Center on Aging and Work, http://agingandwork.bc.edu/documents/RH06_Age&Generations_2009-03-20.pdf.

Raven, C. (2002) Electronic Content Development in a Community Setting, *VINE*, 32 (2), 25–9.

Safer, M. (2007) The 'Millennials' Are Coming, *CBS News*, 25 May 2007, www.cbsnews.com/stories/2007/11/08/60minutes/main3475200.shtml.

Salz, P. A. (2005) Power to the People: do it yourself content distribution, *EContent*, **28** (6), 36–41.

Shirky, C. (n.d.) *Writings about the Internet*, www.shirky.com/.

Summerfield, B. (2008) Cleaning Up the Digital Landfill, *Chief Learning Officer Newsletter*, (July), www.clomedia.com/executive-briefings/2008/July/2265/index.php?pt=a&aid=2265&start=0&page=1.

Sun Microsystems (2009) *Digital Preservation at the National Library of New Zealand: a forward-looking mission*, www.sun-pasig.org/pdf/NLNZ Case Study. PDF.

3

Libraries as places: challenges for the future

Andrew McDonald

Introduction

Many universities and other institutions around the world continue to make considerable investments in imaginatively designed new and refurbished library buildings (Cannell, 2007; Designing Libraries, 2009; Drew, 2009; Edwards, 2009; McDonald, 2002a; Niegaard et al., 2008; Wu, 2003). This is despite some almost reckless predictions about the end of libraries as 'places' due to the rapid growth of networked electronic information and the use of the internet. We are seeing a huge resurgence of interest in creating these new 'places' designed to enhance learning, teaching and research and to 'inspire' succeeding generations of scholars (Watson, 2006, 2007, 2008; Hoare, 2008). Ironically, the welcome advances in information technology, together with significant changes in the way people use public spaces have only served to strengthen the role of libraries as important places in our universities.

A librarian who has been given the exciting responsibility of creating a new building has two significant managerial challenges: developing a compelling vision for the new space and leading the project to make sure the vision is realized. Place making is an enjoyable and creative art, and success requires a thorough understanding of the planning and design process (Khan, 2009; McDonald, 2007a) and an appreciation of the important qualities of creating good 21st-century space (McDonald, 2003, 2006, 2007b).

Although the emphasis in this chapter is primarily on university libraries, the principles discussed are sufficiently generic to relate to other sorts of libraries and, indeed, to learning spaces in general. They are equally relevant to all place-making activities: a major new building or an extension, a refurbishment or an adaptation, smaller projects concerned with making better use of existing space, or a mixture of these.

Let us first explore the nature of the managerial challenge.

The managerial challenge

Shaping new library spaces remains a substantial and complex managerial challenge, arguably the biggest and most important professional challenge the library manager will face. It involves vision and strategy, leadership and management, communication and creativity, and project management with all its associated risks. Many library managers may only have one opportunity to plan a new building in their career, and even though very large capital sums are often involved, they will almost certainly have had little experience or training for managing such a project.

An inspiring vision

We must develop an exciting and compelling vision for our new place. This should go well beyond delivering better-quality services in a more efficient way: the best new buildings transform their institutions, moving the boundaries of what a good library can deliver and creating new opportunities for enhancing learning, teaching and research. Some managers exploit the opportunity to rebrand the service. Our vision should inspire the whole project (Bazillion and Braun, 1994) and influence all the other professionals involved in the planning and design process.

Developing an imaginative vision will be informed by the qualities of good library space discussed later in this chapter and by best practice in library design within the sector. Place making is about creating a new physical environment to facilitate the mission and aspirations of the institution and this will be driven by its mission, ethos and strategic aims. Our responsibility is not only for the immediate future, but also for succeeding generations of scholars: indeed many librarians are planning buildings and important collections for posterity.

Space as a strategic resource

Space is a precious and expensive resource that should be planned and managed within a strategic framework for the development of the university and its library service as a whole. Good library buildings are a key differentiating feature between institutions, defining the host institution and demonstrating its commitment to the student and staff experience. Unfortunately, space has sometimes received less professional attention than collections, digital resources, systems, finance, staffing and the other resources which the librarian manages. Quite simply, good, well-planned space enables the library to fulfil its mission and underpins the development of all other library resources. On the other hand, poor space often conflicts with what readers and library staff are trying to achieve and inhibits the library's ability to fulfil its aims in an efficient way. More seriously, poor space can constrain the development of the service.

Leadership and transformational change

Playing a leading role throughout the whole planning and design process requires all manner of leadership skills. As well as excellent strategic planning, communication, influencing and negotiating skills, the library manager requires presence, integrity, resilience, empathy, patience and humour. It involves managing relationships with many professionals whom we may not have encountered before, developing an inclusive approach that embraces and harnesses the creativity and contribution of the whole team. It requires flexibility and the ability to think on your feet.

Planning new space is about creating and then managing a great deal of change in order to develop an entirely new service that can deliver new levels of quality, impact, responsiveness and efficiency. Indeed, it is a unique opportunity to transform the culture and organization of the library and to influence the attitudes and behaviour of the user community. The library manager must lead the institution through this period of considerable change – on the one hand, managing creativity, ideas and expectations, and on the other, dealing with the effects of change, uncertainty and disruption.

Managing the process

Space planning is not primarily about architecture and taste, or about bricks and mortar, but it is about the responsible library manager seeking to create an attractive new library that works very well and lasts a long time. Planning libraries is simply good management and, as Mason (1996) reminds us: 'good management of the library building planning will make a better building'. He goes further and emphasizes that library managers 'must make sure they are in control of the management'. Successful projects are as much about managing people, culture change and creativity as they are about buildings, space and processes. When it comes to planning new spaces, people sometimes demonstrate irrational feelings and unusual behaviours about territory, status and power.

During the challenging time of a building project, the library director will experience a whole spectrum of managerial emotions: from exhilaration to exhaustion, from fun to frustration, and from satisfaction to insanity. A wide range of managerial skills will be tested: politics and diplomacy, boldness and understanding, direction and ego massaging, trouble-shooting and crisis management, negotiation and compromise, and communication and collaboration. Library managers often find they need to take a particularly determined and persistent approach to ensure that the design delivers what is required. When compromises are needed, they should always be made with the interests of the library and its users in mind. Understanding the processes, priorities and culture of our estates departments and the construction industry is not always easy.

Communication and creativity

A major project is a massive communications exercise involving a whole range of interested parties and professionals (Carmack, 1992; McDonald, 2007a). Within the parent organization there are the governing body, corporate managers, estates professionals, IT experts, library users and library staff. The architect, contractor and library building consultant are key players beyond the institution. Productive and yet sensitive relationships with donors and funding bodies are critical. Increasingly, IT and networking experts are assisting with planning effective integrated electronic environments, and acoustic specialists are advising on ways of managing the growing problem of noise in libraries. Consultants may be called upon to assist with furniture and interior design, artwork, signage, lighting, disability access, security, health and safety, environmental control, transport, landscaping, and preservation and conservation needs. Influencing the early part of the planning and design process is particularly important, since this is when many of the key decisions are made.

Planning new space is an enjoyable and creative process which, inevitably, has its 'creative tensions'. It is a complex human process about which not everyone will or should agree. There are no prescribed solutions for planning library buildings: no one knows all the answers and no two projects are the same. Indeed, different architects and planners will often develop very different design solutions to a particular set of requirements. Architects, creative professionals and librarians must all bring their vision and respective skills to this creative process.

The architect's role is 'to translate the dreams and hopes of the library project team into reality' (Carmack, 1992). Architects, particularly famous ones, tend to have a strong vision about the 'artistic interpretation of space' (Rockwell, 1989). The librarian must have an equally distinctive view about what is required, and must articulate this clearly to the architect and all those involved in the project, and must make sure the design delivers what is required. Communication is vitally important in a creative process and 'there is no reason why an architect who is willing to listen to his client cannot design an efficient, technologically-sound building that is also a credit to its creator' (Bazillion and Braun, 1994). Many regard a good brief as the key to success (Faulkner-Brown, 1993; Holt, 1989; Revill, 1996). At its best, the brief is a strategic as well as a descriptive document, providing a good starting point from which the planning team can develop their requirements in a flexible way. As a rule, the best libraries emerge when there has been a strong shared vision and good communication between all those involved in the process, especially between the architect and the librarian.

Project management

Like all project management, space planning involves taking decisions, normally a large number of them, within a finite time scale and within the resources available in order to achieve project aims. The new library must be delivered on time and within budget, and it must be affordable both in capital and in recurrent costs. As the representative of the parent body, the library manager must manage the project in a responsible way, ensuring a good balance between imaginative solutions, hard-nosed decisions, pragmatic financial management and appropriate compromises. As well as inspiring the process with an imaginative vision, the library manager must pay considerable attention to detail throughout the entire project.

Some risks

There are considerable political, professional and financial risks involved in leading a major project. It is the library manager who will have the responsibility for providing services to users in the new building, and it is the library manager's name that is invariably linked with the success or failure of the project. Well-planned new buildings can transform the learning, teaching and research experience in an institution and will stimulate demand for library services, sometimes by as much as fivefold (Jones, 1999). Sustaining these new levels of usage will present a significant challenge to our management and resources, not least our staffing levels. Poorly planned space will attract criticism from both the user community and other involved parties, and will have a profound effect on the morale of library staff and the reputation of their leader.

Qualities of good library space

McDonald (2006; 2007b) suggests that good library space has a number of important qualities. An understanding of each of these attributes will help us to develop an exciting vision for the new library and will inform the whole planning and design process. The challenge for architects and planners is to strike an effective balance between all these qualities, creating new places with a certain 'wow' factor that take library services to a new level, inspiring our users and capturing the spirit of the university. Ideally, new space should be:

- functional
- adaptable

- accessible
- varied
- interactive
- conducive
- environmentally suitable
- safe and secure
- efficient
- suitable for information technology.

These generic qualities help to define what planners should be striving for in their new libraries. They are the critical issues that should be addressed in the brief and discussed with the planning team throughout the process, and they form a set of criteria against which design solutions can be assessed. Indeed, they are the very qualities that set academic libraries apart from other building types.

Clearly, the priority given to each of these qualities will depend on the mission and culture of the institution, and the role and aims of its library service. They are intended as an indicative set of qualities and should never be taken as a prescriptive set of solutions. Inevitably there are tensions and even conflicts between these qualities, as well as within each of them, and they all have resource implications.

We will now go on to consider each of these defining qualities in a little more detail.

Functional

space that works well, looks good and lasts well

Clearly, we should design libraries which are functional, easy to use and economical to operate. New space must enable the library to fulfil its role and facilitate the delivery of high-quality services. Functional interests should take priority over any purely aesthetic considerations, but it is important for our libraries to look really good too. The design should recognize the crucial importance of people, books and information technology, and the dynamic relationship and complex interactions between them. It should achieve a balance between the needs of the teaching, learning and research communities. New space must also enable the service to respond to the changing needs of the academic community and developments in information technology.

The 'people-centred' approach to planning (Wu, 2003) recognizes that libraries are essentially about people, or rather, about the way in which people interact with the collections, information technology and services they need. The user should be at the centre of the whole process, and as Dowlin (1999) confirms: 'The magic of libraries is in connecting minds . . . and successful library buildings in the 21st century will enable those connections to happen'. Today's diverse students have high expectations of library space, demanding personal spaces, a technology-rich environment and social learning opportunities. Our researchers and academics similarly call for better access to digital resources and both silent and interactive spaces (Hoare, 2008). As Bennett (2005) reminds us, planning should be driven by learning rather than library operations. Learning and research are social processes, requiring library spaces where users can meet, collaborate and work in groups. Indeed university libraries have become important 'third places' where people meet outside home and work (Florida, 2000).

Adaptable
flexible space, the use of which can easily be changed
Paradoxically, one of the few certainties in planning new libraries is the almost guaranteed uncertainty about future use, particularly in relation to information technology, organizational structures, user behaviour and unforeseen developments. The rate of change in higher education in the United Kingdom (UK) is exponential, but is full of opportunity (Guardian, 2008). It is therefore important to achieve a high degree of flexibility in the building so that the use of space can easily be changed with the minimum of disruption, often merely by rearranging the furniture, shelving and equipment.

Achieving long-term flexibility can, however, be more costly than delivering short-term functionality, and planners are now more pragmatic, seeking an appropriate balance between cost and adaptability requirements (Taylor, 1994). Agility and adaptability are perhaps more realistic goals than flexibility in a rapidly changing environment (Heppel et al., 2004). The golden architectural rule that 'form follows function' remains important, but creating wholly flexible spaces can lead to an overly neutral environment that lacks the essential 'wow' factor referred to earlier. As different uses evolve, well-planned, versatile spaces can continue to be effective and even provoke change without losing their architectural character (Muscogiuri, 2009). The growth of digital resources, often at the expense of printed collections, has challenged the traditional view that libraries should always be extendible. Many libraries are now creating social learning spaces from space previously occupied by printed collections.

Future-proofing is an imperfect art, but one fundamental question is how far ahead we should plan. As Brand (1994) reminds us: 'All buildings are predictions. All predictions are wrong.' But any predictions about the size and nature of buildings for the future will depend upon how we envisage library services will be delivered in the networked learning and information age. One library director reflects on this dilemma: 'You can't be sure how these spaces will be used. You are just creating the opportunities for things to happen' (JISC, 2006, 13). Brown (2009) broadens the challenge, suggesting that future-proof design strives to create places that are 'lovable, responsive, energy productive, resource effective, disaster resistant, and perpetually significant'. Jones (1999) warns against planning for more than 15 to 20 years ahead because of the pace of change in information technology, e-learning and higher education and, in particular, the uncertainty about the impact of electronic storage of the need for space. While others may prefer much longer planning periods, pragmatists may suggest that we should look as far ahead as we can, or perhaps as far as we can afford.

Accessible
social space which is enticing, easy to use and promotes independent discovery

The library is the central academic focus of the university and plays a strong social role in the learning and research processes within the institution. It should be as accessible as possible, encouraging people to make full use of the services it provides. It must cater for the growing number of increasingly demanding 'customers' and their various learning and research styles, and for traditional and electronic modes of delivery. The library should be both visible and transparent, and a familiar architectural language will promote the accessibility and readability of the building: an imaginative design will captivate and retain users (Muscogiuri, 2009).

Access and communication routes should be as clear and straight-forward as possible, with a self-evident layout facilitating independent study. Great progress has been made in providing simple and attractive signage systems located at users' decision points, complemented by digital signs, plasma screens and even audible signs.

The design of busy entrance areas has changed, particularly as libraries have installed smart access control systems and self-service systems. The growth of 24-hour, 7-day access requires attention to the security and robustness of the building and its collections, furniture and equipment, as well as to the safety of readers and staff.

The design must meet the current legal requirements for access by those with disabilities and learning differences, not least because good design for disabled people is generally good design for the able-bodied. The law (UK DDA, 1995) requires institutions to make 'reasonable adjustments' to ensure access by disabled people and makes 'discrimination' against disabled people unlawful. The challenge is to remove architectural barriers to access. Recent disability discrimination legislation has led to significant improvements in access to libraries by people with disabilities and learning differences: it has also had the effect of increasing space requirements in our buildings, often by as much as 20%.

Varied
with a choice of different learning and research spaces and for different media

We should provide a variety of study environments to suit the growing diversity of our users and their different styles of learning and discovery, and give our users the freedom to choose their preferred space. Students should be encouraged to learn at their own pace and in their own time, with provision not only for silent, contemplative and independent learning, but also for group, collaborative and interactive learning (Scottish Funding Council, 2006). Some readers like a quiet study environment with good acoustic and visual privacy; others prefer an 'active' or noisy social learning environment. Indeed, the provision of more social spaces in our libraries is an important trend: some libraries have cafés, lounges and meeting places for students, all designed to encourage collaborative pedagogy (Sens, 2009). Students require spaces for discussing ideas, writing reports and preparing presentations (Ball et al., 2009). The 'hybrid library' must, of course, provide access to both traditional and electronic resources, and an increasing amount of space is devoted to technology-rich services (both wired and wireless provision), with associated information skills training and technical support.

In some cases, interiors have become more like an extension of the living room, providing the 'emotional space' for social interaction within the academic community. Designs have been influenced by trends in retailing, theme parks and entertainment and the need for 'food and computers with everything'. Zones for different modes of study are increasingly common and these areas can be differentiated by architectural clues, such as height, layout, style of furniture, lighting, colour, materials, types of technology and even temperature levels (JISC, 2006). Semi-private or group study environments have been achieved within open spaces with interestingly designed furniture, such as learning pods, screens and canopies (Watson, 2006). Views about the most appropriate colours for learning and scholarly work vary, both in relation to the 'hot' colours required for lively interactive areas and the rather 'cooler' colours appropriate for quiet, contemplative study. One design challenge is to create 'ethnically inclusive' spaces that reflect the growing diversity and ethnicity of our user communities. However, these are complex design issues, and there are tensions between creating flexible and well-defined spaces, and in providing personal spaces in public and social areas within one building.

While many new libraries remain 'stand-alone' projects, others have been planned as innovative 'joined-up' services. Several libraries incorporate a range of non-traditional activities into their building, such as learning cafés (Boone, 2003, 2004), student support services and other social learning spaces. Some universities are providing integrated, one-stop student services, emphasizing their role as the natural hub of the whole campus (Watson, 2006). Others are building joint facilities with partner bodies with whom they are working to broaden participation in learning. In the USA, some new facilities have been built with student services, health centres and other academic services (Blumenstein, 2009; Fox and Jones, 1998). Joint university and public libraries have been built in Scandinavia and the USA (Fox, 2005) and are planned in the UK (Collins, 2009). Exciting new joint amenities are emerging from the closer working relationship between libraries, museums and archives.

There are huge opportunities in planning these multipurpose 'places', but also significant funding, political and organizational challenges.

Interactive

well-organized space which promotes contact between users and services

We must achieve an appropriate balance between the space for collections, services, readers and information technology. A well-designed library will present an appropriate hierarchy of spaces and routes that not only makes optimum use of the space available, but also promotes interaction between people and encourages the use of its services. Enquiry points, group-study spaces and information skills rooms are all key areas of interaction in modern libraries, and planners are experimenting with their design.

Indeed attitudes to the provision of services are changing. Some designs are reflecting a more integrated, customer-friendly approach (McDonald, 2002b), moving away from what may be regarded as an overly complex, 'silo' model of service provision influenced as much by supplier interests as by those of customers (Watson, 2006).

Conducive

attractive space which motivates and inspires people

As the academic heart of the university, the library should convey a sense of quality, value and 'place'. The ambience should be conducive to academic work and reflection, and should encourage and inspire use. Readers, many of whom study for long periods and in increasing numbers, should feel both comfortable and safe.

Imaginative architecture, exciting features and varied internal spaces all contribute to the ambience of the environment. This can be further enhanced by paintings, sculptures, stained glass, internal gardens and other 'cultural artwork', sometimes contributed by students themselves. An investment in a high standard of furnishings and finishes will also create this sense of quality and will withstand heavy use over an extended period with the minimum of maintenance. The library should be a particularly pleasant place in which to be, and much more than an unimaginative 'swotting shed' with high-density, regimented study places.

Noise, particularly from readers themselves and computer clusters, is an increasing problem in libraries and planners are paying considerable attention to the 'acoustic comfort' of new buildings. Indeed, acoustic consultants are now often part of the planning team. Ironically, effective noise management is even more important in buildings where social interaction is encouraged, because it enables users to interact with each other without disturbing others who require silence. There are several approaches to controlling noise in new buildings: using architectural features that encourage silence, enclosing potentially noisy activities, zoning areas and using suitable sound-absorbing floor and ceiling finishes. Markham (2008) suggests introducing appropriate background noise, ensuring physical separation between noise sources and noise-sensitive areas and distributing sound-absorbing materials within the library.

One fundamental dilemma is the design of the staircases in buildings. Some new buildings are designed around an open central staircase for transparent access and airflow considerations, while in others planners have enclosed the staircases to contain the inevitable noise associated with readers moving up and down the building. Atria are increasingly common in naturally ventilated buildings and introduce welcome natural light into the interior, but they too can allow the flow of unwanted noise around the building.

Environmentally suitable
with appropriate conditions for readers, books and computers

Sustainable design, both inside and outside the building, is an important recent trend. Key considerations are the materials used, energy use, water use, lighting, roof design, and heating and ventilation. Rogers and Kuzyk (2009) point to the importance of green products, emissions control and energy conservation. High standards in a building's environmental performance are recognized by national awards, such as the Building Research Establishment Environmental Assessment Method (BREEAM) award in the UK (BRE, 2009). To achieve a 'very good' rating, new buildings must meet 20% of their energy requirements from renewable sources. Students are drawn by green buildings and by universities that take an active interest in environmental issues (Sens, 2009).

Suitable environmental conditions are required not only for the comfort of readers, but also for the efficient operation of some computers and the preservation of library materials. Ideally, temperature, humidity, dust and pollution levels should all be controlled within agreed levels for the building. Natural or passive ventilation, now common in new buildings, provides an affordable, sustainable and a people-friendly solution. Any building or energy management system fitted should be designed to accommodate the lowest common denominator of building management.

The ambient lighting, whether natural or artificial, should be sufficient both for book stacks and reader places, and must take account of the growing use of computer terminals by readers and library staff. Task lighting or individual table lights upgrade the lighting at the reader's desk and are increasingly used to define and differentiate study spaces. Large glazed areas have meant that users can enjoy exterior vistas and natural daylight, but double and even triple glazing, tinting, solar film, blinds or architectural shading are necessary to alleviate the worst effects of noise, solar gain and solar glare (Gallina and Mandyck, 2009). Although glass technology has improved tremendously, energy considerations are leading to more modest fenestration in some buildings. Atria can introduce welcome light and natural ventilation to the centre of large buildings.

Safe and secure

for people, collections, equipment, data and the building

People need to 'feel' safe and secure in the library and this can be achieved by 'reassuring' architecture complemented by various techno-logical solutions for enhancing security (Muscogiuri, 2009). There are security risks associated with the building, its users, collections, equipment and data (Quinsee and McDonald, 1991). The design must conform to current health and safety legislation, and particular attention should be paid to the ergonomic design of workstations, securing IT equipment and to operation during non-standard working hours. Unfortunately, good security measures can sometimes conflict with convenience, aesthetics and even safety.

Efficient
economic in space, staffing and running costs

New libraries must operate as efficiently and economically as possible, and most universities will stress the need for minimum running and maintenance costs. In recent years space utilization and efficiency and life-cycle costs have come under close scrutiny, and projects need to demonstrate value for money in relation to the large capital sums involved. The UK Higher Education Space Management Group (2005a, 2005b, 2005c; 2006a, 2006b, 2006c, 2006d, 2006e, 2006f, 2006g and 2007) provides useful tools to help universities manage their space in an efficient and sustainable way that meets their pedagogic, research and support needs.

Universities may consider the economics and desirability of extending and refurbishing existing buildings as an alternative to constructing new libraries (Drew, 2009; Fox and Cassin, 1996; McDonald, 1993). Existing buildings may have a symbolic, emotional or architectural significance within the university, and refurbishment may be consistent with established campus plans (Jones, 1999). Retail outlets are becoming available for conversion to library use, as a result of the economic downturn. Planners may also consider the economics and convenience of housing certain less-used collections in on- or off-campus stores, often organized on a collaborative basis with other institutions. At the same time, some institutions are comparing the relative life-cycle costs of developing electronic libraries rather than traditional libraries, taking acquisition, storage, management and disposal costs into account.

Suitable for information technology
with flexible provision throughout the building

New space must allow the library and its users to benefit fully from the rapid advances in information technology. We must plan buildings to reflect tomorrow's technologies rather than today's (JISC, 2006), surpassing the demands of the internet and social networking generation (Fox, 1999). Technology is now so embedded that it is 'fading in to the foreground' (JISC, 2007). Even though less than 30% of reader places in libraries in the UK have open access workstations at the moment (SCONUL, 2009), the number of computers, peripheral devices, mobile devices and portable machines continues to grow apace. Nevertheless, the ultimate challenge in a fully networked library is to have the capability to provide a fully networked computer or other device at virtually any point in the building, and with an environment conducive to its use (McDonald et al., 2000).

In designing spaces for effective, technology-rich learning, we must recognize the exciting but considerable challenges presented by trends in e-learning, mobile learning, visual and interactive learning, and in supporting learning (JISC, 2006). The impact of IT is pervasive, affecting virtually every university space, and so provision should be planned within the context of the university's strategies for learning and teaching, research, ICT, information, estates and sustainability. Effective planning relies on the combined wisdom not only of architects and librarians, but also of the computer, networking and e-learning specialists who are increasingly becoming members of the planning team. A suitable proportion of the building budget, typically around 10%, should be devoted to ICT provision to fund the cabling, wireless access, active equipment, connections and hardware required, together with suitable safety, security and environmental measures.

A genuinely flexible IT support infrastructure will enable network access throughout the library, often with a blend of hard-wired and wireless provision. Most new libraries are fully wired up with cabling and trunking around the whole building. Docking stations enable readers to connect their laptops to the network, although we note that only 6% of study places have network connections at the time of writing (SCONUL, 2009). Wireless networking is commonplace now that it has become faster and cheaper, often complementing wired provision. Some planners are concerned about relying entirely on wireless technology because of the capacity of what is essentially a shared service to meet intense simultaneous demand from a large number of PCs. Growth in the use of portable and mobile devices in teaching and learning confirms the need for power throughout the new space, if only for recharging purposes. This is notwithstanding the health and safety concerns relating to the use of personal devices in public buildings.

Planners may choose to wire up all the study places, or they may economize by connecting only a certain proportion of them. Computers are often arranged on tables around the perimeter, where they can easily be served from the wall, but are sometimes placed in the centre of the building to avoid problems of solar glare and gain. In many buildings, computers are simply placed on ordinary tables and this gives the most flexible arrangement, but in others specially designed computer furniture is used. Provision should be made for both standing and seated readers and for collaborative use. In any case, the design of workstations for readers and library staff should respect the appropriate health and safety regulations, particularly in relation to adjustable chairs and screens, and make suitable provision for wire management, for both safety and aesthetic reasons.

Our aim should be to arrange the PCs in an attractive way and provide a high-quality e-learning environment. We should compare the merits of distributed PC provision, close to the collections and other information sources, and separate clusters of machines with the benefit of centralized management and support. Machines can be arranged in separate rooms or in open-plan areas, and clusters often double as teaching areas. Personal, silent spaces need equally good connectivity as group spaces (Ball et al., 2009). Folkestad (2009) draws our attention to different physical arrangements of computer tables to support the increasing need for collaborative learning. In designing the layout, there is an inevitable tension between providing the maximum number of machines and creating a conducive space for learning. Large clusters generate considerable noise and heat, and care must be taken to ensure fire protection and security.

More space than ever before is now devoted to IT services and support and to information skills training. Self-issue and -return systems are radically changing the way in which we design entrance areas and counters, since readers can undertake circulation transactions themselves virtually anywhere in the building. Some libraries no longer have a formal issue desk, providing smaller, lower and friendlier help desks for dealing with enquiries. Radio frequency identification technology is now commonplace, and the use of mechanical book sorting devices, smart card-entry systems and self services are all having an effect on the overall design.

Our approach to planning technology-rich learning spaces is affected by developments in computer technology and network architecture. There is a move to thin client technology, where the application software, data and processing power reside on a network server rather than the client's computer, and in appropriate circumstances this can improve flexibility and sustainability. Mobile technology, cloud computing and green computing are all important influences: indeed, environmentally friendly computing solutions are likely to become a legal requirement.

Conclusion: the library as a 'place'

The future of the library as a physical 'place' has been a matter of considerable professional speculation and debate. Despite some hasty predictions about the imminence and inevitability of the virtual library, universities around the world continue to create new libraries to support learning, teaching and research, often, as it happens, with growing printed collections. Rather than libraries becoming replaced by ICT, the technology has moved into libraries.

Many new libraries are landmark buildings on campus, with a strong 'sense of place', and they have facilitated a 'step change' in support for learning, teaching and research in their institutions. These new buildings continue to provide the 'place' where people can come together to undertake a number of important activities. They come in increasing numbers to study, learn, reflect, interact and exchange ideas. They consult the collections, retrieve information and use the computers provided. They seek the assistance and support of information professionals, and they make use of the whole range of managed services provided. The buildings are often the hub for distributing networked services to off-campus users, and house growing traditional collections and special collections of important research and heritage materials. Importantly, these 'places' help to overcome the 'digital divide' by providing access to information for the information 'have-nots'.

Although the balance between these activities is certain to change, the library building remains the important 'place' where all these essential services can be conveniently provided, even in the virtual age (Hurt, 1997). It is interesting that many of the most automated libraries in the world are still buildings, and most often very pleasant ones too. While older buildings may have accommodated technology, today's new libraries are formed by it (Martin and Kenney, 2004). It is likely that, in the medium term, physical and virtual space will be equally important and the main challenge will be in providing a blended service where the virtual and actual spaces are complementary, influenced by the number and diversity of new technologies.

Libraries remain amongst the most socially inclusive, enduring and well-used 'places' in modern society and so their design must encourage and inspire people (Hoare, 2008). While many crave the silent libraries of the past, others stress the importance of design for interaction and collaboration (Sens, 2009). Indeed, libraries have become important 'third places' where people go for social interaction beyond home and work (Florida, 2000).

Creating good new buildings is critical, not only to the future of our universities, but also to the intellectual capital of our countries. We are witnessing unprecedented and dynamic change in society, higher education, technologies and management. New learning technologies and student-centred approaches have transformed our thinking (Hoare, 2008). Our learning futures will be shaped by new educational ideas, imaginative technology and inspired architecture (Watson, 2007, 2008). Current designs are influenced in particular by social learning, broader access, sustainability and acoustic comfort. These trends, and the considerable challenges they present to planners, are likely to continue at an ever-increasing pace.

Tomorrow's libraries will look and feel very different 'places' from yesterday's buildings. The places we create today will encourage even greater use, stimulating as much as a fivefold increase in demand (Jones, 1999), and will remain lasting tributes to the leadership and vision of those responsible for their planning.

if you build it, he will come.   (*Field of Dreams*, 1989)

References

Ball, D., Beard, J. and Dale, P. (2009) *Small Changes – Big Difference: Bournemouth University Library and its learning community*, Paper presented at the IFLA Conference on Libraries as Place and Space, Turin, August 2009, www.ifla2009.it/online/wp-content/uploads/2009/06/Final.Ball.pdf.

Bazillion, R. J. and Braun, C. (1994) Academic Library Design: building a 'teaching instrument', *Computers in Libraries*, 14 (2), 12–16.

Bennett, S. (2005) *Righting the Balance, Library as Place: rethinking roles, rethinking space*, Council on Library and Information Resources Publication 129, (February), 10–24.

Blumenstein, L. (2009) The Heart of the Campus, *Library Journal*, Fall (Library by Design), 34.

Boone, M. D. (2003) Monastery to Marketplace: a paradigm shift, *Library Hi Tech*, **21** (3), 358–67.

Boone, M. D. (2004) The Way Ahead: learning cafés in the academic marketplace, *Library Hi Tech*, **22** (3), 323–8.

Brand, S. (1994) *How Buildings Learn: what happens after they're built*, Viking-Penguin.

Brown, W. M. (2009) Future-proof Design, *Library Journal*, Fall (Library by Design), 1–10.

Building Research Establishment (BRE) (2009) *BRE Environmental Assessment Method* (BREEAM), www.bre.co.uk/page.jsp?id=829.

Cannell, S. (2007) SCONUL Library Design Awards, *SCONUL Focus, ***42**, 92–4.

Carmack, B. (1992) Outline of the Building Planning Process: the players. In Martin, R. G. (ed.), *Libraries for the Future: planning buildings that work*, American Library Association (Library Administration and Management Association), 25–9.

Collins, T. (2009) Innovative £60m Library Approved for Worcester, *Birmingham Post,* (28 July), www.birminghampost.net/news/west-midlands-education-news/2009/07/28/ innovative-60m-library-approved-for-worcester-65233-24252636/.

Designing Libraries (2009) *Designing Libraries: the gateway to better library design*, www.designinglibraries.org.uk/.

Dowlin, K. E. (1999) San Francisco Public Library. In: Bisbrouck, M-F. and Chauveinc, M. (eds), *Intelligent Library Buildings: proceedings of the 10th seminar of the IFLA Section on Library Buildings and Equipment, The Hague, Netherlands, August, 1997*, Saur.

Drew, M. (2009) *Renewing our Libraries: case studies in re-planning and refurbishment*, Ashgate.

Edwards, B. (2009) *Libraries and Learning Resource Centres*, 2nd edn, Elsevier.

Faulkner-Brown, H. (1993) *The Initial Brief,* IFLA Section on Library Buildings and Equipment.

Faulkner-Brown, H. (1998) Some Thoughts on the Design of Major Library Buildings. In Bisbrouck, M.-F. and Chauveinc, M. (eds), *Intelligent Library Buildings: proceedings of the 10th seminar of the IFLA Section on Library Buildings and Equipment, The Hague, Netherlands, August, 1997*, Saur.

Field of Dreams (1989) Film directed by Robinson, P. A., written by Kinsella, W. P., and Robinson, P. A., and produced by Frankish, B. E., Gordon, C. and Gordon, L., Gordon Company.

Florida, R. (2000) *The Rise of the Creative Class: and how it's transforming work, leisure, community and everyday life*, Basic Books.

Folkestad, J. E. (2009) Promoting Collaboration: the physical arrangement of library computers, *Library Hi Tech News*, **26** (1/2), 18-19.

Fox, B.-L. (1999) Structural Ergonomics, *Library Journal*, **124** (20), 57.

Fox, B.-L. (2005) A Storm Rains on Our Parade, *Library Journal,* **130** (20), 44–58.

Fox, B.-L. and Cassin, E. (1996) Beating the High Cost of Libraries, *Library Journal*, **121** (20), 43–55.

Fox, B.-L. and Jones, E. J. (1998) Another Year, Another $543 Million, *Library Journal*, **123** (20), 41–3.

Gallina, C. and Mandyck, C. (2009) Light Done Right, *Library Journal*, Fall (Library by Design), 1–9.

Guardian (2008) *Libraries Unleashed,* (22 April), 1–7 (Guardian Newsprint Supplement).

Heppel, S., Chapman, C., Millwood, R., Constable, M. and Furness, J. (2004) *Building Research Futures*. A research project at Ultralab within the CABE/RIBA 'Building Futures' programme, http://rubble.heppel.net/cabe/final_report.pdf.

Hoare, S. (2008) *Libraries Unleashed: buildings need to inspire, Guardian*, (22 April), 2.

Holt, R. M. (1989) *Planning Library Buildings and Facilities – from Concept to Completion*, Scarecrow Press.

Hurt, C. (1997) Building Libraries in the Virtual Age, *College and Research Libraries News*, **58** (2), 75–6, 91.

Joint Information Systems Committee (JISC) (2006) *Designing Spaces for Effective Learning: a guide to 21st century learning space design*, www.jisc.ac.uk/media/documents/publications/learningspaces.pdf.

Joint Information Systems Committee (JISC) (2007) *Student Expectations Study: key findings from online research discussion evenings held in June 2007 for the Joint Information Systems Committee*, www.jisc.ac.uk/publications/documents/studentexpectationsbp.aspx.

Jones, W. G. (1999) *Library Buildings: renovation and reconfiguration,* Association of Research Libraries, Office of Leadership and Management Services, Washington (Issues and Innovations in Transforming Libraries, SPEC Kit 244).

Khan, A. (2009) *Better by Design: an introduction to planning and designing a new library building*, Facet Publishing.

McDonald, A. C. (1993) The Refurbishment of Libraries – What Should You be Looking For?, *Aslib Information*, **21** (1), 32–5.

McDonald, A. C. (2002a) Celebrating Outstanding New Library Buildings, *SCONUL Newsletter*, **27**, (Winter), 82–5 (Society of College, National and University Libraries).

McDonald, A. C. (2002b) Planning Academic Library Buildings for Customers and Services. In: Melling, M. and Little, Y. (eds), *Building a Successful Customer-service Culture: a guide for library and information managers*, Facet Publishing.

McDonald, A. C. (2003) Creating Good Learning Space. In: *Libraries with Oomph: PFI for higher education libraries: Papers delivered at a Seminar*, Nabarro Nathanson.

McDonald, A. C. (2006) The Ten Commandments Revisited: the qualities of good library space, *LIBER Quarterly: The Journal of European Research Libraries*, **16** (2), http://webdoc.gwdg.de/edoc/aw/liber/lq-2-06/mcdonald.pdf.

McDonald, A. C. (2007a) How Was it for You? The building and design process in practice. In: Latimer, K. and Niegaard, H. (eds), *IFLA Library Building Guidelines: developments and reflections*, Saur (International Federation of Library Associations and Institutions, Section on Library Buildings and Equipment).

McDonald, A. C. (2007b) The Top Ten Qualities of Good Library Space. In: Latimer, K. and Niegaard, H. (eds), *IFLA Library Building Guidelines: developments and reflections*, Saur (International Federation of Library Associations and Institutions, Section on Library Buildings and Equipment).

McDonald, A. C., Edwards, V., Range, P. and Webster, D. (2000) *Information and Communications Technology in Academic Library Buildings*, Standing Conference of National and University Libraries (SCONUL Briefing Paper).

Markham, B. (2008) The Right Kind of Quiet, *Library Journal*, Fall (Library by Design), 32.

Martin, E. and Kenney, B. (2004) Library Building 2004 – Great Libraries in the Making, *Library Journal*, **129** (20), 70–2.

Mason, E. (1996) Management of Library Building Planning, *Journal of Library and Information Science*, **22**, 14–28.

Muscogiuri, M. (2009) *Scenario and Strategies of Design for the Libraries of the 21st Century, Paper presented at the IFLA Conference on Libraries as Place and Space, Turin, August 2009*, www.ifla2009.it/online/wp-content/uploads/2009/06/Final.Muscogiuri.pdf.

Niegaard, H., Lauridsen, J. and Schulz, K. (2008) *Library Space: inspiration for buildings and design*, Danish Library Association.

Quinsee, A. C. and McDonald, A. C. (1991) *Security in Academic and Research Libraries*, Newcastle University Library.

Revill, D. (1996) *Working Papers on Architects' Briefs*, Standing Conference of National and University Libraries (SCONUL Working Paper).

Rockwell, E. (1989) The Seven Deadly Sins of Architects, *American Libraries*, April, 307.

Rogers, M. and Kuzyk, R. (2009) Green in Lean Times, *Library Journal*, Fall (Library by Design), 10–11.

Sens, T. (2009) Twelve Keys to Library Design, *Library Journal*, Spring (Library by Design), 34.

Society of College, National and University Libraries (SCONUL) (2009) *Annual Library Statistics 2007–08*, Society of College, National and University Libraries.

Taylor, S. (1994) *Building Libraries for the Information Age: based on the proceedings of a symposium on Future of Higher Educational Libraries, King's Manor, York, 11–12 April*, Institute of Advanced Architectural Studies, University of York.

UK Disability Discrimination Act (DDA) (1995) Her Majesty's Stationery Office (Public General Act).

UK Higher Education Space Management Group (2005a) *Drivers of the Size of the HE Estate*, HEFCE, www.smg.ac.uk/documents/drivers.pdf.

UK Higher Education Space Management Group (2005b) *Review of Practice Report*, HEFCE, www.smg.ac.uk/documents/reviewofpractice.pdf.

UK Higher Education Space Management Group (2005c) *The Cost of Space Report*, HEFCE, www.smg.ac.uk/documents/costofspace.pdf.

UK Higher Education Space Management Group (2006a) *Impact on Space of Future Changes in Higher Education*, HEFCE, www.smg.ac.uk/documents/FutureChangesInHE.pdf.

UK Higher Education Space Management Group (2006b) *Managing Space: review of English further and HE overseas*, HEFCE, www.smg.ac.uk/documents/FEandoverseas.pdf.

UK Higher Education Space Management Group (2006c) *Promoting Space Efficiency in Building Design*, HEFCE, www.smg.ac.uk/documents/PromotingSpaceEfficiency.pdf.

UK Higher Education Space Management Group (2006d) *Review of Space Norms*, HEFCE, www.smg.ac.uk/documents/spacenorms.pdf.

UK Higher Education Space Management Group (2006e) *Space Management Case Studies*, HEFCE,
www.smg.ac.uk/documents/casestudies.pdf.

UK Higher Education Space Management Group (2006f) *Space Management Project: a summary*, HEFCE,
www.smg.ac.uk/documents/summary.pdf.

UK Higher Education Space Management Group (2006g) *Space Utilisation: practice, performance and guideline*, HEFCE,
www.smg.ac.uk/documents/utilisation.pdf.

UK Higher Education Space Management Group (2007) *Implementing SMG Guidance,* UK Higher Education Space Management Project, HEFCE,
www.smg.ac.uk/documents/Implementing%20SMG%20Guidance%202007.pdf.

Watson, L. (2006) The Saltire Centre at Glasgow Caledonian University, *SCONUL Focus,* 37, (Spring), 4–11.

Watson, L. (2007) Building the Future of Learning, *European Journal of Education*, 42 (2), 255–63.

Watson, L. (2008) Libraries for the 21st Century. In: Weaver, M. (ed.), *Transforming Learning Support Models in Higher Education: educating the whole student*, Facet Publishing.

Wu, J. (2003) *New Library Buildings of the World*, 2nd edn, Shanghai Scientific & Technological Literature Publishing House.

4

Web 2.0: redefining and extending the service commitment of the academic library

James G. Neal and Damon E. Jaggars

Introduction

Web 2.0 advances the capacity for communication, collaboration, and contribution. By promoting social interaction and content exchange, Web 2.0 responds to 'human' objectives. People want to be successful. They want things to turn out well, and to achieve their personal goals. People want to be happy. They care about their well-being and contentment. People want to be productive, achieving results and realizing benefits. People want progress, a sense of betterment and forward movement. People want relationships, satisfying personal connections and attachments. People want experiences, sometimes as observers and sometimes as participants. People want to have impact, to influence events and people, and to have a significant effect. How can academic libraries tap into these 'human' interests and build more responsive and effective service programmes?

Web 2.0 and library users

Web 2.0 advances the focus on the interests of users and the expectations they bring to service environments that are increasingly dependent on digital and network technologies and tools. Users seek customization and personalization, the ability to shape content and applications to their personal interests and styles. They want enhanced openness, a free flow and exchange of information and ideas, without barriers. They seek a self-service capability to control and act on their needs, with minimal intervention by others. They embrace the reality of mutability, of constant change and hybrid approaches and styles. They see the value of collective intelligence and the need to question traditional sources of authority and prerogative. They increasingly understand software not as a product, but as a service, a capability shaped by many for the benefit of all. How can academic libraries leverage these new requirements and embrace the user more actively and iteratively in service conceptualization, development and delivery?

Web 2.0 highlights the shifting requirements that users bring to the technologies that are so integral to their personal and professional lives. Clearly, users want more and better content and access. They want convenience and new capabilities, to do things they never were able to do before. They seek high levels of participation and control over the information and service settings where they work and share. And they expect enhanced levels of individual and group productivity, to get more done with lower and even no cost. Web 2.0 should mean rapid technology development and deployment, never really finalized and always a work in progress. It means perpetual assessment, constantly evaluating and reshaping. It means the erosion of boundaries among creators and consumers and intermediaries, and an expectation of joint and shared jurisdiction and responsibility. How can academic libraries build technology settings and capacities that reflect these values and requirements?

Web 2.0 and library service

Web 2.0 explodes the user community and extends participation beyond the traditional user base that has governed the work of service organizations like academic libraries. Student diversity abounds, and faculty expectations accelerate. Researchers and the world of users on the web present extraordinary disciplinary differences and a new majority of content and service consumers. Local communities have raised expectations, and alumni and supporters seek new relationships and roles. The service interactions of the library combine physical and network spaces, new collecting and application development capacities, new relationships in the classroom and the laboratory, and an anyone, anywhere, anytime, anyhow commitment to support. How can academic libraries extend understanding and resources to an increasingly far-flung and voracious user community?

Web 2.0 enables the academic library to be responsive to key trends and technologies which are influencing the work of higher education. An important annual report, the Horizon Report for 2009 prepared by the New Media Consortium and EDUCAUSE, provides invaluable guidance to academic libraries seeking to advance a 2.0 service capacity (Johnson et al., 2009). Among the trends it cites are the following: the rapid globalization of communication and collaboration, the expanding role of collective intelligence with all its ambiguity and imprecision, the participation and interaction promoted by games as learning tools, the meaningful and intuitive nature of visualization tools, the demand for new and enhanced information and visual and technology literacy, the de-formalism and de-structuring of scholarship, and the expanded focus on assessment and the measurement of quality and impact. The Horizon Report also discusses the critical new technologies that will influence the work of higher education, including: the rampant growth in mobile and multipurpose personal devices, the distributed processing and applications enabled by cloud computing, the power of geo-everything, but especially geolocation and geotagging, the importance of the personal web with customized management of online content, the role of semantic-aware applications which increasingly rely on meaning and context to provide answers, and the availability of smart objects which link the physical world and information. Understanding and applying these trends and technologies will be critical to academic library success in Web 2.0 service development.

Rethinking academic library functions

The academic library will need to rethink its core responsibilities and the way work and services are organized and delivered. What do libraries in the academy do in support of teaching and learning, and research and scholarship? They select, acquire, synthesize, disseminate, interpret, apply and archive information. They enable users to navigate, discover, obtain, understand, use and apply information. How will 2.0 service capabilities reshape, undermine or extend these roles? As libraries take on new purposes as aggregators, publishers, educators, research and development organizations, entrepreneurs and policy advocates, how will this shift their relationships with users and extend and enhance the interest and ability to tap into 2.0 capabilities? Traditional library values are very much challenged by 2.0 developments. The level of communication and sharing enabled by 2.0 raises concerns about intellectual freedom, the level of civility in online and virtual interactions, the maintenance of privacy and confidentiality, the stability, integrity and free flow of information, and the subverting of trust in relationships. Where is the durability, where is the authority, where is the community in the face of constant partial attention and massively distributed collaboration?

What do students want, and how can Web 2.0 help libraries to satisfy these expectations? Students want technology and content ubiquity, supported by point-of-need information and embedded services. They want sandboxes for fun and experimentation, with some balance between anonymity and personal connection. They want social success, academic success and career success. What do faculty want, and similarly how can Web 2.0 enable libraries to be responsive? They want personal advancement and recognition, achieved through contributions to the scholarly literature and high-quality instructional experiences. They want to work on innovative projects, and the ability to connect and collaborate with interesting colleagues and former students around the world. They want excellent laboratory, library and technology support, not limited by time and space.

So in this context of a rapidly evolving academic environment, how do Web 2.0 capabilities fit into a library service programme? The options and opportunities are remarkable: social networking, media sharing, social bookmarking and tagging, wikis, blogs, RSS, mash ups, chat and instant messaging, virtual worlds, widgets, podcasts, games, mobile devices, virtual communities and so on. How do libraries move users from a passive receipt of content and services to a new level of action and participation? Or perhaps better, how do users move libraries to radically democratize their content and services, and eliminate technical, proprietary and economic barriers?

Academic use of non-library tools

Describing the evolving behaviours both demonstrated within and enabled by the use of Web 2.0 social computing technologies, Lorcan Dempsey relates how 'Users are constructing their own digital workflows and identities out of a variety of network services' (Dempsey, 2008).

Scholars grow increasingly reliant on network-based workflows for research and learning; and the entry points to these workflows are becoming increasingly distributed across various platforms and devices. Where academic libraries have concentrated on deploying content and services from a centrally organized website to users' desktops, scholars increasingly live and work in online environments distinct from the library website, utilizing course management systems such as Blackboard and Sakai, social computing platforms like Facebook and LinkedIn, personal web portals such as iGoogle and MyYahoo!, content sharing sites like Flickr and YouTube, social tagging services like Delicious, news aggregators, blogs, locally installed browser plug-ins and widgets etc., etc. As mobile communications platforms mature, these scholarly workflows will continue to diverge from the desktop and toward the handheld computing environment (think iPhone, Google Android, and netbooks).

Academic library users report using Google, Yahoo!, and other non-library search tools far more often than library websites or physical library facilities. In North American research libraries, 73% of faculty and students report daily use of web-based search engines, versus 29% for library websites and just under 15% for physical libraries (Cook et al., 2006). In addition to routinely choosing search engines over physical libraries or library websites to discover and locate information, college students overwhelmingly use search engines as the starting point of their information searches, with 89% starting with search engines, versus 2% with library websites and 2% with online databases (De Rosa et al., 2005).

What does it all mean for libraries?

So what should academic libraries do to respond to their users' move into diffuse network research and learning environments? How do they continue to effectively support scholars and students with high-quality content and services when the once well-worn path from the library website to the user's desktop is decreasingly on the scholar's crowded itinerary? The most obvious response is for academic libraries to proactively move content and services into the network environments where scholars and students live and work. Dempsey describes how 'Libraries have always been eager to "fit in" to their users' lives. In a network-based scholarly environment, this means "fitting in" with evolving network workflows' by embedding library content and services into the various search, discovery, and organization tools to which users increasingly turn to manage their scholarly and personal lives (Dempsey, 2005).

Integrating the library into the new scholarly workflows

If academic libraries hope to support current and evolving information-seeking behaviours, they must integrate into their users' network-based workflows by exposing as much content as possible to search engines, making it discoverable where users are most likely to be working. For example, many academic libraries are exposing their holdings data to web crawlers from Google and other search engines through the OCLC Open WorldCat programme, generating substantial traffic (or 'click-throughs') back to local library catalogues (Gatenby, 2007). Others are registering the link resolvers they use to manage user access to electronic journal content with Google Scholar's Library Links Program, thereby creating links in Google Scholar search results back to full-text content provided locally. Still others are exposing digital collections of various types held in local repositories to search engine harvesters, thus improving the discoverability of these collections for scholars and driving a significant increase in usage of this locally held content (Boston, 2005).

Another method for integrating library content into scholarly workflows is to add unique collections to heavily trafficked content-sharing sites. For example, the Library of Congress has loaded thousands of historical photos into Flickr and is providing increasing amounts of video content on YouTube. This content can be found by users searching Flickr and YouTube but is also indexed by search engines, thus making it discoverable by Google and Yahoo! users as well. The 6,700+ images from the Library of Congress Flickr photo stream receive approximately 800,000 views per month, and one video that had received approximately 20,000 total views in over five years on the library website received approximately 13,500 views in only five months on YouTube (Kroski, 2009).

Academic librarians, curators, and archivists at some institutions are becoming active content contributors to Wikipedia, the heavily trafficked online, user-generated encyclopedia, and another online location where many users begin their research. By creating entries about special or archival collections, or links within existing entries to unique holdings, libraries can expose previously hidden and underutilized content to users at their point of need. Links can be placed in bibliographic entries in Wikipedia articles, referring back to archival finding aids and local digital content, and thus drive increased traffic to a library's website (Lally and Dunford, 2007). As with Flickr and YouTube, Wikipedia articles are crawled and indexed by search engines, often appearing at the top of results lists for many Google and Yahoo! searches. By exposing as much content as possible to search engines, content-sharing services and other network environments where scholars increasingly live and work, academic libraries are better able to get the high-quality content they hold into their users' research, teaching and learning processes at the point of need, and scholars benefit by gaining the abilities to discover and access information heretofore excluded from their preferred workflows.

Technologies for sharing and reusing

Technology publisher and open source software proponent Tim O'Reilly describes Web 2.0 in terms of 'delivering software as a continually-updated service that gets better the more people use it, consuming and remixing data from multiple sources, including individual users, while providing their own data and services in a form that allows remixing by others, creating network effects through an "architecture of participation" . . .' (O'Reilly, 2005). Thriving in this new participatory environment entails providing content in formats that can be easily pushed to, shared with, and reused by users and network platforms. Many academic libraries are enabling users to subscribe to content feeds (news, events, new acquisitions lists, or any other content that can be divided into distinct parts) using RSS (Real Simple Syndication), Atom or other similar syndication services, most often accessed through the user's news reader application or an RSS-enabled web browser. RSS increases the 'portability' of information, 'so that it can be read in different places and used in multiple ways' (Farkas, 2007). The portability of RSS-enabled information allows anyone subscribing to a feed to reuse or recycle it in useful ways. For example, some academic libraries use RSS newsfeeds from their websites to dynamically populate the content found on their institutional Facebook and MySpace profiles. Others use RSS feeds to share new acquisitions lists on subject-based research guides and on course pages in course management systems. Expanding on this approach, the University of Texas at Austin Libraries use a combination of RSS and FriendFeed, a popular service that aggregates and enables sharing across various social networking platforms, to automatically populate its Facebook and Twitter presences by reusing blog posts and news from the library website, photos added to Flickr, and video tutorials posted to YouTube (Sitar, 2009). Supporting this new 'architecture of participation,' some academic libraries have integrated bookmarking and sharing services such as AddThis or ShareThis into their websites, local digital collections and library catalogues. Such services provide tools for users to seamlessly add content to their personal profiles on popular bookmarking services like Delicious, social networking sites like Facebook and LinkedIn, to social news services such as digg and Technorati, and to scores of other social computing services and applications.

The flip side to providing content in formats that users can easily recycle and reuse on other network platforms is for academic libraries to combine functionality from multiple external data sources or services to create hybrid services, or 'mash-ups'. Mash-ups are usually created using open APIs, or application programming interfaces, by which software developers define how external applications can request services or data from network-based applications or databases. Academic libraries have created interesting and useful mash-ups using APIs from Amazon.com to integrate book cover images and other content into their library catalogues. Others have installed the Google Book Search API in their library catalogues, enabling users to view previews, snippets and full text of books scanned by the Google Book Project. Still others have installed the LibraryThing For Libraries service, thus offering users a book recommender service, reviews, ratings and the ability to browse using social tags, all integrated into the library catalogue. Rather than developing these interactive applications independently, libraries can tap into the over 42 million catalogued books, 780,000 reviews, 7 million book ratings, and 54 million tags, created by over 800,000 LibraryThing users to assist local users in discovering information from locally held collections (LibraryThing, 2009).

Social networking the library to its users

Social networking environments such as Facebook and MySpace offer participatory platforms where users socialize, share information, content and build relationships. Creating an active presence in social networking environments offers academic libraries the ability to promote research support and instruction services, news and events, in online environments where students, and increasingly faculty, spend more and more of their time both working and socializing. A recent study from the Pew Internet & American Life Project reports that 57% of adults aged 25–34 who use the internet have a profile on a social networking site, increasing to 75% for adults aged 18–24 (Lenhart, 2009). Social networking platforms provide tools for libraries to integrate both content and services directly into the user experience at the point of need. Libraries can create applications that allow users to search library catalogues, article databases and FAQs, connect to virtual reference services and view video tutorials. Libraries can add news feeds, photos, video, information about events, and anything else that might create meaningful connections with their users. Similarly, web portal platforms such as iGoogle, MyYahoo! and Netvibes offer academic libraries the ability to create customized applications (known as 'widgets' or 'gadgets') that users can include on their personal web start pages with their news feeds, e-mail, calendar, to do lists and other productivity services. Once installed, these widgets allow users to search library catalogues and article databases, connect to chat reference services and learn about library events from the comfort of their customized web space.

Closer to home, academic libraries are actively integrating library services and content into course management systems like Blackboard and Sakai. Students spend large amounts of time interacting with course management systems: accessing syllabi, assignments and course readings; and communicating with other students in course-specific discussion forums and chat rooms. Academic libraries have responded by locating subject-based research guides, course reserve materials, relevant new acquisitions feeds, and links to virtual reference services directly onto specific course pages.

Plugging the library into browsers

Scholarly and personal workflows are increasingly becoming network-based, and the primary user interface to the network is the web browser. Whether it's Microsoft's Internet Explorer, Mozilla Firefox, or Apple's Safari, the web browser is *the* tool through which users work and play on the web. Recognizing this fact, many academic libraries have created browser plug-ins that users can download and install to enable library catalogue searching directly from the browser search box. Taking browser customization a step further, others offer localized versions of the LibX toolbar, which enables library catalogue and article searches, integration with federated search platforms like ExLibris's MetaLib, and the ability to quickly and easily launch searches in configured databases by simply copying text found on the web. Many academic libraries are also enabling their users to connect to locally held electronic resources found in articles on the web. After a library has registered its link resolver with OCLC, users can download and install the OCLC OpenURL Referrer add-on to their Firefox or Internet Explorer browser; and links from bibliographic citations found in web-based resources like Google Scholar and Wikipedia are created, linking back to locally provided journal articles and other content.

Services to mobile library users

As internet-based social computing platforms break down geographical barriers to personal connection and interaction, mobile computing technologies, such as smart phones and netbooks are breaking the static connection between network-based workflows and the personal computer desktop. The emergence of functional mobile computing technologies enables ubiquitous ('anywhere, anytime') access to e-mail, chat, texting, web-browsing and an increasing number of useful network services and applications. A growing number of mobile technology users report using the internet from their mobile devices; in 2009, 23% accessed the internet daily from their cell phone or other mobile device, up from 14% in 2007 (Horrigan, 2009). As smart phones, PDAs and other mobile devices become more powerful with the growing improvement of the mobile web experience, the percentage of users accessing the internet via mobile devices will continue to increase. Academic libraries are beginning to take notice of this trend and have begun experimenting with service offerings geared toward the mobile user. Adding to their telephone, e-mail and chat services, some academic libraries are beginning to offer reference service to mobile users through SMS (Simple Messaging Service) or text messaging. Services such as libraryh3lp and Text a Librarian have sprung up to provide the technical infrastructure to support text-based services for mobile library users. Some academic libraries are creating simplified versions of their library catalogues and websites, optimized for use on the small screens found on cell phones and other mobile devices. OCLC has released an iPhone application (or 'app') enabling users to search WorldCat and locate resources at their local academic or public library. Similarly, a few intrepid libraries have created customized iPhone applications of their own, allowing users to search the local library catalogue and access virtual reference services from the popular smart phone platform. The Kindle, the portable e-book reader from Amazon.com, is being used in a number of pilot projects in academic libraries to supply textbooks and other course materials to students. And many academic libraries are loading podcasts of lectures, tours, orientations and tutorials onto both iTunes U and YouTube, which can be downloaded to and accessed from users' compatible devices.

The library as a Web 2.0 organization

These illustrations and discussions indicate clearly that academic libraries are stepping up to the challenges and opportunities of Web 2.0 services. Experiments and pilots are important, and will remain a fundamental component of the healthy user programme, but how do we mainstream Web 2.0 culture, thinking and action into the core of the library programme? A critical element is rethinking organizational structure and purpose. We can think of an organization as individuals and groups carrying out roles and working together to achieve shared objectives within a formal social and political structure and with established policies and processes. Organization is the tool through which goals and priorities are established, decisions are made, resources are allocated, power is wielded, and plans are accomplished. A Web 2.0 organization considers carefully how administrative responsibility and authority are distributed and shared, how operations and procedures are integrated and flexible, how policies and norms are designed and enforced, and how fluidity and vitality contribute to productivity and success.

Academic libraries are increasingly embracing organizational models which support 2.0 thinking and action. They are moving away from conventional administrative hierarchies and academic bureaucracies, to a combination of centralized planning and resource allocation systems, loosely coupled academic structures, and maverick units and entrepreneurial enterprises. The key characteristics which support a 2.0 culture are: decentralization, distribution, adhocracy, complexity, informality, innovation and collaboration. Academic libraries must redefine the physical, expertise and intellectual infrastructure, while promoting and understanding the geography, psychology and economics of innovation.

The Web 2.0 librarian

Another critical element is rethinking the ways the academic library workforce is attracted and developed. The 2.0 library advancing 2.0 services needs new skills, but also a new attitude. It is essential that the role of professional education be rethought, and that the recruitment and employment of staff be re-engineered to embrace a wide range of academic and professional credentials and a more fluid definition of job responsibilities. This will have a wide impact on the values, outlooks, styles and expectations of the library organization. And it will influence academic community understanding, recognition, respect and support for the work of the library. We need to redefine our expectations for the professional working in the library, with a particular focus in the following areas: a commitment to rigour, a commitment to research and development, a commitment to evaluation and assessment, communication and marketing skills, political engagement, project development and management skills, entrepreneurial spirit, resource development skills, leadership and inspirational qualities, a commitment to continuous improvement, an embracing of ambiguity, a sense of adventure, and deep subject or technical expertise. An academic library cannot thrive as a 2.0 service organization without a staff that is dominated by these essential qualities and characteristics.

Conclusion

The 2.0 academic library is focused on the demands of heightened accountability and assessment, involving its users routinely and aggressively in the development and evaluation of services. Assessment is not just a product of institutional and government expectations and mandates, but also reflects an energized approach to new measures of user satisfaction, success, impact, cost effectiveness, design for usability and market penetration. The 2.0 academic library builds new strategies for marketing products and services, seeking to match the capabilities of the organization with the needs and wants of the communities served. This means not just maximizing support for current users, but also extending the market and developing new markets, and diversifying the product line. Marketing also assumes the ability of the library to move its capabilities to the places where its current and prospective users work. The 2.0 library pursues new arenas for collaboration with other libraries, with other parts of the university and with new partners in the corporate sector. A new and sometimes radical focus on the mass-production work of the library, on the special centres of excellence, on new technology infrastructures, and on new initiatives like 2.0 services requires a new approach to combinations, to sustainability and business planning, to legal and governance structures, to the application of risk capital, and to a competitive spirit. Can the 2.0 library of the future be defined in the neat historical context of an individual institution?

What are 2.0 academic libraries focused on as they confront the extraordinary current context of rapidly shifting user behaviours and expectations, redundant and inefficient library operations, a mandate to achieve scale and network effects through aggregation, the new economic and fiscal realities and the urgency of systemic change? How do they build 2.0 services as they construct the digital library, a combination of quality content and functionality, create content management portals and virtual disciplinary communities, assess the role of the massive search engine libraries, preserve and archive the content, support the course management system and expansion of online learning, support the needs of big science and enrich research through text- and data-mining services, transform scholarly communication, advance the open access and repository movements, support the globalization goals of the university, rethink library space planning and identity, and develop and attract new resources?

References

Boston, T. (2005) *Exposing the Deep Web to Increase Access to Library Collections*, http://ausweb.scu.edu.au/aw05/papers/refereed/boston/paper.html.

Cook, C. et al. (2006) *LibQUAL+® 2006 Survey*, Washington DC, Association of Research Libraries, 166.

Dempsey, L. (2005) *In the Flow ...*, Lorcan Dempsey's Weblog: on libraries, services and networks, http://orweblog.oclc.org/archives/000688.html.

Dempsey, L. (2008) *Stuck in the Middle ...*, Lorcan Dempsey's Weblog: on libraries, services and networks, http://orweblog.oclc.org/archives/001700.html.

De Rosa, C. et al. (2005) *Perceptions of Libraries and Information Resources*, OCLC, 1–17.

Farkas, M. (2007) *Social Software in Libraries*, Medford NJ, Information Today Inc., 50.

Gatenby, J. (2007) Accessing Library Materials via Google and Other Web Sites, *BiD: textos unversitaris de biblioteconomia i documentació*, 19, www2.ub.edu/bid/consulta_articulos.php?fichero=19gatenb.htm.

Horrigan, J. (2009), Wireless Internet Use, *Pew Internet and American Life Project*, www.pewinternet.org/Reports/2009/12-Wireless-Internet-Use.aspx.

Johnson, L., Levine, A. and Smith, R. (2009) *2009 Horizon Report*, The New Media Consortium, www.nmc.org/pdf/2009-Horizon-Report.pdf.

Kroski, E. (2009) The Library of Congress Talks Digital Initiatives, *Library Journal Online*, www.libraryjournal.com/article/CA6675049.html?rssid=191.

Lally, A. and Dunford, C. (2007) Using Wikipedia to Extend Digital Collections, *D-Lib Magazine*, 13 (5/6), www.dlib.org/dlib/may07/lally/05lally.html.

Lenhart, A. (2009) Adults and Social Network Websites, *Pew Internet and American Life Project*, www.pewinternet.org/Reports/2009/Adults-and-Social-Network-Websites.aspx?r=1.

LibraryThing (2009) *LibraryThing Zeitgeist*, www.librarything.com/zeitgeist.

O'Reilly, T. (2005) Web 2.0: compact definition, *O'Reilly Radar,* http://radar.oreilly.com/2005/10/web-20-compact-definition.html.

Sitar, M. (2009) Social Networking at the UT Libraries, *TIS Lab Blog*, http://blogs.lib.utexas.edu/tis/?p=144.

5

Second Life and libraries: boom or bust?

P. Charles Livermore (SL: Hopalong Oh)

Introduction

Second Life (SL) is arguably the most popular and well known of what are known as multi-user-virtual-environments (MUVEs). While awareness and knowledge of MUVEs is growing there are still many who have only a vague idea of what they are and how they relate to the future of libraries and higher education. In 2008 Educause added a section on SL to its '7 things you should know about . . .' series,[1] which provides a useful framework for this discussion.

> Launched in 2003, Second Life is the largest virtual world, with tens of millions of square meters of virtual lands, more than 13 million registered users (or 'residents'), and a thriving economy. . . . Developers of Second Life continue to refine the application, adding functionality and increasing the level at which aspects of the environment – such as the flowing of water, the movement of trees in the wind, the way light changes during the course of a day – reflect those of the real world. Residents of Second Life exist 'in-world' through personal avatars, [animated figures that can walk, run and fly] and can spend time in any of a vast number of locations (or 'islands') that have been created for purposes including education, socializing, entertainment and commerce.
> (Educause, 2008)

The costs of a Second Life

One question that arises early in any discussion of SL is that of cost. It is possible to participate in SL without any expenditure of money. There is no cost for the SL program download, nor for the avatar and its use. While some areas of SL are blocked from entry by their owners, most areas are open to the public at no cost. Additionally, many interest groups have been organized. You can join multiple groups at no cost and receive notification of their activities. Most of these activities – poetry readings, plays, dances, classes, discussion groups – are also available at no cost. And there are locations called 'sandboxes' on which you can build and script objects to store, at no cost, in your inventory. 'Sandboxes' are regularly cleaned of the objects created there. You must own, be given owner privileges or rent property in SL in order to permanently place objects. Owning land costs money. An educational 'island' of 16 acres recently sold for US$700 with an upkeep fee of US$70 a month. People who own an island can rent smaller portions of it to other individuals.

What you need to know about SL

Here is a summary of SL and comments on other things you should know about it.

Who's in SL?

Churches, countries, businesses, schools, universities.

According to a 2007 article, 'More than 150 colleges in the United States and 13 other countries have a presence in Second Life' (Foster, 2007a). In my own explorations, I have visited the SL campuses of Vassar College, Princeton University, Rutgers University, Georgia State, New York University, Penn State and Bowling Green State University, to name but a few. In 2003 the Alliance Library System opened a library in Second Life (Second Life Adds a Library Space, 2007). When I visited the Alliance Library in 2008 I was told that there were about 40 individuals from around the world who volunteered their time at the library and were able to provide services for approximately 70 hours per week. What are not included in these numbers are the individual faculty members and librarians who participate in SL without the direct affiliation of their college or university. I am one who falls into this latter category.

How does SL work?

A user downloads a free program from Linden Labs (http://secondlife.com) for installation on his or her computer. An avatar (a computerized figure which represents you) is provided. You take ownership of your avatar in an introductory area. Basic movements are explained and exploratory exercises are provided. Once the introductory tour is completed you are able to search for the areas you'd like to visit. SL provides a search mechanism for finding places, people, land sales, groups etc. A shortcoming of the search mechanism is that it relies on an island's owner to enter appropriate descriptions of their island. These owner-created descriptions are frequently inadequate. However, once you have located an island of interest you are able to create a 'landmark', enabling easy return to that location.

One observation is that students and faculty find their first experiences in SL frustrating because of the learning curve involved. To resolve this issue it is important that libraries and reference sites provide basic tutorials outlining the essential skills necessary for surviving with ease in SL.

Why is SL significant?

SL allows for members, no matter where they are, to meet and interact face to face (albeit avatar-face to avatar-face). 'The stronger attraction for many academics and researchers is the extent to which the environment serves as a legitimate surrogate for the real world, allowing users to inhabit personas and situations that are otherwise unavailable to them' (Educause, 2008, 2). A visit to the Globe Theatre[2] provides the possibility to see a production of Shakespeare – and for the adventurous, the possibility of performing in the Globe Theatre. While many may never experience the beauty of the Sistine Chapel, Vassar College has brought the semblance of the experience to us.[3] Nicholas Adams, an art historian at Vassar College, says 'the re-creation of the Sistine Chapel on Vassar's virtual campus looks cartoonish because the frescoes' colors and textures are off. . . . Art historians can't take this seriously' (Foster, 2007b, A25). Adams misses the point. Vassar has created a three-dimensional re-creation of the Sistine Chapel and visitors to the real-life chapel have commented on how accurate the depiction is. No matter how accurately the frescoes are shown in printed art publications, they will not have the same impact as a visit to Vassar's SL reproduction.

What are the downsides of SL?

Hardware downsides

The primary downside is the technology. A high-speed internet connection is required, which excludes many who have older, slower computers or who rely on dial-up internet service; older, slower machines are unable to handle the high graphics required by SL; and even newer machines are not immune from technical difficulties. Crashes still occur regularly, if not frequently. My avatar occasionally develops complete paralysis, preventing me from moving, talking etc. However, I have never crashed while giving a class in SL, and Kate Bulkley of the *Guardian* predicts that 'We are probably one PC development cycle – so 18 months – away from where every machine with Vista or Mac OS X should be able to run SL' (Bulkley, 2007, 5).

People downsides

And, just as in real life, there are SL individuals who find joy in disrupting the lives of others: they are called 'griefers'. On a few occasions I have found myself captured in a cage, box or other contraption and have been forced to log out of SL in order to free myself. On another occasion an individual appeared in my SL library wearing a huge phallus. I advised him that his 'attire' was inappropriate for the site. After several warnings I threatened to report him to Second Life (yes, SL has a disciplinary procedure). It turned out that the person was a student in my class. He later apologized to me, indicating that he wasn't aware of his appendage. I was sceptical. This was early in my SL experience. In SL an avatar's normal view is from about six feet behind. This provides an excellent view of the back of his or her head. It takes an effort to see how you appear from the front, and many individuals don't learn this technique for weeks. The individual in question could easily have added the offending 'item' to his attire unaware. A lesson here is to be very careful of what you decide to 'wear'. Check your front before you venture forth in public!

What are the implications for teaching and learning in SL?

This is the key question for libraries and universities. Students meet on their computer in 3D virtual environments, interacting with their fellow students. Co-operation, team building and discussion are key elements in these worlds. This is not new. Many universities are already involved in virtual learning environments (VLEs) which offer and expect this behaviour. Blackboard, eCollege and Jenzabar are but three. Blackboard reported that 150 of the 229 schools in the 2005 *U.S. News & World Report* ranking of top colleges and universities used Blackboard to 'create a networked learning environment' (U.S. News & World Report's Top Ranked Colleges and Universities Use Blackboard, 2005, 1).

What distinguishes SL from these VLEs is the third dimension, the availability of your own visual representative in the form of your avatar, and a more robust environment in which to interact.

Human interaction with computers

In 1996 a research project examined the relationship between individuals and their computers. Its goal was to determine whether individuals would accept computers (or avatars) as team-mates. The conclusion was that not only did the participants accept computers as team-mates, but the relationship between human and computer was the same 'as the effects of being in a team with another human' (Nass et al., 1996). If we can accept a computer as a team-mate it should be easy to participate in groups with avatars as team-mates. In fact, in 1995 Nass (Nass et al., 1995) explored this very issue and demonstrated that 'the social rules guiding human–human interaction apply equally to human–computer interaction'.

A 2006 article in *Educause* stated that

> campuses can expect the boundaries between virtual and brick-and-mortar learning environments to continue to blur. Students and instructors will need access to their virtual learning environments while seated in their brick-and-mortar classrooms.
>
> As campuses accept the notion that virtual spaces are actually classrooms, they can begin to apply the same care and consideration to decisions about course management systems and campus portals as they do to decisions about new construction and renovation.
>
> (Graetz, 2006, 446)

In 1980 Papert wrote that learning to communicate with the computer could be a very natural process, similar to learning how to speak French by living in France. And once we learn to communicate naturally with computers, it may be that this will change how we use the computer to learn other things.

Second Life librarian – a beginning

My involvement in SL began in 2007. I learned that one of my colleagues had acquired an SL island and was involving his students in an exploration of the very active SL business community. Some of his classes were conducted online, others involved real-world classroom attendance. Many of the assignments required research using library databases. It occurred to me that a library presence on his island would allow an exploration of SL as an effective library instruction/reference vehicle.

When I started, I knew very little about building useful objects in SL. All structures in SL are based on seven basic shapes which can be enlarged, twisted, warped, hollowed, cut, coloured and textured. Buildings, trees, plants, chairs, tables, stairways, aeroplanes etc. are all created with these basic shapes. My first project was building a snowman. When I had completed my snowman I was delighted even with its crooked carrot nose!

Building and acquiring tools of the trade

But, whilst it introduced me to building and scripting basics, my snowman wasn't going to be of much use in my library/reference presentations. I visited islands that contained educational elements I wanted to include on my site. I enhanced my scripting and object-building skill and managed to build an inadequate slide presenter. Slides could move forward but I didn't have the skills to build a fully functional slide screen – so if I needed to go back one slide I was obliged to cycle through the entire presentation! I wasn't happy with this, so I searched and found a slide presenter I liked and bought one for $1,500 Lindens (the currency used in SL – approximately US$5) which allowed me to create as many slide presentations as I needed. Among the various options of buying, finding and begging I was able to put together an environment that included the teaching elements I wanted. What I discovered was the extreme willingness of other avatars (individuals) to share their knowledge and their creations.

Creating a presence

When I first started building in SL I created buildings with elevators and roofs. These buildings abound throughout SL. Since avatars can fly, there is no functional value in creating elevators. And since no one can get wet in SL, why have roofs? In fact, recently I had a meeting with two of my colleagues under the sea, with the fish and other sea creatures swimming among us. None of us drowned, nor required towels when we emerged from the water. My library is now located on roofless pods. I do have ramps connecting related pods, so as to make it easier for students who have not yet mastered flying to move from one pod to another; these ramps also help to define related pods. I recently added railings to the sides of the ramps, as those new to SL kept walking off the ramps and falling to the ground. While it is understandable that some may wish to keep the conventions of the real world, my goal is to use the imaginative possibilities of SL to create learning environments that may enhance the SL learning experience.

As the liaison person between the library and distance education faculty, and being aware that one of the stated goals of the university is to make our materials and services equally available to both campus and distance students, I saw SL as an additional way of bridging the distance gap and providing a 'face-to-face' experience for students who might never visit the real-life campus. SL fits with our goal of seamless service to distance students.

I approached the faculty member who owned the SL island and discussed my thoughts about creating a library presence there. He immediately gave me ownership/building privileges, which allowed me to create a small library. My goal was to create an area that would be open to students 24/7, containing guides and links to the databases and materials they needed to complete their assignments. It would also be an area in which I could meet students to provide 'face-to-face' reference service and to offer information retrieval instruction.

The SL library

The latest version of the site I created[4] (Figure 5.1) contains an array of small pods, approximately 15 feet square.

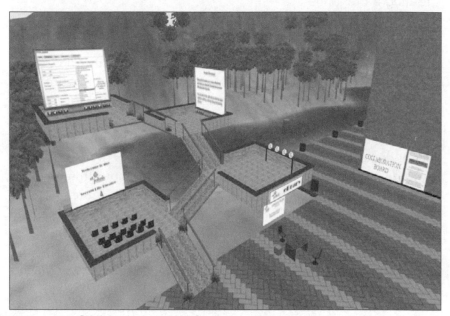

Figure 5.1 *St. John University's SL library presence*

Level 1 contains a small theatre with seats and a screen for library instruction and reference demonstrations. A slide show has been created highlighting the library resources available for each of the students' assignments and for each database of value to an assignment. The presentation also includes possible search techniques to obtain the information students require. The screen is equipped with a pointer, enabling me to easily indicate important points.

Level 2 contains an information bar which provides internet links to the various databases and information sources that are appropriate for use in the assignment in question. At the moment these links take you out of SL and onto the internet. As MUVEs advance, my hope is that database searching can occur within SL and provide an opportunity for real-time demonstrations, in addition to the slide presentations.

Level 3 offers a slide-show tutorial designed to introduce students to SL skills. Specifically, it explains the various ways an avatar can travel in SL: walking, running and flying. In addition to travelling, SL offers a variety of means for viewing the environment – this slide show demonstrates the 'out of body' means of viewing the world around you. The introduction is critical for those new to SL, as 'newbies' come to SL with the minimum of skills. Students have commented on their ignorance of SL features. If we wish students to experience the best of SL, it is critical to reduce their frustrations with regard to the movement of their avatar (Calongne, 2008, 37–48).

Level 4 provides 24/7 student-controlled access to the slide presentations that were conducted in person in the Level 1 theatre. Given the small area of each of the levels, only a limited number of slide presentations can be present at one time. SL, however, has a mechanism called a holodeck. (From Wikipedia we learn that a holodeck 'is a simulated reality facility located on starships and starbases in the fictional Star Trek universe'.) SL allows each island a certain number of units for building the objects found on the island. These units are called 'prims' – short for the word primitive. To minimize the number of prims used on an island at any one time it is possible to create a holodeck in which to store the slide presentation. Only when the object in the holodeck is activated by a student via a holodeck emitter do the prims become accountable towards the area's 'prim allowance'.

Service from a distance

The university is already positioned to take advantage of an expanding universe of online classes. It has four campuses in the New York area – one on Long Island, and one each in the boroughs of Queens, Manhattan and Staten Island; it has a campus in Rome and there is talk of campuses in other locations around the world. Online courses taught from the main Queens, New York campus using the expertise of the existing faculty are a far more economical solution than duplicating faculty positions in each of these locations.

As a distance education librarian, my role is to make every effort to extend the same library service that we offer in Queens to the other campus locations around the world. All St. John's students have access to our online databases and eBooks, but we only offer full librarian services to each of the New York City locations; the Long Island and Rome campuses have no onsite librarians available. Telephone service to Long Island and Rome is offered via the online telephone service Skype. SL offers the advantage of providing a virtual environment where librarian and student can meet 'face to face'.

Creating teaching materials

To create an SL presentation it was necessary to analyse my reference and library instruction classes and parse the elements into slide-sized chunks appropriate for projection onto a screen. I used a word processor to do this – taking screen shots of each chunk and creating JPG images using a graphics program. These JPGs were uploaded into SL and became the textures used in the presentations. SL uses images such as JPGs for creating textures that can be applied to the surface of any object. The textures on an object can be changed in a specified order, thus creating a slide program. This was the first expense that I incurred: each uploaded JPG cost approximately five cents.

As part of my SL experimentation I learned some basic building and scripting skills. However, it is unrealistic and unreasonable to expect that faculty members will acquire these skills. It is critical that libraries and universities incorporating SL as a part of their mission hire designated individuals with this expertise to work with faculty who wish to incorporate SL into their teaching experience.

Experience with students

For the past two years I have met with students in SL to answer their questions and demonstrate how to use the library's database to find the information they need. I have had meetings with groups as small as one and as large as 15. In the first year, scheduled times for presentations were established and announced in class. This wasn't successful. Many students worked full time and attended evening classes; preset times didn't meet their needs. In the second year a mixed schedule of preset times and appointment opportunities was offered. Appointment times ranged from 7:00 a.m. to 1:00 a.m. This is still in an experimental state; the university has not yet adopted SL as a learning platform. It may be that offering sessions at 1:00 a.m. will be difficult to sustain when SL becomes an accepted learning platform. But for the experimental period this will continue to be offered, and will be evaluated for its sustainability.

Delivering instruction

SL sessions were held using the keyboard chat feature. Students were able to type questions and I could respond immediately. SL provides a chat capture feature: question and answer sessions can be copied and e-mailed to students as a record of their attendance and as a reference of what occurred during the sessions. While students could capture the sessions themselves, this was another SL skill many had not yet acquired.

Sessions lasted for approximately an hour. Fortunately I can type quickly, which reduced the lag time in answering questions. However, I found my fingers getting weary by the end of the sessions (typing was fairly constant). Fortunately, at one SL conference I attended I was given a tool called Speakeasy. It allowed me to type my presentation in advance, line-by-line, into the tool. I was then able to recall the presentation one line at a time by simply clicking on that line. This had the advantages of reducing typing fatigue, allowing for additional detail and, more importantly, reducing the impatience of students waiting for the next line in the presentation to appear. In future sessions I plan to use voice-chat in addition to keyboard-chat. With the availability of Speakeasy I will be able to provide students with a transcript of my spoken presentation.

One element missing from the SL sessions to date was a formal feedback mechanism for evaluating their effectiveness. Students were required, as part of the assignment, to offer a critique of their SL session; however, this frequently resulted in uncritical praise of the process rather than a true evaluation of how valuable the session had been to the assignment. A more formal and effective evaluation process will be a critical element in determining how effective my use of SL is.

One of the challenges of SL locations is to make them interesting places to visit. I am working to find some way of presenting my instruction and reference information in the form of a game – a game that challenges and entertains and, ultimately, informs and educates.

Second life as a game?

A debate that has emerged is whether or not SL is a game. This debate can be read in its fullest in the SLed Archives.[5] From these archives the following two views are offered:

SL lacks inherent gameplay. There are some games in SL, but it is not a requirement of the world itself that one participate in them. Most definitions of what a game is seem to be so broad that many things would qualify as a game that really aren't . . .   (Leigh, 2008)

and:

A colleague and I often quote Marc Prensky's (2006) 'Six Elements of games' from his book 'Digital games-based Learning' when we present on 'games in e-learning':

Elements in a game	Elements of a course
Goals and Objectives	Goals and Objectives
Outcomes and Feedback	Outcomes and Feedback
Competition/Challenge/Opposition	Challenge
Interaction	Interaction
Representation or Story	Information
Rules	Policies

We can see some similarities between games and learning in an academic course environment. Following Bruce's comments, Second Life 'as is' only meets one or two of the elements of games.

(Boufrord, 2008)

The subject of games is important in this discussion because SL can be a wonderful platform for the playing of games. And games are a wonderful platform for learning and teaching:

Computers let us make models that work the way some part of the world does. These simulated models make it easier for us to get things done in the real world by letting the computer do some of the work we otherwise would have to do for ourselves. . . . *Computer and video games can change education because computers now make it possible to learn on a massive scale by doing the things that people do in the world outside of school.* They make it possible for students to learn to think in innovative and creative ways just as innovators in the real world learn to think creatively.   (Shaffer, 2006, 242, my italics)

And lest we think games don't already have an impact on what students are doing, Richard Urban, in the *Bulletin of the American Society for Information Science & Technology*, believes that 'introducing serious leisure concepts to MUVEs could clarify that virtual worlds are not simply games, but an important element for developing library services' (Urban, 2007, 38–40).

Whyville is an MUVE designed to inspire children to learn the concepts of maths and science. And this is being done in a game setting. And some educators believe that virtual worlds are the future for those growing up in the wired generation. 'That's because research has shown that kids engage deeply in virtual environments, gaining a conceptual and ethical understanding of school subjects, according to education experts. And many kids are already comfortable socializing online, so educationally oriented virtual worlds can offer that same sort of stimulus and use that potential to aid learning. There's one big caveat, however: Virtual worlds must have knowledgeable and motivated teachers driving the train' (Olsen, 2009, 4).

Already, 'Seventy percent (70%) of college students reported playing video, computer or online games at least once in a while, and 65% of college students reported being regular or occasional game players' (Jones, 2003, 1–14).

This information about games should come as no surprise. Castronova (2007), in his book, *Exodus to the Virtual World: How Online Fun is Changing Reality*, reports that US$10 billion annually is spent on the digital game industry – about the same amount we spend going to the movies. And 'Today students are native speakers of technology, fluent in the digital language of computers, video games, and the internet. Students, as digital natives, will continue to evolve and change so rapidly that teachers won't be able to keep up. Educators must take their cues from their students' 21st century innovations and behaviors, abandoning, in many cases, their own predigital instincts and comfort zones' (Prensky, 2006, 8–13).

Disruptive innovation

A disruptive innovation is an event so profound that it changes the fundamental manner in which an industry operates (Christensen et al., 2008; McLeod, 2009). The digital camera is one example of a disruptive innovation. Its effect on the Eastman Kodak company offers food for thought for the field of education.

In 1975 Eastman Kodak's stock was selling for about $45.00 a share. In that same year Kodak developed the first digital camera. It weighed 8 lbs and was about the size of a toaster. It was another two decades before it took advantage of that early landmark and entered the digital camera market (Dobbin, 2005). By 2009 Kodak stock had dropped to under US$3.00 per share. A Morningstar report stated:

> Eastman Kodak has done a commendable job attempting to wean itself
> from the rapid declines in its core film-based imaging business by
> pursuing digital opportunities. However, we believe it lacks many of
> the advantages it enjoyed with film, and the competition is more fierce.
> We expect the company to struggle in the digital frontier and fail to
> produce shareholder value.   (Morningstar, 2009)

The digital camera created such a revolutionary change over existing camera technology that it destroyed completely the way the photographic equipment companies conducted business. Kodak has become a second-rate player in the digital camera business. In part, this is because it listened to its customers when digital cameras first appeared – people liked using film, it produced a superior-quality image, they were used to it, they were comfortable, they had the slide equipment they needed and the digital images at the time weren't all that good. So with all this product loyalty, why would Kodak invest the money to change?

But while Kodak's primary customers weren't interested in the digital camera there was an audience lurking who loved the new technology – they were satisfied with the first digital cameras, despite the expensive and the less-than-perfect pictures they produced. But digital camera technology improved, pictures got better and costs were reduced. And the rush to digital hasn't stopped.

Kodak, having remained on the sideline during the steady march to digital, is likely never to regain its foothold as a leader in the photographic field.

I was one of those first digital camera buyers – I noticed the poorer-quality image, but was satisfied with the results – especially at the 4 x 6 image size that was commonly produced when printed to paper. And I loved the convenience: don't like a picture – erase it – want a picture – save it or print it to paper. Once I had that digital camera I never purchased another roll of film. (But I wasn't typical of the customers with whom Kodak was most concerned.)

What has all this to do with libraries, education or Second Life?

The current organization and means for the provision of services of libraries and education were established long before students had access to online classes. Education was gained only by attending the building down the block. You could only get material from the library by physically going to the library.

In the early 2000s Paul Allen of Microsoft founded Apex Learning in the USA to provide online courses for advanced placement. These classes were designed specifically for school districts with low participation in a single school but with sufficient participation over the entire school district. In three years the enrolment for these classes grew more than 300% – from 8,400 in 2003 to 30,200 in 2006. Apex Learning, in 2008, served 4,000 school districts and now offers *core* courses for these same schools. Twenty-five states of the USA have similar programmes (Christensen et al., 2008, 238). Students in high school are growing up with online courses. Their experiences are that online courses are mainstream – they are part of the norm. Based on the current levels of adoption by high schools, Christensen predicts that by 2019, 50% of high school courses will be delivered online. 'In other words, within a few years, after a long period of incubation, the world is likely to begin flipping rapidly to student-centric online technology' (Christensen et al., 2008, 238).

Second Life is a MUVE and it is my belief that MUVEs are a disruptive innovation. If this turns out to be true, then the current means for delivering education and library services may become the Kodak of the very near future.

Conclusion

To borrow a phrase from Niels Bohr, Nobel Prize laureate in Physics, 'Prediction is very difficult, especially about the future'.[6] My belief in the potential of MUVEs (SL being the one I work in) is based on the observation that the young people I see have computer familiarity as part of their earliest experience: they are gamers and have experienced online learning to an extent that most of us of an older generation have not encountered.

Second Life is but one of a number of MUVEs that are currently active. It is, perhaps, the most promising and most inhabited of the ones we have; however, just as we moved from Wordstar to WordPerfect, to Microsoft Word, so we don't know where MUVEs are in the development progression. SL may turn out to be the eight-track tape of the MUVE world, but I agree with Castronova (2007) that to ignore SL, and the MUVEs of which it is one representative, is to ignore a technology that is likely to grow to include hundreds of millions people who are likely to inhabit this existence.

Whatever the new world we will inhabit, there will be new skills and routines to understand and learn. Pioneer librarians in these worlds will likely have to learn how to create the tools needed to practise their craft. The increase in distance education requires new staffing patterns if we are to adequately meet the needs of our distant clients. The university library and its librarians will have to accept the fact that we no longer live in a world that exists only when the brick building is open. We must learn to accommodate the student who only has time at 1.00, 2.00 or 3.00 a.m.

Universities throughout the world are offering distance education classes and even degree programmes over the internet. Students in these programmes may never see their professors, fellow students or even the campus from which the classes are given. 'Few college/university presidents or CIOs [chief information officers] are currently prioritizing the exploration of virtual worlds, but it seems safe to predict that within the next three to five years, a higher education institution without a virtual world's presence will be like an institution without a web presence today' (Collins, 2008, 51–63).

Notes

1   www.educause.edu/7ThingsYouShouldKnowAboutSeries/7495.

2   http://slurl.com/secondlife/sLiterary/18/7/24.

3   http://slurl.com/secondlife/Vassar/128/128/26.

4   http://slurl.com/secondlife/Emgeetee/110/154/24.

5   https://lists.secondlife.com/pipermail/educators/.
6   www.quotationspage.com/quote/26159.html.

References

Boufrord, B. (2008) A Game Or Not a Game?, *SLed Archives*,
    https://lists.secondlife.com/pipermail/educators/2008-September/
    026052.html.

Bulkley, K. (2007) *Technology: today Second Life, tomorrow the world: interview with
    Philip Rosedale: the founder of the virtual world Second Life believes that his company,
    Linden Lab, is at the forefront of the internet's next big revolution – the 3D web*,
    http://proquest.umi.com/pqdweb?did=1272529071&Fmt=7&clientId=
    9216&RQT=309&VName=PQD.

Calongne, C. M. (2008) Educational Frontiers: learning in a virtual world,
    Educause Review, 43 (5), 37–48,
    http://net.educause.edu/ir/library/pdf/ERM0852.pdf.

Castronova, E. (2007) *Exodus to the Virtual World: how online fun is changing reality*,
    Palgrave Macmillan.

Christensen, C. M., Horn, M. B. and Johnson, C. W. (2008) *Disrupting Class: how
    disruptive innovation will change the way the world learns*, McGraw-Hill.

Collins, C. (2008) Looking to the Future: higher education in the metaverse,
    Educause Review, 43 (5), 51–63,
    http://net.educause.edu/ir/library/pdf/ERM0853.pdf.

Dobbin, B. (2005) *Digital Camera Turns 30 – sort of*, (9 September),
    www.msnbc.msn.com/id/9261340/.

Educause (2008) 7 Things You Should Know About Virtual Worlds, *EDUCAUSE
    Learning Initiative*, (7 February),
    www.educause.edu/ir/library/pdf/ELI7015.pdf.

Foster, A. L. (2007a) Professor Avatar, *The Chronicle of Higher Education*, 54 (4),
    A24,
    http://proquest.umi.com/pqdweb?did=1353685291&Fmt=7&clientId=
    9216&RQT=309&VName=PQD.

Foster, A. L. (2007b) Second Life: second thoughts and doubts, *Chronicle of Higher
    Education*, 54 (4), A25.
    http://search.ebscohost.com/login.aspx?direct=true&db=aph&AN=
    26910979&site=ehost-live.

Graetz, K.A. (2006) The Psychology of Learning Environments. In Oblinger, D.G. (ed.) *Learning Spaces*, 6.9–6-10, Educause, www.educause.edu/learningspaces.

Jones, S. (2003) *Let the Games Begin*, www.pewinternet.org/Reports/2003/Let-the-games-begin-Gaming-technology-and-college-students.aspx.

Leigh, M. (2008) *A Game Or Not a Game*, https://lists.secondlife.com/pipermail/educators/2008-September/026042.html, *SLed Archives*, https://lists.secondlife.com/pipermail/educators/2008-September/026042.html.

McLeod, S. (2009) *Disruptive Innovation*, http://k12online.wm.edu/k12online081c03.wmv.

Morningstar (2009) *Eastman Kodak Company*, http://quote.morningstar.com/stock/s.aspx?t=EK&culture=en-US&region=USA&r=570789&byrefresh=yes.

Nass, C. et al (1995) Can Computer Personalities be Human Personalities?, *International Journal of Human–Computer Studies*, 43 (2), 223–39.

Nass, C., Fogg, B. J. and Moon, Y. (1996) Can Computers be Teammates?, *International Journal of Human–Computer Studies*, 45 (6), 669–78.

Olsen, S. (2009) Digital Kids: are virtual worlds the future of the classroom?, *CNET News.com*. www.news.com/2009-1041_3-6081870.html.

Papert, S. (1980) *Mindstorms: children, computers, and powerful ideas*, Basic Books.

Prensky, M. (2006) Listen to the Natives, *Educational Leadership*, 63 (4), 8–13, http://search.ebscohost.com/login.aspx?direct=true&db=aph&AN=19270008&site=ehost-live.

Second Life Adds a Library Space (2007) *American Libraries*, 38 (1), 31.

Shaffer, D. W. (2006) *How Computer Games Help Children Learn*, 1st edn, Palgrave Macmillan.

U.S. News & World Report's Top Ranked Colleges and Universities Use Blackboard, *PR Newswire*, 19 October 2005, www.prnewswire.com/cgi-bin/stories.pl?ACCT=109&STORY=/www/story/10-19-2004/0002287294.

Urban, R. (2007) Second Life, Serious Leisure, *LIS*, 33, http://search.ebscohost.com/login.aspx?direct=true&db=aph&AN=28742224&site=ehost-live.

6

Some new business ideas in the HSS publishing space: what may librarians expect?

Frances Pinter

Introduction

Academic publishers don't like edited volumes. They believe that libraries are more likely to purchase single-authored volumes instead. They groan when academics come along with proposals for edited volumes. Sometimes these are accepted as a tactic to catch the editor and turn him or her into an author of a book-length work that conventional wisdom says will sell more copies. The sprat to catch a mackerel. However, there are some topics that require a breadth of knowledge that surpasses the experience and wisdom of any particular individual. The contents of this book, for instance, would have been impossible for one individual to cover with the depth and experience of the contributors assembled here. And even if such a paragon of wisdom were to exist, by the time the relevant data was assembled, the book would be out of date.

We are all, writers and readers, grappling to understand the fast-moving environment in which we live and operate. Some try to preserve old world virtues, whilst others are steaming ahead into uncharted waters, creating new models and methods – often with unforeseen consequences. The purpose of this chapter is to highlight some of the challenges facing traditional scholarly publishers as they've tried to adapt to the new digital environment. It aims to map out some key concerns from a variety of perspectives and then indulge in some blue-sky thinking as to how the future might look. My thoughts are informed by our attempts at Bloomsbury Academic to build a new business model with flexible licensing practices at its core. It intends to make the best use of both old and new media as they co-exist in the very unstable period of transition that we are in today.

Ring-fencing the discussion

The scope of this chapter is limited to a very specific area of academic publishing: library collections – the prime venue (whether physical or virtual) where scholars and students find content. It deals with humanities and social science (HSS) books, or the 'long form publication' as some refer to books in the online environment. Reference will be made to scientific, technical and medical (STM) and professional publishing. Developments in the scholarly journal world do, of course, have implications for the future of the book. However, the pressures for change and the solutions to the problems are not the same. It would be foolish to attempt a 'one size fits all' model for the wealth of material that publishers produce and that libraries are charged with acquiring, preserving and facilitating access to.

The levers of change

The patchwork quilt of issues around envisaging future library services is made up of a number of very different-looking elements. Key to how HSS books will be made available will be factors outside of the control of any specific sector. We should all be working to facilitate scholarship, though in practice we are all under pressures that seem remote to the core mission. Libraries compete for funding against other equally valid claims on resources; publishers (if commercial entities) answer to their shareholders – university presses to their parent institutions, who tend to reduce rather than increase their support. At the same time, significant investments in digital production, delivery and dissemination are required, just when budgets are shrinking. Meanwhile the consolidation of bookselling (especially the huge power of Amazon to force prices down), the abolition of fixed-price agreements in some countries, the advent of Google Book Search/Book Preview and now the Book Settlement have left publishers reeling. Apart from some STM publishers, very few sectors are really in good financial health.

The traditional reaction in times of downturn was to reduce print runs and increase prices. However, academics are fighting back by placing content directly onto personal/institutional websites or in institutional repositories, so this tactic of price hiking is unlikely to work. The problem is not so much the scarcity of funds; the monograph publishing market in the USA for university press books has been estimated at somewhere between $200 million and $300 million – not an insignificant sum. It is more a case of how these funds are channelled. Underlying this is how we think about copyright and how, with more flexible licensing practices, we might also find more efficient ways of paying for the publishing services that academics still want to maintain. This has implications for libraries, who have an important role to play in the debates over where we want to go and how we get there.

Copyright

Copyright is the 'elephant in the room'. Designed over 300 years ago, it was meant to be a tool to protect the individual author against the powers of the printers who controlled distribution. Remaining largely intact until a few decades ago, copyright is now a football, tossed around by the most powerful players, from multinationals who want to protect their income, to states who look at how their own interests might best be served through making changes to national copyright laws. Some countries use copyright as a bargaining chip when it comes to negotiating trade deals within the World Trade Organisation (WTO) regulations and the specifics laid down by the Agreement on Trade Related Aspects of Intellectual Property Rights (TRIPs) (see Matthews, 2002).

So where does that leave libraries? Fighting their corner in the arena of exceptions and limitations within and outside the scope of fair use/fair dealings. These battles are being fought at both national and international levels. This is because of the way copyright regulation works. Firstly, we have the Berne Convention, the grandfather of international conventions agreed in 1886. Berne spells out the minimum requirements of any domestic copyright legal framework. Regulations within countries vary around these minimal guidelines. The levers that enforce the Berne Convention are not, as one would expect, located at the World Intellectual Property Organisation (WIPO) under the aegis of the United Nations, but rather at the WTO. Many have argued that developing countries have been disadvantaged since the formation of the WTO in 1995, especially in the areas of copyright and patents. In

2007, WIPO initiated its 'Development Agenda', which many hope will address some of the imbalances. However, the fight for even stricter regulation of copyright has received additional impetus since the emergence of widespread access to digital media.

Reflected best in the 1998 US Digital Millennium Copyright Act (DMCA), we see that the lock down of rights in the digital media is actually greater than it is in print or any other analogue form of media. The DMCA criminalizes production and dissemination of technology, devices or services intended to circumvent controls on access to copyrighted works. It also criminalizes the act of circumventing any access control, whether or not there is actual infringement of copyright itself.

Of course, it is quite reasonable for companies that had traditionally invested in the creation and distribution of copyrighted material to want to find ways of controlling copying. Indeed the whole definition of a 'copy' is now an interesting question. The first 'digital' production of anything is a copy or, as is often said, the creation is 'born digital'. Without investing in moving text from typewritten (or even handwritten) format into the digital realm one may rightly ask when the 'added value' kicks in. This becomes an important question when thinking about the relationship between authors and publishers. Digital technologies reduce the cost of entry to markets, so publishers, record labels and film companies can no longer claim a natural right to be the gatekeepers.

The new digital divides

Returning now to publishing, and specifically to HSS academic publishing, the internet has provided many wonderful opportunities for scholars to share their research amongst themselves, with their students and with the world at large. We've all witnessed the huge proliferation of materials, and most people with internet access complain more about information overload than about information deprivation. However, the digital divide will take on a new meaning if means of creating order in this world do not proceed at the same pace as the expansion of content. As the global system of tertiary education continues to expand, there will be even more pressures on publishers to publish and libraries to purchase, catalogue and facilitate access. Not only are academics able to produce more writing and spread their work outside the conventional publishing routes, there now are more academics than ever around the globe.

The potential of the web to make access universal was recognized from the moment it was born. At the tertiary level the most high-profile attempt to open up that which was previously closed came from the Open Access movement. The basic model is that the cost of publishing a journal article could be paid for in advance, by the author (usually out of his or her research budget) and this would enable the publisher to post the article online free of charge. Free at point of use was heralded as a tremendous breakthrough, making it possible for researchers and students all over the world to stay up to date with research developments. Out of this original 'gold standard' came the 'green standard', whereby an article is lodged with an open repository, usually institution based, though sometimes subject based. To date over 4,000 journals are either totally open access or operate a hybrid model whereby the author selects whether to pay for the gold (open access) route or the traditional subscription model.

Publishers, such as Elsevier, fought this model at first, but after a while they came round, realizing that their cash flow was not adversely affected and their bottom-line profits were preserved. Recently, a plethora of new journals have been launched speculatively, and if they do not gather up a sufficient number of author submissions with fees they simply close down. Some of these are so fly-by-night that their names can no longer be found! Despite many publishers' policies of waiving fees for authors from poorer countries, there is potentially a new barrier to entry if authors without the means to pay for open access fees find that the gates to these journals are closed to them.

Nevertheless, mainstream publishers have reconciled themselves to the open access model. For instance, in late 2008 Springer bought BioMed Central – a company yet to make a profit with a turnover of €15 million, for a rumoured $35 million – one of the largest and most successful and respected open access journal publishers.

Licensing

While the debates continue over open and closed access in the realm of subscriptions, librarians are fighting for licenses that are simple, easy to understand and easy to implement.

The transaction costs of the multiplicity of licensing serve only to increase the administrative costs of the library and reduce the amount of funds available to purchase content. Publishers are experimenting with a variety of access models, some of which are so cumbersome that one can only conclude that they will be self-defeating. Taylor and Francis recently developed a model that allows users to purchase print access to content. Users can browse a book for three consecutive 15-minute sessions, though if an ePrint/Copy has not been purchased during this time, then access to that book is denied for seven days. This model also restricts copying to 10 pages per session.

With the advent of digital content free at point of use, there needed to be a way of protecting the rights of both the publisher and the original copyright holder (usually the author, though in some instances it may be the research funding body) and so we began to see the use of open content licences online. The most prevalent ones in use today are the Creative Commons licences, a suite of six licences that provide varying degrees of open use by readers. These are based on a 'some rights reserved' principle that protects the copyright holder and allows a broader range of use than the traditional 'all rights reserved' copyright, where permissions need to be sought for any use above and beyond fair use/fair dealing. See www.creativecommons.org for information on how these licences operate.

Business models for the 'long form publication'

We need to develop a new business model for HSS books. The current journal open access model works best in STM, where articles are short and research budgets are large. With the average research budget for humanities projects being very small or even nil, it is hard to see how the author-side payment would work. We are working with book-length material that is ten to twenty times longer than the average journal article. Although the peer-review costs may be similar, the copy-editing, typesetting and formatting costs are proportionately greater and authors are unlikely to find such funds to bring the content to 'book' publication standard. Even if such funding were available, it would have to fight the legacy perception of these being seen as subsidies – usually associated with vanity publishing – or of material that did not pass muster with the gatekeepers whose role it is (or was) to ensure quality.

In the English-speaking publishing world, HSS relies on two types of publishers: university presses and commercial houses. These fall into a number of categories: very large multinationals with or without trade divisions; large specialist publishing companies; smaller academic publishing houses; and offshoots of scholarly associations. The United States is home to the largest number of university presses, and continental Europe follows thereafter. In the UK we have Oxford University Press and Cambridge University Press dominating the scene, along with a handful of small university presses including Open University Press, Manchester University Press and Liverpool University Press. Oxford University Press had a turnover of $492m in the 2007–8 financial year. Large mainstream academic publishers such as Routledge, Sage and Macmillan are now global entities, and many small presses operate within specialist subject areas. HSS academics still rank university presses higher than commercial presses, especially in the USA. The pressures on these companies are huge. More academics send in proposals, more need to be rejected and costs need to be lowered in light of tightening library budgets. Yet, as print runs fall and unit costs go up, publishers still have to recover the fixed costs incurred in the pre-publication investment in their books.

At the other end of the cycle publishers have sought to reduce stockholding costs – those costs after the pre-publication investments are made – through the new Print on Demand (POD) facilities. If publishers only need to print when an order comes in, rather than printing stock for, say two years, then the financing costs are reduced, stockholding costs disappear and the price of the book should fall. However, this is true only to an extent. The unit cost of POD is still higher than a modest print run by conventional means, and there is still the problem of recovering the cost of the pre-print investment, the so-called 'first copy' cost. Amortizing these costs over an ever-dwindling number of print copies creates even higher prices. The idea of recovering the 'getting to first copy' investment costs through print sales simply does not work any longer.

Added to which, we no longer have a fixed definition of what a 'book' might be – or become. The opportunities to expand, link and morph continuously as a result of reader feedback and collaboration is irresistible. Indeed, younger scholars are embracing the opportunities with great relish.

So what are publishers doing in the HSS sphere? What are the new models that might indicate the way forward? And why don't they seem especially attractive to librarians? Most publishers have to make ends meet through the sale of their intellectual product bit by bit, book by book. Libraries have a choice of what they purchase. These decisions get made through a variety of methods. Some libraries rely mainly on faculty to make recommendations, others buy through library suppliers who carry out a degree of pre-selection and can provide specially tailored book approval schemes. In other libraries it is the librarian who selects directly from information that pours in from a myriad of sources. In fact, most libraries source their books by a mixture of these means. Publishers relying on academic library purchases have to promote widely to get even one copy of a book bought by a university library.

Can open access work for books?

Greco and Wharton (2008) asked what would happen if all the income that American university presses derive from the sale of monographs to US university libraries was pooled and paid directly to the university presses under the provision that the contents of the books were posted online on an open access basis. Publishers would then be assured of covering their 'first copy' costs and would also be free to make some extra profit on any print versions they produced, through either short-run printing or pure POD. This approach would virtually eradicate any risk. In this way readers could be assured of perpetual access and any library that still wanted a print copy would be able to obtain it.

Of course, there was uproar at the mere suggestion of some kind of centrally controlled funding body. The implication was that this would necessitate a rechanneling of funds that had hitherto been part of the library budgets. Sequestering these was simply not an option. However, the article sparked a lively debate, raising many questions around how to move forward.

Academic presses are under increasing pressure to allow the published work to appear online free of charge even after the publisher has invested considerable sums and is uncertain of the return. My own contribution to this volume allows me to post this chapter on my website or 'on my university or corporate networks/intranet, or secure external website at my institution for personal or professional use but not for commercial sale or any systematic external distribution by a third party'. The publisher still hopes this will not erode its sales. However, as search and navigation functions improve, this is unlikely to remain the case.

Testing new business models

A few publishers are conducting some very public experiments. Flat World Knowledge is an American company specializing in business studies textbooks. Its content is available free online under a Creative Commons non-commercial licence. It is then selling the print copy – in black and white or at a higher price in colour. It is selling additional content, such as podcasts, webcasts, study guides and teaching aids. It is even selling the pdf – marketed as 'looking just like the book' as opposed to the free html version that you can copy – but only chapter by chapter. The online copy acts as its own promotion piece. The origination costs are amortized over a notional income per title derived from the sale of the print versions and the additional products that surround it.

It is conceivable that the Flat World Knowledge model might work for basic undergraduate textbooks in markets such as the US, where there is enough wealth for students to purchase textbooks. There is, however, an additional challenge to the library when an enhanced e-copy is being sold. Just what does the library receive when the core content is free, while the add-ons might be very costly and may require updates? And on what basis should these products be sold – perpetual access or annual subscription?

Bloomsbury Academic is the new imprint of the Bloomsbury Publishing Group Plc that is making all its research-based scholarly books available online using a Creative Commons non-commercial licence. The gamble here is that enough libraries will still be requested by academics to purchase a print copy for their collections. If an HSS book is being read 'cover to cover', then reading onscreen is not especially pleasant, and printing out copies of long books, often read only once by one person only and then dispensed with is neither ecologically friendly nor cost-effective. Careful selections for libraries will determine whether this can become a viable revenue stream.

With the Bloomsbury Academic model there is the danger that libraries with limited funds will nevertheless choose not to purchase the print copy, even though they are aware that this is less than ideal for their readers. Perhaps a membership model to support the initiative may prove successful. Unlike Flat World Knowledge we are also selling through the traditional trade channels.

The search for sustainability

So, with budgets stretched, how can publishers find ways of meeting the demands of their authors, their readers and the libraries that serve them – and remain sustainable? At Bloomsbury Academic, we are developing an 'enhanced' e-book product that takes the core content of the book and adds additional functionalities and, in some cases, additional content, and for this we are developing a subscription model. The analogy is with ice cream. Plain vanilla ice cream is the publisher-selected and -crafted, peer-reviewed, edited content which is available in html online, published under a Creative Commons Non-Commercial licence. The printed book takes that vanilla ice cream, adds a wafer and wraps it up – and for this there is a charge. Then there is the ice cream sundae, with chocolate sauce and extras such as nuts, fruit and whipped cream. This is the enhanced e-book – which we will sell to libraries. We believe that with enough sales of ice cream sandwiches and sundaes we will recover the cost of our investment in getting to 'first copy' stage. And by giving away the vanilla ice cream we'll be promoting the book (through the various search engines and our own marketing efforts) to generate enough demand for either the physical book or the enhanced e-book. There is nothing new in this principle, as Chris Anderson (2009) in his book *Free: the future of a radical price* explains. What is different now is that the 'free' can cost so little to make and distribute over the internet. The trick is to publish content that people want and are able to purchase in media that suit their needs and their pockets. The added benefit – that ultimately scholars around the world will have access to at least the vanilla ice cream – is, to mix metaphors, the icing on the cake. And what a wonderful cake it will be when we are finally able to make it on a scale that makes a difference!

The OAPEN project

Open Access Publishing in European Networks (OAPEN) is a European

Commission-funded project that is looking for the answer for HSS books. OAPEN is a 'consortium of University-based academic publishers who believe that the time is ripe to bring the successes of scientific Open Access publishing to the humanities and social sciences' (OAPEN 2009). The partners are: Amsterdam University Press, Georg-August Universitaet Goettingen, Museum Tusculanuum Press, Manchester University Press, Presses Universitaires de Lyon, Firenze University Press, University of Amsterdam and Leiden University. The website continues to state that 'the 30 months project (launched in September 2008) aims to develop and implement an OA publication model for academic books in the Humanities and Social Sciences. The project aims to achieve a sustainable European approach to improve quantity, visibility and usability of high-quality OA content.' At the time of writing this article (spring 2009), the project had only been in existence for six months. The project will produce much useful work in the form of designing workflows and recommending the adoption of common standards and metadata to improve retrievability and visibility of HSS publications and create awareness of the issues surrounding opening up content through a commonly held repository. However, the fundamental issues around how to make the publishing process, which includes selection, peer review, editing, typesetting, formatting, marketing and enabling the production of print copies, i.e. funding the getting to 'first copy' stage, remain unresolved. In discussions with the project manager, it appears there will be an effort to raise 'subsidies' from wherever possible.

Finance models

Subsidies for HSS are notoriously difficult to come by and will only worsen as the world tightens its belt to recover from the financial crisis of 2008–9. They are considered discretionary and, for some, a sign of failure. When a book can't reach the necessary sales of 300–500 copies needed to break even, most people (apart from the author and his or her few readers) conclude that the book isn't worth publishing. Some stand that argument on its head and say that the book doesn't sell more due to its high price and because the publisher does not know how to market or price the book. However, in the case of monographs, it really is the case of supply and demand not working in harmony. The issue is a broader one. The question is, how should we go about obtaining maximum exposure of content so that readers have easy and free access? Some experiments, such as the JISC National E-Books Observatory project have made a first step in testing what happens if you make a textbook available online free of charge within the UK university system (having paid £600,000 for the licenses to publishers for 30 titles, with another 6 titles 'thrown in' for free). The results have been mixed, but it is probably that the project structure still needs a bit of tweaking (see JISC, 2009). Yet the JISC Observatory project is not really an open access project since it is 'open' only to UK university students.

In the case of books, or books that become 'long form publications', there is the additional factor that much research is international. Opening up access on a countrywide basis to those who can afford a country site license would create yet another digital divide. And while researchers send their electronic editions (or links) to colleagues, this would be only a partial solution to full global access to scholarly works and would fall short of the potential for best access practices in the digital realm.

So, who should pay and what mechanisms would need to be in place to pay for getting to 'first copy' stage for content that has a global market? Should the funding be sought in the country of origin of the author or the publisher? Or should there be some global institution – a World Bank for Books? Is this too fanciful?

A role for libraries

One model might be to top-slice library budgets and reallocate them to a central trust. Authors could apply to this pool for funding their publications, or if that is too granular, perhaps a more efficient route would be to allocate funding to universities on a pro rata basis – in line with the publication rate of their faculty. Another option would be to have publishers bid for funding from such a pool to fulfil service contracts for set series or collections. Does this sound fanciful? Well, it is in line with some ideas currently being discussed over how to redistribute some of the BBC's current budget raised from TV licences – by dividing it up and allocating a set amount to some of the smaller channels and production companies on a competitive tendering basis.

Perhaps some of the global professional bodies, such as the International Federation of Library Associations and Institutions (IFLA) and the International Publishers Association could do a deal with Google to fund such co-operation, with countries then paying into the pot the funds they would otherwise allocate for HSS e-book purchases and great techies of Google providing improved search facilities? Perhaps some adaptation of Greco and Wharton's model for the United States would then have much greater impact on world scholarship, if it could be implemented on a global level – would it not?

The above reference to Google may send shudders down the spines of those who oppose the Google Book Settlement. But there is no doubt that resources, both technical and financial, will need to be garnered from large, well-endowed partners to bring about any changes. Librarians have an important role to play in this debate. They have been more successful in creating consortia to further their interests than most other professions. They can use this convening power to help all stakeholders to think out of the box and contribute to finding new ways of making open access work for more than just journals.

References

Anderson, C. (2009) *Free: the future of a radical price: the economics of abundance and why zero pricing is changing the face of business*, Random House.

Greco, A. and Wharton, R. (2008) *Should University Presses Adopt an Open Access {Electronic Publishing} Business Model for All of Their Scholarly Books?*, ELPUB 2008 Conference on Electronic Publishing, Toronto, http://elpub.scix.net/cgi-bin/works/Show?_id=149_elpub2008.

JISC (2009) *Dispelling Myths About E-Books with Empirical Evidence*, JISC National E-Books Observatory Project [online], www.jiscebooksproject.org/wp-content/jc_ebooks_observatory_summary-final.pdf.

Matthews, D. (2002) *Globalising Intellectual Property Rights: the TRIPS Agreement*, Routledge.

OAPEN (2009) Open Access Publishing in European Networks [online], www.oapen.org/.

7

Loosely joined: the discovery and consumption of scholarly content in the digital era

Paul Coyne

Introduction

The library has been a focal point for innovation in digital services since the advent of micro-computing and, latterly, the web. Technology in the library is not new; nor are concerns about the role of technology in the library. However, the advent of the internet, the growth of social networks and the increasingly mobile nature of digital technologies pose new and important challenges and opportunities for academic libraries in how they manage the abundance of information and make it available.

Academic libraries are having to respond to the needs of a new generation of 'digital natives', who see access to social software as a basic human right, yet the need to preserve privacy, reliability and accountability remains fundamental to the sustainability of such institutions.

This chapter will explore the recent history of technological advances in the library and show how the early theoretical 'memex' system proposed by Vannevar Bush in 1945 (Bush, 1945) is only now becoming a reality, with the advent of cloud computing. It will show how the ability to link and access data, increased expectations, a shift to user-centred services and a change in how library space is used are leading to a fundamental restyling of libraries, to a point where Web 2.0 technologies are becoming central to their function rather than add-on facilities.

The concept of Library 2.0 is still not well formed, but it is providing a framework for understanding that adaptability and flexibility are essential to ensuring that academic libraries remain central to the learning experience, provide open access for users and protect and promote quality authorship.

Big, bigger, invisible!

It is commonly asserted that the digital era has brought new challenges and opportunities to the fore. However, problems of growth and the advancement of technology have been identified for some time. In his 1983 paper, James Thompson described the 'End of Libraries' and pointed to advances in micro-computing that then provoked anxiety, and questioned the purpose of the library and the role of the librarian in the electronic age.

Thompson is one of many researchers who recall the earlier work of Fremont Rider (1944) in his seminal article 'The Scholar and the Future of the Research Library'. Steele (2005) reviewed the article in the light of recent advances in digital technology and wrote that Rider believed 'research library growth has continued, without any significant change of rate, either downward or upward, for over thirty decades, and at a rate so uniform over so many years, and so uniform in so many different libraries, that it might almost seem as though some natural law were at work' (Rider, 1944, 15–16). Put simply, Rider believed that, given this historical pattern of growth, research libraries would face insurmountable problems in future years.

Library growth

In his article Rider calculated that American research libraries had, on average, doubled in size every 16 years. Furthermore, by the year 2040 Yale would have 200,000,000 books, on 6,000 miles of shelving; and if by then it still maintained a traditional card catalogue, that catalogue would comprise 750,000 catalogue drawers occupying eight acres of floor space and would need to be serviced by 6,000 cataloguing staff.

We now know that Rider was incorrect in his precise assertions about the doubling of research libraries every 16 years; however, he was right in predicting the implication of relentless growth in publications.

Digital content

As we enter the second decade of the 21st century many of the issues identified by Rider have not disappeared. Libraries and library users have access to more content – in the form of digital information – than at any time in human history. Digital information is, by its very nature, invisible. Growing collections and their implications for the library have been well documented; the means by which libraries might manage the concomitant demands have not manifested themselves as predicted.

Thompson (1983) reports that in 1967 the American Council of Learned Societies (ACLS) concluded, 'Even the most sophisticated electronic circuitry will remain an aid to, not a substitute for, men's minds in contact with books.' In an age when access to digital content via portals and services such as Google's federated search portals is commonplace, such a pronouncement seems a little quaint. Indeed, much of the current discussion focuses on the quality, diversity and reliability of access to digital content in a virtualized environment, rather than exclusively on the issue of collection size.

Collection 'completeness'

A study conducted by Professor Allen Kent Thompson (1983) questions the notion of 'completeness'. The study suggests that from the dawn of the printing press to 1983 some 30 million unique titles had been printed. It goes on to record that the largest of the world's libraries contained no more than 5% of that total.

Later, by the mid-1990s, the advent of the world wide web had a major impact on the library. And while there are many passionate debates with respect to issues of preservation, curation, privacy, provision and, not least, economics, there can be no doubt that it has provoked revolutionary change in how information is accessed and disseminated.

Scholarly publishers, along with library partners and customers, have been most pioneering in providing access to a range of electronic resources. The ease of accessing information from a variety of sources other than the library catalogue or the library shelves has rendered the 'completeness' mission of the library inconsequential. Size no longer matters. Or perhaps it would be more correct to say that size should no longer matter.

Managing information abundance

Although Rider's sometimes controversial solutions to the problems of unchecked growth were not widely adopted – he supported the shaving of books to make them smaller so they would fit better on shelves – others who wrote about how best one might manage a vastly increased store of knowledge and research were closer to the mark. Vannevar Bush, in his remarkable 1945 article 'How We May Think', proposed a device called a 'memex'. The memex could be used to access, organize and contribute to the store of human knowledge. When describing how this machine might work, given the technology of the time, Bush admitted that only the scale of the proposition currently put the idea beyond practical implementation; the important and transformative step was the ability of the memex to tie 'trails' together.

> All this is conventional, except for the projection forward of present-day mechanisms and gadgetry. It affords an immediate step, however, to associative indexing, the basic idea of which is a provision whereby any item may be caused at will to select immediately and automatically another. This is the essential feature of the memex. The process of tying two items together is the important thing.

Remarkably, the memex anticipated the world wide web by 45 years. Yet even the world wide web does not fully meet the vision of the memex. An important dimension has, until relatively recently, remained out of the picture – that of contribution. What is now commonly referred to as Web 2.0, the second phase of the web, is a far more participative version of the world wide web. It is closer to the original visions of both Vannevar Bush and Tim Berners-Lee. The participative web has seen an explosion of growth in the diversity, form and quality of online information, and this explosive growth has profound implications for both publishers, library users and libraries.

What does this mean for libraries in the digital era?

The library in the digital and social era

Cheap and always-available access to the internet, combined with affordable and ever more powerful personal digital devices, has caused expectations to be raised. Students, researchers, faculty and authors expect to be able to access information around the clock, from anywhere in the world and on a range of devices, including smart phones, PDAs and laptop computers. In short, the focus of attention has shifted from the institution to the user. No longer can we expect students and researchers to follow a prescribed workflow; increasingly they demand services that can be incorporated into highly personal learning and research workflows.

Such advances have raised questions about the form and function of library services, and indeed the nature of the library itself, although, as we have seen from Bush and Rider, these concerns are not new. Is there something qualitatively different about the challenges we face today?

Work places or workspaces?

The library of the 20th century was about defining a specialized space for learning and research. However, in the 21st century people are no longer tied to specific spaces for study or learning. Mitchell (2005) suggests that there is a 'huge drop in demand for traditional, private and enclosed spaces' such as libraries and classrooms, and simultaneously 'a huge rise in demand for semi-public spaces that can be informally appropriated to ad hoc workspaces'.

This sentiment, expressed by Lougee (2002) in the concept of the 'diffuse library', recognizes that mobile and participative social technologies have created an information environment that is highly distributed. In addition, ideas of 'openness' have become more robust since the turn of the century – open access, open source, open communities and open knowledge networks. The 'open' movement is characterized by its level of collaboration and its intent to create and share new knowledge with as few barriers to participation as possible. In her paper, Lougee goes on to advance a future role for libraries in the digital era:

> With the incorporation of distributed technologies and more open models, the library has the potential to become more involved at all stages, and in all contexts, of knowledge creation, dissemination, and use. Rather than being defined by its collections or the services that support them, the library can become a diffuse agent within the scholarly community. (Lougee, 2002, 4).

It has been suggested that the ubiquitous presence of the internet, growth of electronic publishing and proliferation of online scholarly journals are the developments that will 'affect the physical and intellectual structure of library buildings in decades ahead' (Bazillion and Braun, 2001). The development of collaborative learning requires that new buildings must 'accommodate group studies, electronic classrooms, "information galleries" and space for faculty to create Web-enhanced courses' (Bazillion and Braun, 2001). The concept of the 'library as place' was reviewed in a report published by the Council on Library and Information Resources and entitled *The Library as Place: rethinking roles, rethinking space* (Freeman et al., 2005).

Digital natives in the library

Does the digital era, then, demand a new, more diffuse or embedded role for the library if it is to continue to serve its highly mobile and distributed user population? Prensky (2001) has coined a term to describe a new generation of users, referring to them as 'digital natives'. He has defined 'digital natives' as:

> the first generations to grow up with . . . new technology. They have spent their entire lives surrounded by and using computers, video games, digital music players, video cams, cell phones, and all the other tools and toys of the digital age. . . . Computer games, email, the Internet, cell phones and instant messaging are integral parts of their lives.

If you are not a digital native, you are a 'digital immigrant' – one of those who may have acquired some form of digital literacy to a greater or lesser degree, but who nonetheless apply to the use of technology the mind-set, techniques and concepts with which older generations grew up.

Lippincott (2005) refers to 'an apparent disconnect between the culture of library organizations and that of Net Gen students', arguing that while the information-seeking behaviours of this generation have altered substantially, libraries have not kept pace in their information-providing practices and in the systems and services that deliver information.

In the 2003 *OCLC Environment Scan: pattern recognition* study (De Rosa et al., 2004), the argument is put more succinctly, when the authors point to 'the indisputable fact . . . that information and content on the open Web is far easier and more convenient to find and access than are information and content in physical or virtual libraries. The information consumer types a term into a search box, clicks a button and sees results immediately. The information consumer is satisfied.' The report also finds that:

- 89% of college students use search engines to begin an information search (while only 2% start from a library website)
- 93% are satisfied or very satisfied with their overall experience of using a search engine (compared with 84% for a librarian-assisted search)
- search engines fit college students' life-styles better than physical or online libraries, and that fit is 'almost perfect'
- college students still use the library, but they are using it less (and reading less) since they began using internet research tools
- despite massive investment in new digital resources, students continue to associate the library with 'books'.

Catering to the natives

However, it would be imprudent to characterize all or even most undergraduates as 'digital natives' and to base future planning and strategies in one particular demographic grouping. Most libraries serve multiple constituencies – academic staff, research fellows and post-graduate students – from different generations. Equally, their interests, values and behaviours in seeking information may be quite different. The library, even in the digital era, has a responsibility to provide flexibility and choice in the way its services are offered.

Robinson (2008) argues that this is in fact what libraries have always done. It is in response to the demands of 'digital natives' that digital services are being developed, so that the needs of this group can be met. Ironically, some of the most effective programmes for meeting the needs of a diverse user base are based upon recent advances in social software, derived from the 'digital native' Web 2.0 movement.

While acknowledging that libraries have ceded ground to internet-based services, the internet developer and research organization Talis also points to possible ways in which the restyling of libraries using Web 2.0 applications could be achieved (Chad and Miller, 2005). Chad and Miller's white paper for Talis summarizes the principles of 'Library 2.0' as follows:

- The library is everywhere, meaning essentially that the library 'is available at the point of need, visible on a wide range of devices, and integrated with services from beyond the library, such as portals, virtual learning environments'.
- The library has no barriers, meaning that the resources which a library holds should be more widely exposed via the web, 'visible to search engines such as Google, and harvestable into new applications and services built by the library and by third parties'.
- The library invites participation, encouraging and enabling library users to participate and contribute to understanding of resources so that ultimately everyone benefits.
- The library uses flexible, best-of-breed systems: to achieve this situation requires new and different relationships with technology partners, relying less on proprietary systems and more on open, compatible and interoperable standards and modules.

Defining 'Library 2.0'

The term 'Library 2.0' is contested. An established definition does not yet exist, despite numerous attempts to come up with one. It is not clear whether an entirely new model is needed, or simply an extension of that which already exists. Holmberg et al. (2009) provide a range of definitions from the literature:

- 'a subset of library services designed to meet user needs caused by the direct and peripheral effects of Web 2.0'

(Habib, 2006)
- 'the combination of Web 2.0 and libraries, together with the libraries' traditions of serving users'

(Wallis, 2007)
- 'an attempt to apply Web 2.0 technologies to the purpose of the

library, together with goals for greater community involvement'
(Lankes et al., 2007).

Maness (2006) provides a more precise definition:

The application of interactive, collaborative, and multimedia web-
based technologies to web-based library services and collections.

According to Maness (2006, 40), a theory of Library 2.0 has four
essential elements:

- it is user-centred
- it provides a multimedia experience
- it is socially rich
- it is communally innovative.

Casey and Savastinuk (2006) state that Library 2.0 is a new library service
model for the digital era, one which focuses on 'user-centered change'
and 'encourages constant and purposeful change, inviting user
participation in the creation of both the physical and the virtual services
they want, supported by consistently evaluating services'. They further
indicate that 'technology can help libraries create a customer-driven 2.0
environment' (ibid., 40), and propose that 'any service, physical or
virtual, that successfully reaches users, is evaluated frequently, and
makes use of customer input' can help libraries create a customer-
driven 2.0 environment (ibid., 42).

Getting mobile

The trends that began with the Web 2.0 social software movement have
been accelerated with advances in mobile technologies and e-book
reading devices. In fact, mobile communication has been more widely
adopted more quickly than any other technology, ever (Castells et al.,
2007).

Hahn (2008) reports that Pew Internet and the American Life Project
'Mobile Access to Data and Information' discovered that the mobile
phone ranks as the most highly valued technology in America, and that
it is the technology which Americans are least willing to part with (see

also Horrigan, 2008). The mobile phone has thus surpassed the internet and television in preference; these results indicate a fundamental societal shift occurring in the years 2003 to 2008. The findings are also consistent with UK and European studies. Chen and Katz (2009) note the findings of the 2008 Carphone Warehouse and LBS [Location-based Services] Mobile Life report that one in three people would want £1 million in return for giving up their mobile phone, and those aged between 16 and 24 would prefer to give up sex for a month rather than do without their handset.

Mobilization in the library

As in the case of the challenges posed by the participative web, the library is already adapting with mobile-ready services. Kroski (2008) provides examples of some of these and other services:

- **Reference/enquiries:** Libraries are offering services through a range of communication vehicles such as chat, instant messaging, texting and e-mail. Should the reference desk take phone calls from people in meetings or study space in the library? Data from an ongoing study of Virtual Reference Services indicate that even where people are physically in the library they may prefer to use chat reference rather than seek out a face-to-face encounter.
- **Presentation and visibility:** Videos and podcasts describing or promoting particular library services, covering library events and so on are becoming more common. Often, these are made available on network-level sites – YouTube, iTunes – where they are more visible.
- **Alerting:** RSS is becoming pervasive. SMS text message and e-mail alerts are also more common. People may be told about events, the status of their interactions/requests and the availability of staff.
- **Syndication:** Many libraries have begun to push applications and content into the diffuse social network environment of their users. RSS feeds, widgets and Facebook applications are becoming more common.
- **Mobile websites:** Some libraries are specifically designing for mobile access. This poses new questions for the library. To gain

maximum coverage, the mobile site needs to be much simpler than a typical library site and it is productive to think what is best to present there.

Networking services, meeting individual needs

As mobile communications add another layer of networks and networking into more of what library users do, they reconfigure one's relationship with time, space and other people, just as earlier networks did, and as described earlier in this chapter in relation to the emergence of the participative web and Library 2.0 services. Dempsey (2009) has written extensively on the issues presented by the emergence of mobile technologies in the library space and suggests that the library may increasingly come to be regarded as a networked service, thus:

> As a growing proportion of library use is network-based, the library becomes visible and usable through the network services provided. On the network, there are only services. So, the perception of quality of reference or of the value of particular collections, for example, will depend for many people on the quality of the network services which make them visible, and the extent to which they can be integrated into personal learning environments. Increasingly, this requires us to emphasize the network as an integral design principle in library service development, rather than thinking of it as an add-on. The provision of RSS feeds is a case in point. Thinking about how something might appear on a mobile device is another.

New challenges are presented by the widespread adoption of highly personal mobile technologies. To begin with, how does one 'mobilize' existing services to work better with the variety of user consumption patterns which are emerging from the digital and social networks? And second, do these changing behaviours require the library to restructure some of the ways in which it thinks about and provides its services?

Dempsey (2009) suggests that to meet these challenges the library must provide a higher level of network- (and mobile-) ready services than now exists.

Currently, libraries provide a thin layer over two sets of heterogeneous resources. One is the set of legacy and emerging systems, developed independently rather than as part of an overall library experience, with different fulfilment options and different metadata models (integrated library system, resolver, knowledge base, repositories) (Dempsey, 2009). Another is the set of legacy database and repository boundaries that map more to historically evolved publisher configurations and business decisions than to user needs or behaviours (for example, metadata, e-journals, e-books and other types of content, which may be difficult to slice and dice in useful ways).

One of the problems here, as identified by Fox (2009), is a lack of standardization. HTTP has become a widely used mechanism since the web has become the most common modality for information access. For example, in the electronic book arena, Amazon is struggling to become the de facto standard for reading in the electronic world with the Kindle. If you have a wireless connection, you can purchase and read a rapidly growing list of books and periodicals from Amazon for the Kindle, no matter where you are. Even the largest texts take only seconds to download. Amazon is able to provide this service because it has established not only a name brand, but a means to maintain and distribute vast quantities of literary data to these mobile devices. This represents the essence of cloud computing (Fox, 2009).

The answer in the cloud

Cloud computing is a synonym for the internet. To say that a library or institution is engaged in cloud computing is to say that it is involved with projects that base applications and computing services on the internet in a widely distributed environment. There are many synonyms for cloud computing: 'on-demand computing', 'software as a service', 'information utilities', 'the internet as a platform', and others (Hayes, 2008, 9).

Cloud computing may be one strategy for libraries seeking to become more embedded in personal and mobile workflows without neglecting their legacy systems and processes and support for their other constituencies. It may not be such a big step, either.

Libraries in the clouds

For many years libraries have submitted electronic MARC records to the OCLC database. It enables the sharing of records between libraries and reduces the time spent cataloguing materials. As Fox (2009) points out, 'OCLC has been functioning as a cloud computing vendor because they provide cataloguing tools over the internet and allow member institutions to draw on their centralized data store. WorldCat is another example of cloud computing architecture drawing on the union catalogue infrastructure they have built up over the years.'

The adoption of cloud computing or software as a service (SaaS) may provide libraries with the means to develop high-order network and mobile services reasonably swiftly. For example, with the library acting as the gatekeeper, institutions could provide their students with mobile access to a list of articles simply by selecting them and giving them a code that would bring up the list from a publisher or vendor 'cloud'. There would be no need to put articles on reserve, and the publisher would watch for copyright infringement. The same could work for pre-print archives, data archives and digital object repositories. Perhaps publishers could co-operate to provide service mash-ups that would combine research data with digital objects, all available on mobile devices in order to distribute course content. Cloud computing provides many opportunities for the diffusion and provision of all sorts of electronic data in creative venues. The creation of document clouds such as DocStore and Scribd suggests that this model may indeed be viable for certain institutions.

Functional examples of this new breed of computing are proliferating. Many established brand names are developing cloud-based services. Amazon provides hosting services for data that are priced at gigabyte-month and CPU-hour rates. IBM has begun developing what it calls the 'Blue Cloud' infrastructure. Google is in the process of implementing what it calls the 'App Engine', which provides a hosted service for applications within its server farms and on a massive and highly redundant storage system (Hayes, 2008, 10). Microsoft has also ventured into this realm with its Azure system, which it calls a 'cloud services operating system'.

Assuring a sustainable future

Although there have been great advances in the network layer that may enable libraries to engage creatively with users in distributed and highly personal settings, there remain important questions of privacy, reliability and accountability. Anticipating these issues, Fox (2009) poses the following questions:

> The benefit of cost and scalability are sometimes out weighed by the possibility of a lack of perpetuity. If the organization supplying the cloud computing infrastructure decides to discontinue their efforts or goes out of business, how much would that affect the parent institution which the library serves? Could the data be easily migrated to another service? How much development time would be required to accommodate that service to the needs of the library?

The question for the library, and for other actors offering information services, is who owns the data that describe the personas, relationships, interactions and history that highly distributed, social and networked services require. The issue of ownership must be addressed and resolved before any enterprise, including the library, can reasonably expect to develop distributed and diffuse services through mobile and web-based networks.

Open data movements and standards

There are indications that open data movements such as the Data Liberation Front from Google, the Open Data Foundation and OpenID may advance the cause of open data standards. Ultimately, this may lead to the Unified Web and a unified web culture in the medium term. Such movements underline the evolution of the web from a global information space of linked documents to one where both documents and data are linked. Underpinning this evolution is a set of best practices for publishing and connecting structured data on the web, known as Linked Data (Bizer et al., 2009). Linked data has become to be regarded as a key component in what is now termed the 'semantic web' or Web 3.0.

The semantic web, in conjunction with the promotion of open data standards atop heterogeneous network layers, offers a neatly satisfying return to the promise of the memex as originally proposed by Bush in

1945 and described earlier in this chapter. Recall that only the scale of the original memex put the idea beyond practical implementation at the time; the important and transformative step is the ability of the memex to tie 'trails' together:

> All this is conventional, except for the projection forward of present-day mechanisms and gadgetry. It affords an immediate step, however, to associative indexing, the basic idea of which is a provision whereby any item may be caused at will to select immediately and automatically another. This is the essential feature of the memex. The process of tying two items together is the important thing.
>
> (Bush, 1945)

The adoption of linked data best practices will lead to the extension of the web, with a global data space connecting data from diverse domains such as people, companies, books, scientific publications, films, music, television and radio programmes, genes, proteins, drugs and clinical trials, online communities, statistical and scientific data, and reviews. This web of linked data will enable new types of applications and could at last deliver the promise of the memex, albeit 60 years after it was first proposed.

This highly distributed, open, social and mobile environment may also provide the answer for one of the long-held axioms of the library, and the question introduced at the beginning of the chapter – that of completeness. The advent of scalable, robust and globalized networked services when combined with open linked data, social networking technologies and collaborative communities could allow even the most modest library to offer its users more than the content available at the Library of Congress, which, by Professor Thompson's calculations, may hold no more than 5% of all titles ever printed (Thompson, 1983).

Conclusion

This chapter started by looking at predictions about the future role, even death, of the library as a consequence of new technologies. As we have seen, such concerns are not new, although there are aspects of the most recent advances that pose new challenges for librarians, publishers and institutions.

The emergence of the participative web at the beginning of the 21st century can now be seen as a highly disruptive social phenomenon that has caused the expectations of students, sometimes referred to as 'digital natives', and of other types of user to be raised – expectations that publishers and libraries sometimes fail to meet. However, as they have done throughout the ages, libraries, librarians and publishers are adapting to the new environment. Although widely debated, the concept of Library 2.0 is an important one. Similar to the Web 2.0 movement, it should be regarded as a cultural shift, rather than a technological advance. The principles of user-centredness and embeddedness within the communities they serve are principles cherished by most libraries.

The trends begun by the Web 2.0 movement have been accelerated by the explosive growth in mobile technology and services – Castells et al. (2007) reports that it is the most rapidly and most widely adopted technology ever. The implications for information access and the reconfiguration of the relationship between student and institution are profound. Dempsey (2009) suggests that libraries must look to develop high-order networked services to serve highly mobile and distributed user populations. Such services will be highly personalized and loosely joined. There are challenges here for the library in brand positioning and the management of such services. Cloud computing may be one route that libraries take in order to provide such services.

Although in its infancy, and with questions of privacy and data ownership yet to be resolved, the infrastructure will soon be in place to provide a rich web of linked data. Such a vision comes far closer to the concept of the web as originally proposed by Tim Berners-Lee and the memex 'trails' of Vannevar Bush. For a perspective on recent and future technological and social advances one must look to the recent past, and in doing so it becomes possible to appreciate how adaptable, flexible and creative library and information professionals have been, and continue to be, in highly disruptive times.

References

Bazillion, R. J. and Braun, C. L. (2001) Classroom, Library and Campus Culture in a Networked Environment, *Campus-Wide Information Systems*, **18** (2), 61–7.

Bizer, C., Heath, T. and Berners-Lee, T. (2009) Linked Data – The Story So Far,
International Journal on Semantic Web and Information Systems (IJSWIS),
http://tomheath.com/papers/bizer-heath-bernres-lee-ijswis-linked-data.pdf.

Bush, V. (1945) As We May Think, *The Atlantic Monthly*, **176** (1), 101–8.

Casey, M. E. and Savastinuk, L. C. (2006) Library 2.0: service for the next-
generation library, *Library Journal*, **131** (14), 3.

Castells, M. et al. (2007) *Mobile Communication and Society: a global perspective*, MIT
Press.

Chad, K. and Miller, P. (2005) *Do Libraries Matter?*, White paper, available at
www.talis.com/downloads/white_papers/DoLibrariesMatter.pdf.

Chen, Y. F. and Katz, J. E. (2009) Extending Family to School Life: college
students' use of the mobile phone, *International Journal of Human–Computer
Studies*, **67** (2), 179–91.

De Rosa, C., Dempsey, L. and Wilson, A. (2004) *The 2003 OCLC Environmental
Scan: pattern recognition*, OCLC.

Dempsey, L. (2009) Always On: libraries in a world of permanent connectivity,
First Monday, **14** (1),
http://firstmonday.org/htbin/cgiwrap/bin/ojs/index.php/fm/article/view/
2291/2070.

Freeman, G. T. et al. (2005) *Library as Place: rethinking roles, rethinking space*,
Council on Library and Information Resources.

Fox, R. (2009) Library in the Clouds, *OCLC Systems & Services*, **25** (3), 156–61.

Habib, M. C. (2006) *Toward Academic Library 2.0: development and application of a
Library 2.0 methodology*, School of Information and Library Science, University
of North Carolina at Chapel Hill, NC, available at
http://etd.ils.unc.edu/dspace/handle/1901/356.

Hahn, J. (2008) Mobile Learning for the Twenty-first Century Librarian, *Reference
Services Review*, **36** (3), 272–88.

Hayes, B. (2008) Cloud Computing, *Communications of the ACM*, **51** (7), 9–11.

Holmberg, K. et al. (2009) What is Library 2.0?, *Journal of Documentation*, **65** (4),
668–81.

Horrigan, J., (2008) *Mobile Access to Data and Information*, Pew Internet American
Life Project,
www.pewinternet.org/pdfs/PIP_Mobile.Data.Access.pdf.

Kroski, E. (2008) *Web 2.0 for Librarians and Information Professionals*, Neal-
Schuman Publishers.

Lankes, R. D., Silverstein, J. and Nicholson, S. (2007) Participatory Networks: the
library as conversation, *Information Technology and Libraries*, **26** (4), 17–33.

Lippincott, J. K. (2005) Net Generation Students and Libraries, *EDUCAUSE Review*, 40 (2), 55-6., www.educause.edu/EDUCAUSE + Review/EDUCAUSEReviewMagazine Volume40/NetGenerationStudentsandLibrar/157965.

Lougee, W. P. (2002) *Diffuse Libraries: emergent roles for the research library in the digital age*, Council on Library and Information Resources.

Maness, J. M. (2006) Library 2.0 Theory: Web 2.0 and its implications for libraries, *Webology*, 3 (2)., www.webology.ir/2006/v3n2/a25.html.

Mitchell, W. J. (2005) *Users, Technology and Space in Libraries in the Digital Age*, http://dspace.mit.edu/handle/1721.1/33023.

Prensky, M. (2001) Digital Natives, Digital Immigrants, *On the Horizon*, 9 (5), 1–6.

Rider, F. (1944) *The Scholar and the Future of the Research Library: a problem and its solution*, Hadham Press.

Robinson, M. (2008) Digital Nature and Digital Nurture: libraries, learning and the digital native, *Library Management*, 29 (1/2), 67–76.

Sidorko, P. E. and Yang, T. T. (2009) Refocusing for the Future: meeting user expectations in a digital age, *Library Management*, 30 (1/2), 6–24.

Steele, C. (2005) No Easy Rider? The Scholar and the Future of the Research Library by Fremont Rider: a review article, *Journal of Librarianship and Information Science*, 37 (1), 45.

Thompson, J. (1983) The End of Libraries, *The Electronic Library*, 1 (4), 245–55.

Wallis, R. (2007) Web 2.0 to Library 2.0 – From Debate to Reality, *New Review of Information Networking*, 13 (1), 53–64.

8

Knowledge management, universities and libraries

Helen Hayes and Philip G. Kent

Introduction

> In this century of creativity and ideas, the most valuable resources
> available to any organizations are human skills, expertise and
> relationships. Knowledge Management is about capitalizing on these
> precious assets in a systematic fashion.
>
> Geisler and Wickramasinghe (2009)

The term 'knowledge management' became popular in the 1990s. This
quote highlights the human and organizational aspects of the concept
and the benefit of the approach for improving innovation and
productivity. Knowledge has contributed to human existence since the
beginning of time and it has been at the heart of universities since their
foundation. Lee (2005) notes that in 1965 management-thought leader
Drucker postulated that knowledge would replace machinery, land
and labour as a primary source of production. The knowledge economy
and growth of knowledge workers evidence this trend. The core strength
of knowledge management is in knowledge sharing that leads to
innovation, change and improvement.

In the 21st century we have cause to reassess the concept, particularly
in the higher education environment. Has knowledge management
delivered all that was promised in the early hype? Libraries and
technology have changed significantly since the early 1990s. Have
libraries and technology delivered as expected against the knowledge

management agenda, and what lessons have we learnt? This chapter examines the current status of knowledge management and its role in higher education and libraries. Drawing on experience at the University of Melbourne and beyond, we suggest that knowledge management principles are still manifest today. Following on from the initial hype, knowledge management is embedded in many activities that perhaps don't acknowledge the label.

Knowledge management

Knowledge management defined

In 2003 Standards Australia brought together practitioners from a variety of disciplines to develop an interim Australian knowledge management standard. This acknowledged that no single discipline owned knowledge management. The definition embodied in the 2005 standard is holistic:

> A trans-disciplinary-approach to improving organisational outcomes and learning through maximising the use of knowledge. It involves the design, implementation and review of social and technological activities and processes to improve the creating, sharing and applying or using of knowledge. Knowledge management is concerned with innovation and sharing behaviours, managing complexity and ambiguity through knowledge networks and connections, exploring smart processes, and deploying people-centric technologies.
>
> (Standards Australia, 2005)

Over time there has been some debate about terminology and whether knowledge can be managed. There is some validity in this, as knowledge is nebulous and difficult to qualify or manage. Despite variations in opinion, the term has gained worldwide exposure – if not achieving full understanding. Consequently, it is preferable to further conversations around the existing term rather than to start again. The scope of the Australian standard encourages organizations to 'develop their own shared understanding' for their own context.

From data to wisdom

The difference between data, information, knowledge and wisdom – including a suggestion that there is an ascending hierarchy from data to wisdom – has exercised a number of authors (Lee, 2005). There is value in not becoming too prescriptive, but rather, focusing on shared benefits and outcomes. In most cases benefits are derived from all parts of the hierarchy. Data provides valuable evidence for increasing useful information which, when combined with human interaction, forms knowledge that gives people the wisdom to make good decisions.

Geisler and Wickramasinghe (2009) put a chronological perspective on the data-to-wisdom continuum. They note that period from 1940 to the 1960s was the 'number crunching' period, whereas the 1970–1980s information era saw the rapid growth of information systems. The 1990s saw the emergence of knowledge management as a discipline assisted through advances in computing power. The current period, from 2000 onwards, is the 'wisdom era' where 'sense making' is sought by managers and widespread applications are available to assist strategic decision making. Technology is the enabler, and not the driver.

Knowledge, technology and people

An early advocate of knowledge management, Broadbent (1997), highlighted that knowledge management is not new and that 'good firms have been practising for many years'. According to Geisler and Wickramasinghe (2009), knowledge management decisions should be based primarily on who (people), what (knowledge) and why (business objective and processes), while how (technology) should be addressed last. This is important, as the technological aspects of knowledge management sometimes overshadow the human dimension.

Some commentators highlight the dichotomy between the 'soft' (people) and 'hard' (technology) aspects of knowledge management. On the soft side, knowledge management has gained prominence through the impact of the baby-boomer generation on the workforce, with large numbers of workers due to retire in the next few years. A number of organizations have a heightened awareness of potential loss of organizational knowledge or know-how and have implemented projects to capture it prior to exits.

Ferguson and Lloyd (2007) highlight an important difference between information and knowledge management:

> A common distinction between information management and knowledge management is that the former is concerned primarily with the management of 'explicit' forms of knowledge, such as policy documents, the contents of databases or corporate records . . . whereas KM represents an attempt to manage all the intellectual assets in an organisation, including the knowledge locked away in people's heads, a significant portion of which is what could be termed 'know how'.

In most organizations enormous amounts of information are either lost or hidden from view. Almost 15 years ago, Lew Platt, former chief executive of Hewlett-Packard, observed that 'if only HP knew what HP knows, we would be three times more productive' (Sieloff, 1999). This became a mantra for the knowledge management movement and companies like Hewlett Packard invested large sums of money to codify knowledge and connect people.

Knowledge management functions

In regard to the practice of knowledge management, early thought leaders Davenport et al. (1997) offer four useful perspectives or knowledge management functions:

- create knowledge repositories
- improve knowledge access and transfer
- enhance the knowledge environment
- manage knowledge as an organizational asset.

This further expands our understanding of the diversity of activities and skills associated with knowledge management.

The 1990s also saw the convergence of libraries and information technology, in some part due to the growth of electronic information as well as the strong connection between libraries and systems development for organizing data and information. In the higher education context, this was noteworthy in the United Kingdom. Australia followed suit in some universities. In the 2000s some universities are deconverging their libraries and IT departments, including the University of Melbourne. This is not an indictment of the past but an acknowledgement that environments and organizations change and that IT permeates all aspects of university work.

The usefulness of knowledge

Returning to the 'soft' side of knowledge management, Metcalfe (2006) highlights that knowledge is only useful when it is shared, transmitted, or acted upon. Collaboration and interaction between individuals is crucial. The cultural aspects of knowledge management pose particular challenges, summarized by Wen (2005):

> How to motivate staff to contribute and share their knowledge is not an easy task. Some staff may not want to share their knowledge for fear that once their knowledge is shared, they might no longer be valued or deemed indispensable.

This perspective that knowledge is power is now being questioned, as organizations build engagement and success around collaboration and knowledge sharing, and performance indicators require this capability.

Knowledge management, universities and libraries

According to Metcalfe (2006), universities are 'obvious sites to explore the implementation of knowledge management principles in the public sector', due to the connection between academia and the production of knowledge. This contrasts with the literature on the private sector, where return on investment and additional revenue from leveraging previous work are key. While universities have different drivers, their role in stimulating the knowledge economy requires that knowledge management principles are embedded in organizational culture so as to achieve results that contribute to the economic, social and cultural well-being of society.

Lee (2005) agrees that:

> Universities and research organizations are themselves knowledge reservoirs. These highly valued intellectual assets, regardless of whether

they are explicit or tacit, should be inventoried, archived, indexed, frequently updated, and made accessible in digital form.

University libraries as custodians of knowledge

As universities were established, libraries were often one of the first organizational units created. At the University of Edinburgh the Library preceded the establishment of the university. Libraries have played a central role in the mission of universities through their historical role as custodians of information and knowledge. Over successive generations, libraries have added value by identifying, organizing, describing and providing systems for accessing knowledge for scholars to explore.

Martell (2009) highlights an early article on knowledge management and academic libraries by Townley (2001). This article ranked fifth in the Ten Most Cited Articles in the prestigious *College & Research Libraries News* from 2000 to 2006.

Branin (2009) points to incredible opportunities for academic libraries to manage the broader knowledge of the university, referring to the growth of institutional repositories to 'meet the knowledge management challenge' by collecting, organizing and preserving a broader range of content created by members of the institution and its affiliates. This is essential not only for the institution but also as a social and public responsibility.

Knowledge management: value and benefits

Most definitions of knowledge management highlight the benefits to the organization, particularly in advancing the mission of the enterprise and in adding value. The benefits of knowledge management are sometimes difficult to articulate. It is helpful therefore that Geisler and Wickramasinghe (2009) have built on the work of others to provide a detailed list of the diverse benefits of a knowledge management approach (Table 8.1).

Geisler and Wickramasinghe (2009) have continued this work with the articulation of metrics that can be collected to evidence the benefits realized through a knowledge management approach (Table 8.2).

Table 8.1 *The eight principles of value of knowledge management*

Category of impact	Examples of benefits
Individual	Improved literacy Improved competence Accomplishment and empowerment
Institution (projects, team, enterprise)	Efficiency of operations Improved decision making Added prestige and credibility
Economy	Improved productivity Cost savings Improved innovation Improved market share
Society	Improved compliance and safety Improved healthcare, energy, transport and social services
Science and technology	Refining and verifying existing knowledge Adding to the pool of science and technology
Knowledge management system	Higher rate of knowledge dissemination Value added to users
Strategy of organizations (growth, competitiveness)	Contribution to growth, survival and competitiveness Contribution to art and science of strategic management
Future	Better forecasts and planning Improved pre-emptive abilities
Source: Adapted from Geisler and Wickramasinghe (2009)	

Table 8.2 *The four 'I's: clusters of metrics of value derived from knowledge management*

Cluster	Illustrative metrics
Infrastructure	Communication tools People skills and development Management support
Innovation	New products and services Lessons learnt New ideas, concepts and methods
Institutional growth and survival	Enhanced productivity Sales and revenues Comparative strategic advantages
Inter-organizational co-operation	Enhanced networks Collaborative efforts with others
Source: Adapted from Geisler and Wickramasinghe (2009)	

Regardless of how knowledge management is defined and its benefits are articulated, there is ample evidence that organizations that have developed a culture of knowledge sharing and collaboration are more likely to succeed. Hubbard et al. (2007) reveal the lessons of a 25-year study of 11 top-performing Australian enterprises. They suggest that the keys to innovation in high-performing companies are the human dimensions of collaboration and adaptability. Kennedy (2009) outlines key insights from high-performing corporations:

- innovation comes from knowledge flows, not stocks
- networks are the oxygen of innovation
- collaboration and adaptability drive the innovation pay-off.

Universities that form clusters of expertise around disciplines or common objectives have been highly successful in gaining recognition and funding support. Such 'centres of excellence' often bring together a range of skills and knowledge to work collaboratively towards an agreed vision. Broad, multi-disciplinary and multifaceted problems, such as addressing future water needs in drought prone areas, require the expertise and collaboration of many professionals, including engineers, scientists, environmental and agricultural experts, ICT and public policy makers. Together they are able to identify and map the entire range of issues and seek intersecting solutions that address all aspects of the problem, such as water purification, water measurement and metering, contamination, desalination, public education and policy-making.

Institutional context for knowledge management at the University of Melbourne

Founded in 1864 by Redmond Barry in the tradition of Oxford and Cambridge, with three professors and 16 students, the University of Melbourne is one of the oldest and most prestigious universities in Australia. Its motto derives from Horace: *Postera crescam laude* 'to grow in the esteem of future generations'. Lieutenant-Governor La Trobe laid the foundation stones of the new University and the Melbourne Public Library on the same day (Reynolds 2009). Both institutions were established to preserve and transmit knowledge. The inscription on the foundation stone of the University declares that it was 'instituted in honour of God, for establishing young men in philosophy, literature and piety, cultivating the talent of youth, fostering the arts, and extending the bounds of science' (Macintyre and Selleck, 2003).

Situated on a historic campus close to the centre of Melbourne, the University has grown into a large and complex institution with 45,000 students and 7,000 staff. It has achieved an international reputation, ranking 38th in the Times Higher Education World University Rankings for 2008 and 73rd in the Shanghai Jiao Tong Academic Ranking of World Universities for 2008.

The Melbourne Model of learning and teaching

In 1996 the University set about a reform agenda by which infrastructure was upgraded and increased, and fee-paying international students were welcomed. Revenues increased, as did international reputation, particularly due to the University's strong performance in research.

In 2005 the *Growing Esteem* strategy was launched. Using the metaphor of the triple helix, the three strands of Research, Learning and Teaching, and Knowledge Transfer reinforce and support each other. The strategy set a horizon of 2015 by when the University will have a sharper research focus, a revised portfolio of highly sought-after degrees, and knowledge transfer activities befitting an externally engaged, public-spirited institution.

The reformed learning and teaching offering has become known as the Melbourne Model. It is centred on six broad undergraduate degrees (arts, biomedicine, commerce, environments, music and science) and a suite of US and Bologna-style postgraduate degrees leading to professional qualifications (e.g. architecture, law) and research higher degrees. In addition to discipline studies, undergraduate students are required to study a quarter of their course across other disciplines through 'breadth' subjects. The Melbourne Model and its implementation from 2008 aroused significant interest and have differentiated the University of Melbourne from other local university offerings.

Vice-Chancellor Glyn Davis explains:

> University educators are now realising that the students of today and tomorrow need to be able to handle more complex knowledge and concepts, and this can be done more successfully at graduate level. At

undergraduate level, today's students need to get deep discipline content and breadth of academic experience and develop the capacity to negotiate their way successfully in a world where knowledge boundaries are shifting and re-forming to create new frontiers and challenges almost daily.

(Fearn, 2009b)

In addition to academic reforms, the University has instituted a number of student-centred initiatives which together create a unique 'Melbourne Experience'. The University's Graduate Attributes,[1] articulated in 2007, state that graduates will be:

- academically excellent
- knowledgeable across disciplines
- leaders in communities
- attuned to cultural diversity and
- active global citizens.

The University is currently reviewing and refining the *Growing Esteem* strategy in order to sharpen institutional priorities (University of Melbourne, 2009). The discussion document 'What are Universities For?' highlights the views of Colin Lucas, former Vice-Chancellor of the University of Oxford. He argues that universities:

are concerned to create and transmit 'useful knowledge'. Inescapably, the definition of useful knowledge is relative: it is partly what serves the broadest purpose of rendering the human condition and the world we live in coherent to us; and it is also partly the preparation of what we do not yet know to be useful knowledge.

In 2008 the Vice-Chancellor established an Information Futures Commission (IFC), which was charged with stimulating a vigorous internal conversation to inform the development of scholarly information and a technologies, services and infrastructure strategy. The foreword to the Commission's consultation paper quotes the *Growing Esteem* discussion paper:

[T]he archetypal image of a university is a community of scholars clustered around a library, drawing on and adding to a growing archive of codified knowledge . . .　　　　　　(University of Melbourne, 2005)

As a result of the extensive consultation process and expert input from international advisers, a 10-year strategy entitled *Melbourne's Scholarly Information Future* was endorsed in July 2008. The strategy includes eight actions organized under the three strands of the triple helix and a series of enablers as follows:

To advance Melbourne's position as a leading research institution we will seek to:
1　Provide an outstanding information environment that facilitates creativity and the development of critical thought and knowledge
2　Disseminate the University's scholarship widely, inviting local, national and international collaboration and communication.

To enhance learning and teaching at Melbourne we will seek to:
3　Equip our students with the critical, ethical and practical capabilities to effectively use scholarly information
4　Equip our staff with the resources, capacity and skills required to create learning experiences of the highest quality.

To distinguish Melbourne through its knowledge transfer activities we will seek to:
5　Unlock the potential of our unique scholarly collections to stimulate engagement between the University and its communities.

Overall we will seek to:
6　Create physical environments that support the development of scholarly communities and facilitate a sense of belonging
7　Provide an information environment that is distinguished by ease of use, equity of access, quality of content and richness of possibility
8　Engage in advanced scholarship of information practice, using this to inform the development of our information partnerships, services, system and infrastructure.
　　　　　　　　　　　　　　　　　(University of Melbourne, 2008)

With this strategy set, it is clear that the University of Melbourne and its Library have considerable opportunities to pursue a scholarly information future rich in knowledge management themes.

Scholarly information futures at the University of Melbourne

Following the development of the strategy, the Library at the University of Melbourne is being reinvigorated. However, there are a number of examples of knowledge management practices since the mid-1990s. While there is no branded knowledge management programme in place, there is evidence to support Broadbent's assertion that such activities are not new.

Creating knowledge repositories

If we return to Davenport's first perspective of creating knowledge repositories, this is an area where libraries excel. Through judicious acquisitions and donations, the University of Melbourne has arguably one of the richest Australian university collections of rare and significant cultural resources. In recent years specially funded projects have reduced cataloguing backlogs to ensure that the research community is aware of these riches and has access to them. The catalogue is not a repository for its own sake, but a knowledge transfer tool to draw scholars to the University and its rich collections.

Economic stimulus funding from the Australian government was provided through the Australian Scheme for Higher Education Repositories (ASHER) initiative. All Australian universities have been encouraged to implement institutional repositories. The University of Melbourne ePrints Repository (UMER)[2] is a knowledge repository to expose publications produced by scholars at our research-intensive institution. The University has commenced discussions on options for open access policies, with a view to determining a University-wide position by the end of 2009.

Digitization projects

Digitization projects were identified by the Information Futures

Commission as an important opportunity to share not only the metadata on the University's rich heritage collections but also full text and images. The Library has digitized various items from cultural collections, including extensive print collections. Three linked projects in 2009 have acted as forerunners in engaging the University community with the potential of digitization. The University Calendars project has digitized content from 1864 to present on all aspects of University life, including lists of professors and students, examination papers, fees and advertisements for regalia. Reports of the Victorian Protector of Aborigines 1860–1900 have been digitized to further knowledge of indigenous history in the colony, and digitized Transcripts of Evidence of the 1939 Bushfires Royal Commission are topical in the light of tragic bushfires in the Victorian countryside during 2009.

Digitization offers great opportunities, but requires careful management of copyright and other issues. According to Purcell (2009):

> Opening the doors of the archives to researchers is a careful balance between access and risk management; however, the positive benefits of making use of existing historical records far outweigh the negatives.

Collaboration tools

Turning to Davenport's third perspective of enhancing the knowledge environment, collaboration tools assist in sharing knowledge and experience. Within the Library, the Learning Environments team has very successfully implemented the Learning Management system. Since online presence for all undergraduate subjects was mandated by the Academic Board in 2007 a high uptake has been achieved and more than 3,500 subjects have been established. Detailed subject information, including information about assessment, readings and resources, is an important element of sharing knowledge within the student learning experience.

To complement the undergraduate learning experience, Sakai@ Melbourne is a platform of aggregated technologies that support online collaboration for our researchers and research higher degree students. In partnership with the Melbourne Graduate School of Research, a learning portal for research higher degrees was developed. This common service platform has been optimized for project teams, including internal and inter-institutional collaborations. At June 2009 over 1,477 users (431 external and 1,046 internal) were collaborating on over 200 project sites. Tools such as templates, wikis, calendars, announcements, forums and e-mail archives facilitate knowledge sharing and support rich-research communities.

The nearby Victoria University Library has implemented a new initiative through hiring a team of 'student rovers' to assist other students. This necessitates sharing within the trusted community of practice of rovers. The programme receives oversight and mentoring from an academic practice leader. A wiki provided opportunities for handovers between rovers, and an opportunity for reflective learning. Geisler and Wickramasinghe (2009) cite debriefings of air pilots after missions as a similar opportunity for extracting tacit knowledge.

While Web 2.0 technologies can be instrumental in knowledge environments, libraries around the world have been upgrading physical learning spaces to facilitate collaborative and individual learning as well as enhance the student experience. The University of Melbourne has adopted a precinct approach to providing student-facing services. In 2009 the Eastern Precinct was opened, incorporating an upgraded Library, student learning environments with 24/7 capability, and unsupervised collaboration spaces adjacent to casual outdoor spaces and a centre for student advice. These spaces have been very popular in supporting different learning contexts and group work, increasingly part of the academic experience.

The literature is rich on the importance of a sharing culture and on stimulating innovation and new ways of working. As a result of the Information Futures Commission, cultural change will be stimulated through a round of Innovation Grants. Terms of reference were finalized for bids in the second half of 2009. Approved projects will be co-funded to encourage experimentation with new forms of scholarly communication and stimulate creativity and collaboration.

Managing knowledge as an asset

The fourth of Davenport's knowledge management perspectives is to manage knowledge as an organizational asset. The ability to share simple or transactional information such as company wide data networks, groupware, intranets and schedulers is an important enabler. Handzic and Zhou (2005) point to such systems as being integral to developing knowledge networks. A project at Melbourne to bring structure to the shared computer drive has facilitated easier access and a standardized approach to retrieving records within the Library. Building on advice from records management professionals within the Library, a common structure and vocabulary for headings ensures a standard approach by different sections of the Library.

As Melbourne is a research-intensive University, stored research data, as a knowledge asset, provides considerable opportunities to evidence past research. It may also be used for future analysis and re-work. In the spirit of the institutional repository movement, the Government has identified the need for a strategic national approach to exposing and providing access to data from publicly funded research. The Australian National Data Service (ANDS) initiative (http://ands.org.au/) will allocate funding for strategic projects to 'seed the research data commons'. The University of Melbourne Library is collaborating with the ANDS project to trial processes for gathering metadata on rich sources of research data so as to facilitate knowledge and collaboration within research communities.

Within the University, the Library plays an important role in e-research initiatives. According to Branin (2009):

> The new and rather daunting responsibilities emerging in science librarianship include participation on research teams, science data curation, and helping manage the whole life cycle of scientific information from research and discovery to publication and data archiving. This sounds like the fruition of knowledge management to me.

A related project involving the Library will redevelop research systems for greater strategic value. Consolidation and linking of data and information on research metrics and performance (e.g. bibliometrics) will provide a strategic view of research to support future decision making. Value is added by means of a new view of existing knowledge.

Knowledge transfer at the University of Melbourne

The Objects of the University include:

> To undertake scholarship, research and research training of
> international standing and to apply that scholarship and research to
> the advancement of knowledge and to the benefit of the well-being of
> the Victorian, Australian and international communities.

When the University launched its *Growing Esteem* strategy, it highlighted
the University's role as a public-spirited institution. At the same time,
it established knowledge transfer as a core activity (sometimes referred
to as a 'third stream' activity) alongside research, and teaching and
learning. In doing so the University made a public commitment to its
important role in contributing to the benefit of communities, locally,
nationally and internationally. The public assertion of these values
ensures that the University builds knowledge transfer into the
organizational culture through its planning, development and review
processes, ensuring that these objectives are given equal weight alongside
teaching and research.

Interaction with external communities

Knowledge transfer is defined within the University as the direct two-
way interaction between the University and its external communities,
involving the development, exchange and application of knowledge and
expertise for their mutual benefit. It involves three key elements, which
are to:

- generate intellectual capital in ways that are mutually beneficial
  to the university and the partners with whom it engages
- be linked to the University's teaching and research activities
- be characterized by their responsiveness and relevance to
  economic, social, environmental and cultural issues.

The capacity of universities to make significant contributions to the
converging global demands of the 21st century depends in large part
on their ability to engage in a continuous cycle of knowledge
development and innovation through collaboration and engagement with
industry, governments and community groups, combined with the
ability to leverage leaders, thinkers and knowledge to achieve tangible
benefits for society. Knowledge transfer occurs when organizations

collaborate to achieve shared objectives by exchanging knowledge and expertise. The outcomes of these collaborations are more significant than either partner could achieve on its own.

The authoritative Science and Technology Policy Research Unit (SPRU) at the University of Sussex defines 'third stream' activity as 'the generation, use, application, and exploitation of knowledge and other university capabilities outside academic environments' (University of Sussex, 2002). The Victorian [Australia] Minister for Skills and Workforce Planning, in his April 2009 Media Release states:

> Victoria's universities . . . serve as leading institutions to produce
> knowledge and skills needed by graduates entering the workforce, and
> by industries competing in the global economy.

This emphasizes the importance of universities as major contributors to the knowledge economy, alongside industry and business.

The Cutler (2008) report on Australia's capacity to innovate, *Venturous Australia*, states:

> Entrepreneurs, policy-makers, researchers, workers, and consumers are
> all part of the innovation system. One way to make the system
> stronger is by strengthening its constituent parts. The other is by
> strengthening the links between these parts.

The NESTA Research Report UK (Kitson et al., 2009) describes the 'connected university' model that focuses on a much wider range of interactions with business. This engagement turns academic excellence into economic impact. The model applies not only to research-oriented universities but also to further education for local and wider economic benefit, and involves building networks with local firms, nurturing local clusters and creating national and international connections.

Universities' rationale for knowledge transfer

Knowledge transfer involves a wide range of activities with external organizations and communities, from joint research to providing cultural experiences or public debate and, improving the educational prospects of communities.

Knowledge transfer has suffered from a similar misunderstanding in terms of definition and means of execution as has knowledge management. Knowledge transfer is not new, but the renewed focus on it elevates its importance in universities and ensures that it is done well. Fearn (2009a) writes:

> They have avoided it, complained about it and questioned its merits, but now academics have a genuine reason to get involved in Knowledge Transfer – it is good for their careers. Research into the London-based knowledge-transfer projects in the arts and humanities found that early-career academics have much to gain from getting involved in schemes that involve external partners such as theatres and galleries.

Fearn (2009a) identifies the benefits of knowledge transfer as profile building, demonstrating leadership, networking opportunities, and recognition for academic staff as potential speakers and collaborators and responsible advocates for their profession.

The benefits of knowledge transfer at the University include new research opportunities, greater innovation, wider networks that lead to industry–research collaborations and funding, a faster route to market, attracting staff and students to the University, closer relations with government, enhanced reputation and standing, improved teaching results, more relevant curriculum, and greater employment opportunities for students.

Mechanisms for knowledge transfer

In a similar way to knowledge management, knowledge transfer requires excellent systems and processes to ensure that it provides significant value to the University. Sieloff (1999) notes that in spite of the early informal attempts to share knowledge within Hewlett Packard:

> the need for more explicit and deliberate strategies for managing knowledge has only recently become clear, as the disruptive technology of the Internet and the World Wide Web triggered an explosion in the availability of information and knowledge, but did nothing to expand our limited attention capacity.

The culture of organizations will only change with the right incentives and systems to support the new environment. Universities that plan to develop a strong culture around knowledge transfer must develop systems and processes to identify, manage and reward faculties and staff for their efforts. Systems are needed that enable universities to know who their partners are, the useful knowledge and assets that they have, how to engage with these partners, and how to collaboratively identify new opportunities for both the partner and the university. Rewards and recognition systems are needed, such as promotion criteria that recognize and reward good practice. For academic staff who are unused to creating opportunities through partnership and collaboration, staff development opportunities and tools may be required, as well as networking opportunities where common interests can be discussed with potential partners.

Knowledge transfer mechanisms at Melbourne

The University of Melbourne has developed a range of mutually beneficial partnerships with industry, government, not-for-profit organizations and community groups, leading to results that the University could not have achieved on its own. In addition, it has created collaborations and partnerships around themes that are important to its mission. One example is the newly established Melbourne Institute for Indigenous Partnerships (MIIP). The MIIP will play a key role in co-ordinating the development of the wide range of indigenous programmes that are supported by the University and its affiliates and will be a significant link to the indigenous communities across Australia. The Institute is a co-ordinating mechanism that draws on expertise from a range of faculties and disciplines. MIIP operates as a virtual institute, bound together by a governance structure and a program director to provide strategic leadership for its members. Through the director and its associate members, the Institute will lead the development of a more co-ordinated university interface with Australian governments and with business and non-government sectors in relation to indigenous development.

The same philosophy underpins the creation of a number of virtual research institutes that draw together expertise to create cross-disciplinary strength that will seek answers to major social, economic and environmental issues. These institutes will produce a step-wise change in cross-disciplinary capacity, providing leadership and co-ordination that transcend individual disciplines. The institutes will seek significant new partnerships and increase the University's response to external priorities. To date, three institutes of this type have been established: the Melbourne Energy Institute, the Melbourne Institute of Materials and the Melbourne Sustainable Societies Institute.

The Melbourne Model ensures that the curriculum provides broad, cross-disciplinary subjects to graduate students. Cahill (2009) quotes the Deputy Vice-Chancellor Research:

> My understanding is that in the best US universities now more than 50 per cent of PhD students are enrolling in interdisciplinary projects and we're going to find our way to enable that trend.

In addition to research- and teaching-led collaborations, the University has developed strong cultural and community engagement in the communities in which it has presence. One example is the annual, neighbourhood Carlton Community Day, held by the University to encourage newly arrived refugees to enjoy the amenities of the University campus for sport and recreation and to raise aspirations in the local community for university study and personal development.

Another exciting initiative was the Festival of Ideas in June 2009. The theme of 'Climate Change/Cultural Change' recognized that Australia is on the sharp edge of climate change. Over six days, more than 50 outstanding thinkers led a programme that comprised evening keynote lectures which led on the next day to challenging panel discussions, debates, forums and seminars across the University campus on climate change and cultural changes within Australian society. The festival sought responses to the impact of climate change on our community – societal, political, economic, medical, geographic and creative.

Community outreach programmes help to acknowledge the place of the university within its region, through its understanding of regional needs, the industries that the region supports and the importance of universities to the fabric of society.

These initiatives created greater opportunities, through collaboration and partnership, to enhance teaching, extend the boundaries of research and address the current and future needs of a knowledge economy. This is at the heart of being an externally engaged, public-spirited university.

The University Library has established many connections to external communities, including business and government. The digitization of the transcripts of the 1939 Bushfire Royal Commission has demonstrated that the Library can assist current policy makers to learn from history. Further digitization projects include a plan to digitize a vast quantity of business archives, in partnership with the CPA (Certified Practicing Accountants), to provide valuable material for lawyers, economists, historians and policy makers.

Recognitions

In 2006 the Library won a Knowledge Transfer Award for the Howship Project. Benjamin (2006) reports on this project, between the Archives and the Benalla & District Family History Group. A collection of 1,250 dry glass negatives created by William John Howship was digitized and catalogued in the University of Melbourne Archives' photographic Image Catalogue, UMAIC. The collection was made accessible nationally and internationally through the PictureAustralia gateway[3] 'further enhancing the collection's profile'.

The project forged an important partnership between the University and the Benalla community which was highly beneficial for both parties. A community-based project to identify and add stories to the images was assisted by access to members of the local community, some of whom were descendants of those depicted in the photographs. The project was extended to students from Benalla College, who assisted as part of their community service. One benefit was in evidencing past risks. Photographs of flooding in the township were useful knowledge for avoiding future risk.

Another Knowledge Transfer Award, the Redmond Barry Fellowship, was recently awarded to journalist Andrew Dodd for a history of John James Clark, who arrived in Melbourne and worked as an architect in the 1850s, from the age of 14. Clark designed many of Melbourne's most prominent buildings and played a role in the development of the public libraries in Sydney and Melbourne. The annual Fellowship facilitates the production of a literary work using archival materials and sources from the University Library and the State Library of Victoria. The work will shed further light on the architectural history of the new colony and will lead to greater understanding of the wealth of material held in the State

Library and the University Library. This is collaboration between two important libraries to advance research and build greater understanding of their collections.

Conclusion

Libraries and the universities that they support are built by knowledge workers whose roles are not just about preparing students for the professions and extending the frontiers of research, but also to contribute to the knowledge economy.

Creating and exchanging knowledge and intangibles through interactions within and beyond their institutions is the heart of what universities and their members do. This activity narrows the gap between information and innovation and between innovation and application. The resulting increase in productivity is both incremental and transformational.

The dimension of knowledge creation that has been acknowledged through knowledge management is the human dimension – the sharing of knowledge between people in organizations and through knowledge transfer – the sharing of knowledge between organizations, including between universities and industry, governments and communities.

By developing systems and supporting services that enhance the capability of universities to form collaborations, both internally and externally, universities will thrive in the engine-rooms of innovation.

Geisler and Wickramasinghe (2009) offer a useful model for determining evidence of the knowledge-based enterprise:

- flexible structure
- informal processes
- enhanced communications network
- culture favouring the transaction and exchange of knowledge
- senior management cognizant of the key role of knowledge and supportive of its applications in the enterprise
- structures and processes devised to transact in knowledge, such as joint ventures and exchange of personnel with other enterprises
- knowledge considered a key strategic asset of the enterprise.

The University of Melbourne, as evidenced in this chapter, exhibits many of these characteristics. While the knowledge management label is not used to describe these activities across the University, these characteristics are nevertheless evident through the vision that is embodied in the Triple Helix. The principles of knowledge management flow from strategic documents to performance measurement and programme reviews.

In a rapidly changing external environment, universities require assistance to better manage their corporate and institutional knowledge and information. Within changing structures and collaborative approaches, libraries in partnership with other university groups have an opportunity to develop new services that may require the skills of other groups. By being broadly focused, libraries can become trusted consultants in the larger work of the institution. This requires deep understanding of the research priorities of key academics and of the learning requirements for both on-campus and online teaching, and recognition of where partnerships with other libraries, other research organizations and business will produce significant benefits for the university.

Librarians are able to facilitate the adaptation of existing knowledge in multiple ways. This includes managing information as well as data for researchers. Increasingly library staff are becoming trusted partners in the academic enterprise in both knowledge management and knowledge transfer by helping to locate new sources of information beyond traditional resources and forming alliances to share knowledge and information held within and beyond the institution.

The Library has many opportunities, through cultivating an outward-facing and opportunistic approach, constantly refining and reviewing priorities to add value to the mission of the University and the Library. There are opportunities for innovation and to add greater value to a range of core programmes outside existing Library work, such as marketing of data and repository management.

The Library supports information access for alumni and is key to building University-wide knowledge systems such as the database of academic expertise found in the 'Find and Expert' database and made available to external groups from the University's website.

Partnership building is an important aspect of this work, not only to attract gifts and donations, but also to negotiate access to collections that may not be openly available to academic staff. In 21st-century organizations, collaboration and partnership is a valued asset when applied internally to enhance the business of the university, and externally to enhance the opportunities for new research and learning.

Let us return to the original premise of whether knowledge management has achieved its original vision. Knowledge management and knowledge transfer are not new concepts. Definitional debates should not cloud the reasons why organizations should focus on knowledge management. The difference is that by refocusing on what can be achieved by using these using knowledge management concepts, and by working collaboratively to achieve common goals, we achieve the capacity to resolve issues that are complex and extraordinary by harnessing the skills and 'know how' of others to achieve common goals.

To answer the questions posed in the introduction, the evidence at the University of Melbourne suggests that, despite the hype, a knowledge management approach when applied to gathering, organizing, sharing, exchanging and accessing knowledge, has transformed the University's business of research, learning and teaching, and knowledge transfer. In conclusion, the experience at the University of Melbourne is that knowledge management is embedded in many activities that perhaps don't acknowledge the label. Libraries and technology have delivered against the knowledge management agenda by providing enabling capacity to achieve organizational goals.

Notes

1   www.unimelb.edu.au/about/attributes.html.
2   www.lib.unimelb.edu.au/eprints/.
3   www.pictureaustralia.org/index.html.

References

Benjamin, J. (2006) Uni helps Benalla Recover Rich Legacy in Early Photographic Image Collection, *UniNews*, 15 (5), (April),
www.lib.unimelb.edu.au/collections/archives/publications/howship.htm.

Branin, J. (2009) What We Need is a Knowledge Management Perspective, *College and Research Libraries*, 70 (2), 104–5.

Broadbent, M. (1997) The Emerging Phenomenon of Knowledge Management, *Australian Library Journal*, 46 (1), 6–24.

Cahill, S. (2009) The Ideas Man, *The University of Melbourne Voice*, 5 (3), (8 June–12 July), 4.

Cutler, T. (2008) *Venturous Australia: building strength in innovation*, Cutler and Company.

Davenport, T. H. and Prusak, L. (1997) *Information Economy: mastering the information and knowledge environment*, Oxford University Press.

Fearn, H. (2009a) Knowledge-transfer Boon for Fledgling Scholars, *Times Higher Education*, (23–29 July), 23.

Fearn, H. (2009b) The Wizards of Oz, *Times Higher Education*, (8–14 January), 36–9.

Ferguson, S. and Lloyd, A. (2007) Information Literacy and Leveraging of Corporate Knowledge. In: Ferguson, S. (ed.), *Libraries in the Twenty-First Century: charting new directions in information services,* Topics in Australasian Library and Information Studies, Number 27, Charles Sturt University, Centre for Information Studies.

Geisler, E. and Wickramasinghe, N. (2009) *Principles of Knowledge Management: theory, practice and cases*, ME Sharpe.

Handzic, M. and Zhou, A. Z. (2005) *Knowledge Management: an integrative approach*, Chandos.

Hubbard, G., Samuels, D., Heap, S. and Cocks, G. (2007) *The First XI: winning organisations in Australia*, 2nd edn, Wiley.

Kennedy, N. (2009) *The Hidden Dimensions of Innovation*, Hargreaves Institute Presentation, 11th March, www.abfoundation.com.au/research-knowledge/presentations/243.

Kitson, M., Howells, J., Braham, R. and Westlake, S. (2009) *The Connected University: driving recovery and growth in the UK economy*, NESTA (National Endowment for Science, Technology and the Arts) Research Report: April.

Lee, H.-W. (2005) *Knowledge Management and the Role of Libraries*, www.white-clouds.com/iclc/cliej/cl19lee.htm.

Macintyre, S. and Selleck, R. J. W. (2003) *A Short History of the University of Melbourne*, Melbourne University Press.

Martell, C. (2009) A Citation Analysis of College and Research Libraries Comparing Yahoo, Google, Google Scholar, and ISI Web of Knowledge with Implications for Promotion and Tenure, *College & Research Libraries*. Pre-print anticipated for publication September 2009, www.ala.org/ala/mgrps/divs/acrl/publications/crljournal/preprints/preprints.cfm.

Metcalfe, A. S. (2006) *Knowledge Management and Higher Education: a critical analysis*, Information Science.

Purcell, A. D. (2009) Making the Most of Your Historical Assets, *Information Management*, January–February, 46–8.

Reynolds, S. (2009) Libraries, Librarians and Librarianship in the Colony of Victoria, *Australian Academic & Research Libraries* 40 (1) 15.

Sieloff, C. (1999) If only HP Knew what HP Knows: the roots of knowledge management at Hewlett Packard, *Journal of Knowledge Management*, 3 (1), 47–53.

Standards Australia, (2005) *Knowledge management – a guide*, AS 5037, Standards Australia.

Townley, C. T. (2001) Knowledge Management and Academic Libraries, *College and Research Libraries*, 62 (1), (January), 44–55.

University of Melbourne (2005) *Growing Esteem,* http://growingesteem.unimelb.edu.au/_data/assets/pdf_file/0009/86688/2005finalgrowingesteem.pdf.

University of Melbourne (2008) *Melbourne's Scholarly Information Future: a ten-year strategy July 2008,* www.informationfutures.unimelb.edu.au/commission/reports.

University of Melbourne (2009) *Refining our Strategy: a discussion paper that invites involvement and response,* May, http://growingesteem.unimelb.edu.au/about/refining_our_strategy#Refining.

University of Sussex, Science and Technology Research Unit SPRU (2002) *Measuring Third Stream Activities*, Final Report of the Russell Group of Universities, April.

Wen, S. (2005) *Implementing Knowledge Management in Academic Libraries: a pragmatic approach,* www.white-clouds.com/iclc/cliej/cl19wen.htm.

9
Libraries and the management of research data

Martin Lewis

Introduction

Perhaps the starting point for any discussion about libraries and research data is to ask whether managing data is actually a job for university libraries. The answer to this question is 'yes and no'. 'Yes', in the sense that data from academic research projects represents an integral part of the global research knowledge base, and so managing it should be a natural extension of the university library's current role in providing access to the published part of that knowledge base. 'No', because the scale of the challenge in terms of infrastructure, skills and culture change requires concerted action by a range of stakeholders, and not just university libraries.

This assessment, from the perspective of the United Kingdom (UK) in 2009, is not a prescription for inaction on the part of university libraries, however. On the contrary, libraries have a key role to play in developing both the capability and the capacity of the higher education sector to manage research data assets. Some of them are already doing so; and, as for the rest of us, we need to take steps to understand the landscape even if we lack the resources to make immediate progress locally.

As with any emerging area, the management of research data is still evolving. In this chapter, by 'research data management' we mean the storage, curation and preservation of, and provision of continuing access to, digital research data – in other words, most of the processes at the centre of the Digital Curation Centre (DCC)'s Curation Lifecycle Model, as well as in the lower half of the outer circle (Figure 9.1). Perhaps more simply, this is *not* just about the storage of data, which is how the subject is sometimes represented and how the requirement to 'do something' about research data is often manifested locally.

It's worth taking a little time to reflect on how the management of research data sits alongside the other relationships that the modern university library has with its academic community. We'll then consider what the drivers are for investing time and effort in managing research data, before looking in more detail at what contribution university libraries can and should be making.

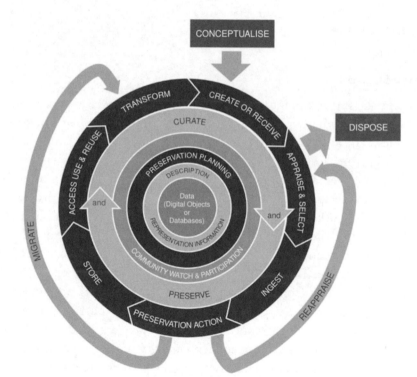

Figure 9.1 *The Digital Curation Lifecycle model*
Source: Reproduced with permission under a Creative Commons licence. CC-NC-BY-SA DCC.

Libraries and their relationship to researchers

As the other contributors to this book demonstrate, university libraries in many countries have, in general, been very successful in engaging with the rapidly changing learning and teaching agenda on their campuses (and off them as well). From information literacy to the development of bold, new, technology-enabled learning spaces, they have re-engineered the relationship with their teaching colleagues, improved the student learning experience and raised expectations. And at the risk of over-generalization, we might contend both that these successes have been evident in universities across the spectrum of research-intensiveness, from new universities without a significant research base, to the big research elite universities of the Russell Group in the UK; and that a similar general re-engagement with researchers has been notable by its absence, even within the Russell Group universities.

Despite libraries' progress over the last decade in transforming access to the research literature through provision of e-journals and resource-discovery tools – and perhaps in part *because* of it – libraries have become more distant from their research customers, especially their STM (science, technology and medicine) research colleagues. The Research Information Network (RIN)'s report *Researchers' Use of Academic Libraries and Their Services* (RIN, 2007) represents a valuable snapshot of the nature of the researcher–librarian relationship: it notes the decline in visits to the physical premises of libraries in recent years, especially by STM researchers, and the weak link in such researchers' minds between the digital content they use and the library's role in providing it. In the late 1980s and early 1990s, it was not unusual for larger university libraries to be conducting several thousand mediated online bibliographic searches per year on behalf of their researchers, the majority of them involving a detailed client interview, with the useful secondary outcome that the library liaison staff involved would have a good picture of the client's research. While no one would suggest a return to mediated access to the research literature as a way of improving research liaison, not least since the size of the research community has increased enormously since the early 1990s, the challenge of re-engaging with researchers to understand their developing knowledge management needs is clear. And the need for progress with the research data management task requires that this re-engagement takes place.

Why manage research data?

But why do we need to manage research data in the first place? Library managers contemplating multiple demands on limited resources deserve an answer to this question, even though it may seem redundant to the relatively small cadre of data managers in the workforce; and moreover, they in turn need to be able to articulate the answer to university managers when discussing institutional approaches to the challenge.

The answer is in part a prosaic one: the volumes of data being generated by researchers are growing rapidly (for once, there may be a case for accurate use of the word 'exponential'), not least as a result of the increasing use of e-research tools (see the following section); and research funders are increasingly likely to require researchers to deposit their research data (research funders' policies on data deposit are now included in the SHERPA 'Juliet' database maintained by the UK Open Access project, SHERPA[1]).

More powerfully, the rewards of managing research data include significant potential benefits for academic research itself:

- the ability to share research data, minimizing the need to repeat work in the laboratory, field or library
- ensuring that research data gathered at considerable cost is not lost or inadvertently destroyed
- the retrieval, comparison and co-analysis of data from multiple sources, with the potential of leading to powerful new insights
- the ability to check or repeat experiments and verify findings – particularly important amid growing national and international concern about research integrity
- the emergence of new research themes – and in particular cross-disciplinary themes – from re-analysis of existing data or comparisons with new data: increasingly, data may become the starting point for new research as well as representing a result of current research.

To this list of drivers should be added the public access argument (also used in relation to open access to published research papers): that society as a whole benefits from access to the fruits of publicly funded research, a sentiment expressed in the Organisation for Economic Co-operation and Development's (OECD) *Principles and Guidelines for Access to Research Data from Public Funding*, which states:

> Sharing and open access to publicly funded research data not only helps to maximise the research potential of new digital technologies and networks, but provides greater return from the public investment in research. (OECD, 2007)

Even those institutions in which research data management has not been actively discussed are likely to find it growing in a priority as researchers whose funding carries a requirement to manage post-project data outputs approach the latter stages of their projects.

e-Research and research data management

The UK's e-Science Core Programme

Management of the data outputs of research projects is not a requirement that has just emerged in the last few years: it is over 40 years since the UK Data Archive was established at the University of Essex, and many university libraries have long held collections of paper-based surveys and other data outputs. However, it is the growth of digital research data that has driven recent interest in long-term curation and storage. In the UK, the government-funded e-Science Core Programme, which ran for about six years from 2001, has raised the profile of this issue, to the extent that research data management is sometimes seen as a challenge exclusively linked to e-science or e-research (the term e-research is more inclusive of the non-science disciplines, which are increasingly using the techniques and tools of e-science).

The e-Science Core Programme was administered by the Engineering and Physical Sciences Research Council (EPSRC) on behalf of Research Councils UK (RCUK), and aimed to establish the toolkit – including infrastructure, middleware and documentation – to facilitate wider uptake of e-research. The UK's seven Research Councils also established e-science programmes, with ring-fenced funding, to promote e-science within their disciplinary areas. The Core Programme also funded demonstrator projects to enable researchers to understand the scope and capability of e-research.

Announcing the eScience Core Programme in 2000[2], the then Director-General of the Research Councils, Professor Sir John Taylor, said: 'e-Science is about global collaboration in key areas of science, and the next generation of infrastructure that will enable it'.

We can characterize e-research from the vantage point of nine years later as:

- data-intensive: generating and often *using* large volumes of data
- collaborative: involving researchers across multiple institutions, often transnationally
- grid-enabled: using high-capacity networks and middleware.

Although data management was not directly addressed in the first phase of the Core Programme, the implications of large-scale e-research projects for data management were soon apparent. The term 'data deluge' was used by the Core Programme's leadership to describe the challenge ahead (Hey and Trefethen, 2003). Additionally, the Joint Information Systems Committee (JISC) commissioned a report on the curation of eScience data (Lord and Macdonald, 2003) that made a number of recommendations about the need to develop national capability and capacity. It highlighted the role of the Digital Curation Centre, co-funded by the second phase of the Core Programme and by JISC, as a source of expertise and advice for the higher education sector, and made some trenchant comments about the need for a coherent national approach to the challenge:

> There is a lack of a government-level, overall strategy for data
> stewardship and data infrastructure to which science administrators
> can refer, still less to support the researcher in their evolving roles and
> duties with regard to data curation.
>
> (Lord and Macdonald, 2003, 5)

The need for long-term investment appeared to have been recognized by the UK Treasury in its *Science and Innovation Investment Framework 2004–2014* (HM Treasury, 2004). This developed the concept of a national 'e-infrastructure' to support world-class research and innovation, and the Office of Science and Technology (OST), then part of the Department of Trade and Industry, was asked to lead on e-infrastructure. The OST set up a working group, with six sub-groups being asked to explore different aspects of the challenge. These were:

- data and information creation
- preservation and curation

- search and navigation
- virtual research communities
- networks, computer[3]and data storage
- AAA (authentication, authorization and accounting), middleware and DRM (digital rights management).

As can be seen, data management featured prominently in the work of the sub-groups. An opportunity to feed their work directly into the UK government's 2007 Comprehensive Spending Review was missed, however: and when the overarching report was finally published in 2007 (Pothen, 2007) it did not attempt to quantify the level of investment needed to develop and sustain a national infrastructure for the management of digital research data. This brief historical overview of UK developments sets the scene for discussion of the UK Research Data Service (UKRDS) feasibility study in a later section, an initiative in which higher education librarians have played a significant role.

International developments

The UK's e-Science Core Programme helped to get the UK into something of a leadership position in the early years of e-research. Since one of the key benefits of e-research is the facilitation of global collaboration, however, we should note that other countries have also been exploring and investing in e-research. The US National Science Foundation (NSF) has set out a clear vision for future investment in 'cyberinfrastructure' (NSF, 2007a). Unlike the UK, it moved quickly to announce investment funds for digital research data curation through its DataNet programme, the call for which was issued in 2007 (NSF, 2007b). The call document sees a key role for what it terms 'library and archival science' in the new partnerships that it envisages for DataNets. Two DataNet projects have so far been approved: the Data Conservancy led by Johns Hopkins University Library, and the DataNetONE consortium led by the University of New Mexico. The National Science and Technology Council's Committee on Science set up an interagency working party on digital data in 2007, which has recently reported. This sets out a roadmap for a series of co-ordinated national activities, and includes the clear statement that:

> We envision a digital scientific data universe in which data creation, collection, documentation, analysis, preservation, and dissemination can be appropriately, reliably, and readily managed. This will enhance the return on our nation's research and development investment by ensuring that digital data realize their full potential as catalysts for progress in our global information society.
>
> (Interagency Working Group on Digital Data, 2009)

Australia has also moved relatively speedily to develop an e-research road map; and has set up the Australian National Data Service (ANDS), following a report on the data management implications of e-research which is also an excellent overview of the challenge (ANDS Technical Working Group, 2007).

Closer to home, there are significant efforts on a European Union-wide (EU) basis to progress a shared understanding of and commitment to the development of a pan-European e-infrastructure. The European Strategy Forum on Research Infrastructure (ESFRI) advises the EU Council on investment in major components of the e-infrastructure, including large-scale facilities, and published a roadmap for future development in 2006 (a revised version is in preparation). The e-Infrastructure Reflection Group (e-IRG) acts as a think-tank for major European players. It currently has a research data management task force, which is undertaking a survey of data management initiatives; at the time of writing its report is expected shortly.

Back in the UK, the e-Science Core Programme has ended. Interest in e-research remains high, however, as evidenced by the scale of the programmes at the UK's 'All Hands Meetings' organized each year by the National e-Science Centre (NeSC). Increasingly, e-research is becoming more mainstream, as more research acquires the characteristics of e-research, and the growth of digital data-intensive research in the humanities and social sciences has been particularly noteworthy. Moreover, librarians contemplating the research data landscape are realizing that effective data management is needed for smaller-scale projects – the 'long tail' of research that doesn't involve massive data volumes, but whose data outputs have the potential to inform future research.

What libraries can do about data

For those managing academic libraries or information technology (IT) services, one of the most difficult issues relating to data management is working out what needs to be done locally, and what might best be done nationally or internationally. The current absence of a coherent national framework for data curation in the UK does not mean that there is no provision. Many subject areas are covered by well-developed data management facilities run by national or international data centres, reflecting disciplinary differences in the academic culture around deposit and reuse of datasets, and these represent a significant asset for the UK in terms of the knowledge base of data management. The facilities include the European Bioinformatics Institute, an agency of the European Molecular Biology Laboratory based in the UK; the network of data centres run by the Natural Environment Research Council (NERC); the UK Data Archive, and the Economic and Social Data Service (ESDS) which it hosts; and the Cambridge Crystallographic Data Centre. There are, however, large gaps, particularly following the demise of the Arts and Humanities Data Service in 2008, a development which has raised concerns about the degree of reliance that can be placed on external agencies as persistent guardians of research data for the long term. The need to fill these gaps was one objective of the UKRDS feasibility study.

In the meantime, there are several areas where libraries can and should be active in relation to research data. In most of these areas they will want to work in partnership with other campus agencies, notably IT services, and also research offices and those responsible for research governance (such as a Pro-Vice Chancellor for Research). Nine such areas can be grouped handily into a pyramid for ease of reference (Figure 9.2 on the next page), but they are intended to be neither exhaustive nor definitive. In general, the activities lower in the pyramid are areas of early engagement and which may be appropriate for the highest number of university libraries, regardless of the scale of the research base of the parent institution.

Develop library workforce data confidence

We consider issues about the research data management workforce below; this heading is about raising the general level of awareness of the

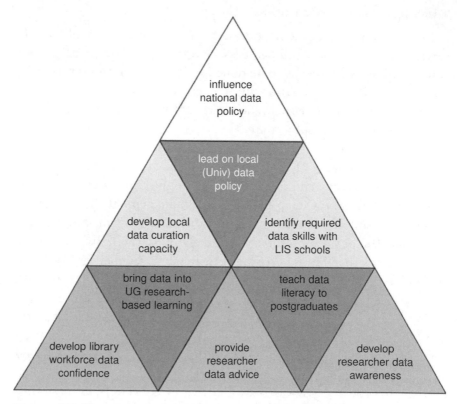

Figure 9.2 *The research data management pyramid for libraries*

existing academic library workforce in relation to both e-research and data management issues, with the objective of equipping staff to hold conversations with academic colleagues and research students on these topics. The target audience is primarily academic liaison librarians, but other library staff, such as systems teams, repository managers and e-resource managers may also benefit from an improved level of knowledge about and understanding of the data management landscape. There are a number of ways in which this can be achieved.

First, library staff have a professional responsibility to update their own knowledge about data management. There is now a wealth of reading available on the subject, not only from the sources already mentioned, but also as a result of a number of recent studies and projects funded by bodies such as JISC and RIN in the UK. Liz Lyon's report for JISC, *Dealing with Data* (Lyon, 2007), is an excellent overview of the current state of play and articulates the policy and operational challenges of data management very clearly. RIN has set out a series of principles for data management (RIN, 2008a), and along with JISC and NERC has commissioned a report on researchers' attitudes and practice in relation to data management (RIN, 2008b). JISC has also commissioned a report on the costs of data preservation (Beagrie et al., 2008) which, in addition to providing help for managers who are trying to assess the resource implications of providing data management capacity, also contains a helpful analysis of the different tasks involved in managing data. It's also important for library liaison staff to ensure that they are up to speed on the policies of the principal funders of research in their universities, not only in relation to open access to published outputs, but in relation to data; and that they are aware of the existing national and discipline-based data centres and repositories.

Second, there is an increasing number of externally organized workshops and courses dealing with data management. Research Libraries UK and the Society of College, National and University Libraries (SCONUL) have organized a number of workshops aimed at academic librarians, based in part on a needs analysis (Martinez, 2007); and the DCC has organized short courses for data managers, as well as a series of international conferences on digital curation. Third, networks of professional practice are beginning to emerge in the UK, such as the DCC Associates' Network and the Research Data Management Forum. There is still a need, however, to reach out to those university library staff for whom research data is barely on the radar, and this must be a short- to medium-term priority if libraries are to become fully engaged with data management.

Provide researcher data advice

University libraries may not (yet) have in place the capacity to provide local data management for digital datasets, but once they have engaged with the issue, and once their liaison staff have enhanced their knowledge of the landscape, they can start to provide advice on data management to researchers, both informally and through the development of more formal content on library websites. Many libraries already provide advice on open access and other aspects of scholarly communication, and data management should be seen as a natural extension of this role. Quite often, academic requests for assistance may occur as requests to IT services for data storage, so it is important that libraries and IT services have a joined-up approach. Such storage requests may be made rather late in the data lifecycle, but they are a way of starting to identify research teams and individuals whose research is data-intensive. Initially the level of advice that libraries may be able to provide will be limited: as the workforce develops its confidence, it will expect to influence the ways in which researchers approach data management *before* research projects start, and ideally at the proposal-writing stage.

Develop researcher data awareness

In parallel with the provision of advice to individual teams or researchers, there is a role for university libraries in raising awareness of the challenges of data management within their institutions, and initiating discussion about it through a range of channels. In most institutions there will be a very wide range of interest in data issues, from researchers who have given little if any thought to the fate of the data they generate, to those working in areas with well-established cultures of data curation. The RIN report on data publication (RIN, 2008b) highlights this diversity, and also draws attention to some of the disincentives for researchers to expend time and effort on data management. These include lack of familiarity with data management techniques, concern about the volume of requests for information/clarification, uncertainty about whether they have all the permissions needed to publish their data, anxiety about subsequent unauthorized modification or misinterpretation, and a feeling that they themselves may be able to extract further publications from the data. Libraries embarking on local data management advocacy need to consider these points carefully, and ensure that their messages are aligned with those of other institutional players, notably, research administrators.

Teach data literacy to postgraduate research students

Most UK university libraries have some involvement in research training, either through formal research training programmes or through less formal channels, although relatively few of them cover research data management (RIN, 2008c). In theory at least, this should be a natural development of libraries' information literacy role, one that is now well established and understood. Research training for postgraduate research students is a key area of contribution in relation to research data management because it presents an opportunity to influence the way in which future researchers approach data when planning their research. The term 'data literacy' is often understood to mean 'statistical literacy'; but for this purpose we mean developing in postgraduates an understanding of the way in which, as future researchers, they will generate and use data, how they need to describe it in order to facilitate future retrieval, how they might approach the identification of data appropriate for preservation, and what options may be open to them for the subsequent storage and curation of their data.

Bring data into undergraduate research-based learning

This is a logical extension of the development of data management skills for postgraduate students. Many undergraduate programmes include a dissertation requirement that will give students experience in the generation of data, and this is an opportunity to start to develop good practice among those who move on to research careers. However, effective management of research data on a wider scale may also bring pedagogic benefits for undergraduate education, by enabling students to access and use real research data in an educational context, an approach that aligns well with the use of problem-based and enquiry-based techniques in the curriculum. Using real research data to enhance students' learning experience will also be of interest to research-intensive universities, for whom provision of 'research-led' learning is an important differentiator in the undergraduate marketplace.

Develop local data curation capacity

Assuming that a combination of advocacy and research-funder policies effectively influences researcher behaviour, should libraries invest in actual data storage and curation capacity? The business case for such investment remains a challenging one, particularly when library budgets are under pressure from the need to sustain current services, to innovate in a wide range of areas (some of them described elsewhere in this book) and to meet the inflationary pressures associated with content procurement.

However, an increasing number of case studies are available to inform decisions by library and institutional managers, many of them taking institutional repositories (IRs) as a starting point for data curation. In the UK, the DISC-UK DataShare project followed the journey from conventional IR to data repository in three big, research-intensive universities (Rice, 2009), each of them using a different repository platform. Purdue University Library in the US has developed a distributed institutional approach to data curation through its Distributed Data Curation Centre (D2C2) (Brandt, 2007; Mullins, 2007). Toolkits to facilitate the introduction of a managed approach to research data are also starting to become available, among them the Data Audit Framework (Jones et al., 2008), which has been trialled at four UK universities.

Identify required data skills with library and information science schools

While the existing library workforce can make a significant contribution to getting research data curation on the institutional map, even libraries with well-developed IRs are likely to find that they need additional skills in order to provide significant data curation capability locally. There is a role here for library managers in identifying the skills gap and working in partnership with library and information science (LIS) schools to develop new training and development resources. Not every university library will need or want to be active in this area, but there is a sense among many university library directors that professional practice has actually changed faster than the curricula of the LIS schools that supply new entrants to the workforce; and consequently libraries have a role to play in providing the evidence base for the development of new data management courses. We'll return to this theme below.

Lead on local data policy

The informal contacts with researchers and other research stakeholders discussed earlier represent an opportunity for the library to exercise a degree of policy leadership more formally at university level. University research and innovation committees, and even senior management teams, need to understand the nature of the data management challenge and the benefits of a coherent (but not necessarily uniform) approach across the institution. They may also need to approve a business case for any investment in this area, and their commitment will be crucial in helping to bring sceptical researchers on board. In this respect, it is not only subject staff and repository managers who need to be data literate: library directors need to be able to articulate both the challenge and the preferred solutions with their senior colleagues. The DISC-UK DataShare project has produced a policy guide for institutions embarking on the extension of their existing IRs to support data deposit (Green et al., 2009).

Influence national data policy

Librarians can and should expect to be players in their national policy arenas for research data – where these exist. Their influence has been especially apparent in Australia, where librarians are well represented on the ANDS Steering Committee; and Liz Lyon, Director of the UK's library research organization UKOLN, has been a member of the US National Science Foundation's Advisory Committee on Cyberinfrastructure. In Canada, the multiagency Research Data Strategy Working Group, led by the Canada Institute for Scientific and Technical Information, included several university library staff among its membership. The working group has recently published a detailed gap analysis of Canadian research data management provision (Research Data Strategy Working Group, 2008). UK university librarians were not heavily involved in the OST's e-infrastructure sub-groups in 2006, but they have played a major part in the UKRDS feasibility study.

In the next two sections we look at two key non-technical strategic challenges: funding and policy; and workforce development.

Funding and policy

It is clear from the studies conducted so far that providing effective data management throughout the data lifecycle requires non-trivial invest-ment. The return on this investment comes from higher-quality research, from easier and therefore cheaper access to existing data, from a reduc-tion in the need to repeat data-generating investigations and from the facilitation of new research topics and insights. But who should pay?

In the UK, this question has proved much harder to resolve than the technical challenges of data curation. In a provocative interview in 2004 in the journal of the UK's professional library association, Professor Tony Hey, then Director of the e-Science Core Programme, criticized university librarians for failing to engage with the need for long-term management of digital research data (Library and Information Update, 2004). There was some uncomfortable justification for his views, since up to that point librarians had been largely unaware of the growth of grid-enabled research and did not generally see the management of the associated data outputs as being within their professional domain. That has certainly changed: both Research Libraries UK and its US equivalent, the Association of Research Libraries (ARL), set up task forces on e-research in 2005, and few librarians would now argue that research data is an inappropriate area for professional and management attention. On the other hand, the UK Core Programme offered no funds for institution-level data management, and the e-research community probably did not appreciate the resource constraints under which university libraries worked, nor the broad front on which change and innovation was taking place elsewhere in libraries, not least in support for learning and teaching.

From the libraries' perspective, growing awareness of the scale of the investment needed, coupled with uncertainty about the demand from researchers for data management, and lack of confidence both about their ability to engage with researchers and in the capabilities of their workforces, has been a significant disincentive for involvement. Additional uncertainty has been generated in the UK by the patchy provision of national-level facilities: will the disciplinary gaps be filled nationally, perhaps by the Research Councils or national agencies such as the British Library or JISC, eventually obviating the need for major local investment? Finding the resources to initiate and develop IRs has not been straightforward for many libraries, and they may feel that extending IRs to include large volumes of data, with metadata, preservation and access challenges an order of magnitude more complex than those posed by e-prints, is not a good use of their resources.

The UKRDS feasibility study

Frustrated by the failure of the OST e-infrastructure process to spark policy leadership from government or from the research councils, Research Libraries UK and its IT services equivalent, RUGIT (the Russell Universities Group IT Directors forum), developed a joint bid to the Higher Education Funding Council for England (HEFCE) in 2007, for funding for a feasibility study for a national research data management service. The bid was submitted under HEFCE's shared services programme, on the grounds that although data management was in its infancy in most universities, it would be cheaper to invest in a national framework than to have every university in England develop the necessary capability and capacity locally. The bid was successful, and the UKRDS feasibility study was completed at the end of 2008 (UK Research Data Service, 2008, 2009). The study confirmed, first, that even conservative assumptions about the cost of local research data management centres yielded significant savings for a national approach; and second, that rather than establishing a monolithic central agency, a UKRDS should be an enabling framework that would facilitate a mixture of appropriate local and national provision, identifying gaps and commissioning additional capacity as required, with a registry of researchers' data management plans as a core component of the service.

The final report recommended that funding should be allocated for an initial two-year 'pathfinder' phase. Rather than pilots, the pathfinders would be live components of the UKRDS service, involving a subset of research-intensive universities, at least one Research Council and one of the existing national data centres. At the time of writing, a bid for the pathfinder phase is being developed by the UKRDS project team. One of the political dimensions of this challenge, and one which the UKRDS study has already encountered, is the UK's unusual 'dual support system' for research funding (Adams and Bekhradnia, 2004). Dual support means that universities receive two separate streams of public funding, one from the Research Councils, relating to specific projects and programmes, and one from HEFCE and its Welsh and Scottish equivalents, intended to provide for discretionary and 'blue skies' research, but increasingly linked to the provision of basic research infrastructure. While some of the seven Research Councils top-slice their own funding in order to operate national data centres, others see data management as an infrastructural cost which should be on the university side of dual support. This continuing discussion in the UK's corridors of power demonstrates that the development of a sustainable business model for research data management is key to scaling up capacity to meet the needs of 21st-century research.

Workforce development

While it may be heartening to hear non-librarians expressing confidence that librarians' renowned metadata skills equip them to be the research data managers of the future, knowledge of MARC, AACR and even Dublin Core does not represent a licence to curate research data. Neither does liaison librarians' knowledge of the bibliographic landscape of their territories mean that they can expect to advise scientists on data collection formats. Developing librarians' *data confidence* will enable them to have conversations about data with researchers, and the importance of this step should not be underestimated. However, the next level of engagement and support for research data will require new skills, or new combinations of skills, and new roles.

JISC commissioned a major study from consultancy Key Perspectives on the development of 'data scientists' (Swan and Brown, 2008), a slightly unfortunate charge, since, as the authors note:

> In practice, there is not yet an exact use of such terms in the data community, and the demarcation between roles may be blurred. It will take time for a clear terminology to become general currency.

Swan and Brown see several differentiated but partly overlapping roles emerging to support research data management, from the data creators (the research scientists), through data scientists (data experts working closely with researchers, and often with the same domain subject background) and data managers (typically information technologists) to data librarians (usually based in academic libraries and managing local data collections). Corrall (2008) identifies three overlapping skill domains in which the hybrid data professionals of the future will work, which she terms 'context' (i.e. academic research), 'conduit' (primarily technology) and 'content' (library and information science). There are so far very few data librarians in UK universities (Swan and Brown (2008) estimate the total at five), and most of them are associated with institutions that have distinctive specialist roles or collections (Macdonald and Martinez, 2005). Data scientists and data managers can be found in national data centres, and in some cases attached to big research teams in universities.

Clearly, few if any university libraries are likely to be able to go out and recruit a team of data scientists and data managers to cover their university's disciplinary spectrum. The need for domain subject knowledge for data scientists is itself a powerful argument in favour of national-scale solutions, at least for some disciplines: large data centres are more likely to be able to create a critical workforce mass, and to be able to give their data specialists a reasonable career structure. This is already the case in some areas, such as bioinformatics: the European Bioinformatics Institute has a staff bigger than most university libraries. Data scientists may also be attached to big research groups, either as permanent team members or on a per-project basis, in which case they may be supported as direct costs by research funders.

It is likely or even probable that data scientists will not come from traditional library backgrounds; they are more likely to be career researchers for whom a period as a data scientist is part of a longer-term research career track. But their posts may come into existence in part because effective liaison between the library and the research team has already highlighted the project's data management requirements and resulted in the inclusion of a data scientist post in the grant proposal. Who might have provided that advice? Perhaps the university library's data librarian, who may also have a role in the management of locally held datasets for smaller projects, a requirement that may continue even if the large-scale gaps in national provision are plugged in the future.

This scenario implies a need for several types of training and development:

1   Award-bearing programmes, probably at Masters level, for career data scientists and data managers intending to achieve career-track positions in large data centres.
2   Short-course provision, not necessarily award-bearing, but probably accredited, for career researchers interested in project-based data science and management roles.
3   Training for data librarians: in the short term, the demand here is likely to be for post-qualification training among members of the existing library workforce; as the requirement for such posts increases, there may be demand for data-oriented postgraduate

LIS courses for new entrants intending to specialize or retrain in data librarianship, though take-up may depend on the extent to which data librarians can (and want to) progress into more senior academic library roles. An early exemplar is the MS specialization in Data Curation offered by the Graduate School of Library and Information Science at the University of Illinois at Urbana-Champaign (n.d.) (which also offers an MS in Biological Informatics).

There is also likely to be demand, in line with the *data confidence* theme, for some of the course content in these programmes to be available to mainstream academic library staff as continuing professional development modules.

Conclusions

It should by now be apparent that the 'yes and no' answer with which we started is far more 'yes' than 'no'. But there remain many questions, not all of which will find answers before library managers find themselves having to make difficult decisions about how much time and resource to invest in managing research data. Anna Gold, in an excellent review article on libraries and e-research, notes that:

> In sum, it is fair to say there is still a substantial amount of uncertainty about the roles libraries can play in scientific data management, reflecting an environment of ongoing experimentation and negotiation (and perhaps some wishful thinking). (Gold, 2007)

This is still true, and arguably not just in relation to science data. Among the remaining uncertainties are the following:

1 How rapidly will demand from researchers for data management grow?
2 Will more research funders mandate deposit of data outputs?
3 How will the data management requirement be funded?
4 Will researchers be interested in data scientist/data manager roles, and will the academic community recognize this as a mainstream research career route and not a dead end?

5 Will data storage/curation/access capacity develop at national and international level, and how quickly?

From a UK perspective, there is a further pressing question: will a policy lead be taken by any of the major research stakeholders in a position to effect change? In 2003, as we noted earlier, Lord and Macdonald observed a lack of overall strategy for data management and the associated infrastructure. Over five years later, Professor Sir Ron Cooke, outgoing chair of JISC, commented:

> More investment and policy leadership is required for the curation of research data, including international collaboration, to build a layer of academic and scholarly resources readily available to all. This should be a priority for DIUS [Department for Innovation, Universities and Skills], RCUK [Research Councils UK] and others where clear policy leadership is urgently required. (Cooke, 2008)

These questions will not be answered in the very short term. The difference librarians have made in the last five years or so, however, is that they are now well placed to influence many of the answers. This positions the profession to add significant value to an area that, over the course of the next decade, is set to move from being on the fringes of professional concern to being a core component of libraries' support for the academic research mission.

Acknowledgement

I am grateful to Professor Sheila Corrall, Department of Information Studies, University of Sheffield, for discussion and comments.

Notes

1 www.sherpa.ac.uk/juliet/index.php.
2 www.rcuk.ac.uk/escience/news/firstphase.htm.
3 www.nesc.ac.uk/documents/OSI/index.html.

References

Adams, J. and Bekhradnia, B. (2004) *What Future for Dual Support?*, Higher Education Policy Institute,
www.hepi.ac.uk/downloads/6%20Dual%20Support.pdf.

ANDS Technical Working Group (2007) *Towards the Australian Data Commons: a proposal for an Australian National Data Service*, The Department of Education, Science and Training,
www.pfc.org.au/pub/Main/Data/TowardstheAustralianDataCommons.pdf.

Beagrie, N., Chruszcz J. and Lavoie, B. (2008) *Keeping Research Data Safe: a cost model and guidance for UK universities*, Joint Information Systems Committee,
www.jisc.ac.uk/media/documents/publications/
keepingresearchdatasafe0408.pdf.

Brandt, D. S. (2007) Librarians as Partners in E-research: Purdue University Libraries promote collaboration, *College & Research Libraries News*, **68** (6), 365–7, 396.

Cooke, R. (2008) *On-line Innovation in Higher Education: submission to the Rt Hon John Denham MP Secretary of State for Innovation, Universities and Skills*, Department for Innovation Universities and Skills,
www.dius.gov.uk/higher_education/shape_and_structure/he_debate/~/
media/publications/O/online_innovation_in_he_131008.

Corrall, S. (2008) *Research Data Management: professional education and training perspectives* [presentation], Research Data Management Forum, November,
www.dcc.ac.uk/events/data-forum-2008-november/presentations/07.pdf.

Gold, A. (2007) Cyberinfrastructure, Data, and Libraries (Parts 1 and 2), *D-Lib Magazine*, **13** (9, 10),
www.dlib.org/dlib/september07/gold/09gold-pt1.html,
www.dlib.org/dlib/september07/gold/09gold-pt2.html.

Green, A., Macdonald, S. and Rice, R. (2009) *Policy-making for Research Data in Repositories: a guide*, EDINA and [Edinburgh] University Data Library,
www.disc-uk.org/docs/guide.pdf.

HM Treasury (2004) *Science and Innovation Investment Framework 2004–2014*, HMSO,
www.hm-treasury.gov.uk/spending_sr04_science.htm.

Hey, T. and Trefethen, A. (2003) The Data Deluge: an e-science perspective. In: Berman, F. et al. (eds), *Grid Computing: making the global infrastructure a reality*, Wiley,
www.rcuk.ac.uk/cmsweb/downloads/rcuk/research/esci/datadeluge.pdf.

Interagency Working Group on Digital Data (2009) *Harnessing the Power of Digital Data for Science and Society. Report of the Interagency Working Group on Digital Data to the Committee on Science of the National Science and Technology Council*, www.nitrd.gov/about/harnessing_power_web.pdf.

Jones, S. et al. (2008) The Data Audit Framework: a first step in the data management challenge, *International Journal of Digital Curation*, 3 (2), 112–120.

Library & Information Update (2004) Why Engage in E-science?, *Library & Information Update*, 3 (3), 25–7.

Lord, P. and Macdonald, A. (2003) *e-Science Curation Report: data curation for e-Science in the UK: an audit to establish requirements for future curation and provision, prepared for the JISC Committee for the Support of Research*, Joint Information Systems Committee, www.jisc.ac.uk/uploaded_documents/e-sciencereportfinal.pdf.

Lyon, E. (2007) *Dealing With Data*, Joint Information Systems Committee, www.jisc.ac.uk/media/documents/programmes/digitalrepositories/dealing_with_data_report.pdf.

Macdonald, S. and Martinez, L. (2005) Supporting Local Data Users in the UK Academic Community, *Ariadne* [online], 44, www.ariadne.ac.uk/issue44/martinez/intro.html.

Martinez, L. (2007) *The e-Research Needs Analysis Survey Report {for the} CURL/SCONUL Joint Task Force on e-Research*, www.rluk.ac.uk/files/E-ResearchNeedsAnalysisRevised.pdf.

Mullins, J. L. (2007) *Enabling International Access to Scientific Data Sets: creation of the Distributed Data Curation Center (D2C2)*, Purdue University, http://docs.lib.purdue.edu/lib_research/85/.

National Science Foundation (NSF) (2007a) *Cyberinfrastructure Vision for 21st Century Discovery*, www.nsf.gov/pubs/2007/nsf0728/index.jsp.

National Science Foundation (NSF) (2007b) *Sustainable Digital Data Preservation and Access Network Partners (DataNet): Program Solicitation NSF 07-601*. National Science Foundation, Office of Cyberinfrastructure, www.nsf.gov/pubs/2007/nsf07601/nsf07601.htm.

Organisation for Economic Co-operation and Development (OECD) (2007) *Principles and Guidelines for Access to Research Data From Public Funding*, OECD, www.oecd.org/dataoecd/9/61/38500813.pdf.

Pothen, P. (2007) *Developing the UK's E-infrastructure for Science and Innovation: report of the OSI e-infrastructure Working Group* [Joint Information Systems Committee], www.nesc.ac.uk/documents/OSI/report.pdf.

Research Data Strategy Working Group (2008) *Stewardship of Research Data in Canada: a gap analysis.* Research Data Canada, http://data-donnees.gc.ca/docs/GapAnalysis.pdf.

Research Information Network (RIN) (2007) *Researchers' Use of Academic Libraries and Their Services*, RIN, www.rin.ac.uk/files/libraries-report-2007.pdf.

Research Information Network (RIN) (2008a) *Stewardship of Digital Research Data: a framework of principles and guidelines*, RIN, www.rin.ac.uk/files/Research%20Data%20Principles%20and%20 Guidelines%20full%20version%20-%20final.pdf.

Research Information Network (RIN) (2008b) *To Share or Not to Share: publication and quality assurance of research data outputs*, RIN, www.rin.ac.uk/files/Data%20publication%20report,%20main%20- %20final.pdf.

Research Information Network (RIN) (2008c) *Mind the Skills Gap: information handling training for researchers*, RIN, www.rin.ac.uk/files/Mind%20the%20skills%20gap%20REPORT%20July %2008.pdf.

Rice, R. (2009) *Final Report {of the} DISC-UK DataShare project*, Joint Information Systems Committee, http://ie-repository.jisc.ac.uk/336/1/DataSharefinalreport.pdf.

Swan, A. and Brown, S. (2008) *The Skills, Role and Career Structure of Data Scientists and Curators: assessment of current practice and future needs*, Key Perspectives, www.jisc.ac.uk/media/documents/programmes/digitalrepositories/ dataskillscareersfinalreport.pdf.

UK Research Data Service (2008) *Report and Recommendations to HEFCE*, (December), www.ukrds.ac.uk/HEFCE%20UKRDS%20Final%20Report%20V%201. 1.doc.

UK Research Data Service (2009) *The Data Imperative: managing the UK's research data for future use.* Joint Information Systems Committee, www.ukrds.ac.uk/UKRDS%20Report%20web.pdf.

University of Illinois at Urbana-Champaign, Graduate School of Library and Information Science (n.d.) *Master of Science – Specialization in Data Curation*, www.lis.illinois.edu/programs/ms/data_curation.html.

10

The leadership of the future

Liz Wright

The slot in culture that I'm most closely associated with is one in which charlatans declare that they know the future. My job is to sit near that slot and when people approach me I say, 'Only charlatans say they really know the future'.

William Gibson (2007)

Introduction

We live in an age of uncertainty and widespread turbulence, where 'the rate of change is the biggest change' we face (Brockman, 2004), yet where our ability to predict and prepare for the future has never been more important to the survival of our organizations and our endeavours.

Whoever can most accurately predict the future can create a future-ready workforce, adapt organizational systems, reconstruct processes that interface better with clients and stakeholders, and generally rethink their product, their production methods, their supply chain, their mode of product delivery and their product marketplace before their hungry competitors. Strategic and operational innovation is a key to competitive success in the 21st century: effective creation and leadership of the cultures that create innovation are vitally important. This applies in an academic library context as well as in the commercial sector.

Leaders need to anticipate the future. As well as helping us to prepare for the future, this type of focus helps us to make sense of the present: 'A global futures perspective can help leaders make sense out of the chaotic patterns of change in the external world' (Johansen, 2009). Yet Kouzes and Posner (2009) comment that being forward looking is the one leadership competence that leaders today are least capable of demonstrating. We must rectify that. Leading with an eye firmly fixed on the future, 'future watching' for new ideas, directions, trends, inventions and models, must become a thoroughly widespread capability, practised continually across the organization through every means possible, if organizations are to compete and innovate successfully.

Many of the innovations of the future are visible in the green shoots of the present. For some proactive, far-sighted organizations, new forms of leadership are already here; for most, they will be here within the next 5–10 years, for as the visionary writer William Gibson famously commented, 'the future is already here – it's just not evenly distributed' (Gibson, 1999).

The most successful organizations of the future will be those that can identify early indicators of directions that will become mainstream, and get there faster than their competitors. These organizations may be the followers of the new initiatives, or they may be their creators. Leadership Capability is already a source of business-competitive success: it will become even more so in the next 10 years (the 2010s), especially in the global universities of the future.

This chapter will explore the current and future states of leadership, suggesting that leaders need to develop a personal leadership model to cope with the pressures of the future leadership environment. It makes predictions about the main forces for change that will affect organizations in the next 5–10 years, and the likely implications for leaders and organizations, and suggests the Star Cluster Model for the development of leadership capabilities in the 21st century.

A personal view of leadership

> If your actions inspire others to dream more, learn more, do more and become more, you are a leader. (John Quincy Adams)

My life has always centred on leadership. As a little girl with two long plaits, I remember getting strange looks from my friends about how I spent my pocket money – not on magazines and clothes, but on books on Winston Churchill and Admiral Horatio Nelson. A weird child! But it always seemed to me, as the youngest child in a Welsh working-class family, struggling to survive with no father, that leadership was important.

It was the leadership of my mother, working long hours as a night sister, that helped us to survive. My mother had extraordinary leadership skills – her vision, her ability to see a way through radical and painful personal change, her constant encouragement for us to create a better life through education, was an inspiration to me. She taught me my first and greatest lesson about leadership: leadership is about creating a brighter, stronger future, through a strong vision linked to determined action.

Later, I saw how leaders could make or break their organizations, create happy or unhappy workplaces and contribute to peoples' psychological and physical anguish. I saw successful organizations ruined within months by the actions of rash, immoral or arrogant leaders with excessive power and narcissistic tendencies. I also saw organizations at the brink of disaster after years of bad leadership rescued by new leaders who used their skills, energy and imagination for positive change. Leaders could create outstanding power in their people, and in themselves, because of the way that they used their skills.

To me, outstanding leadership creates the breath and spirit of humanity. It helps us define who we are, and who we want to be; to decide on the lives we can live in the future; and how we will interact with our world so as to be more than we currently are. Leadership makes a difference to those around us too – helps them to see life differently, boost their skills and find new energy. Most of all, it stimulates new horizons, new paradigms and new hope for the future. We need it more than ever for the 21st century.

Leadership today: somewhat confused!

Last week, there were 122 million references on Google on a search of 'Leadership'. Today, there were 123 million. A million additional references added in just seven days, illustrating the obsession that we currently have about leaders and their leadership. There are dozens of references to leadership and leaders on the internet daily, in the newspapers, on the TV, on the radio and in the coffee shops and eating houses of the world's cities – conversations mostly about politicians and business leaders, but also about scientific, social, educational, cultural and military leaders.

Leadership is 'a central concern of all the social sciences and most of the humanities' (Maturano and Gosling, 2008) as well as a source of much debate in the leadership 'industry'. We watch heroic leaders in films and on TV as they save mankind from aliens, vampires, the darker forces of humanity or ourselves. We analyse real leaders in historical dramas, considering how they acted, thought, behaved, led others and made mistakes. In our cultural fantasies we continually create and recreate images of powerful leaders in every walk of life, and put them to the test – their morality, their problem-solving ability, their blend of thinking and action, and their commitment. We are obsessed by the leadership image, and its potential to transform our lives.

Yet, as always, reality is somewhat different. Contemporary leaders often seem barely able to cope with the demands placed on them. Meg Munn (2006), then UK Parliamentary Under Secretary of State, commented that management and leadership was 'one of the UK's significant skill gaps', adding that public trust in leaders in businesses and governments was at a low ebb. A recent report commented that 'many of our current leaders were trained in the last decades of an industrial era in hierarchical organizations typified by command and control' (Business in the Community Report, 2009, 3). Similar criticisms of current leadership skills can be found in current leadership literature of Australia, the USA and Europe.

Leaders are criticized for being out of step with the times and operating old paradigms of leadership; using mechanistic, hierarchical, command and control styles, and other 'structures of domination', thereby encouraging the spread of competitive and individualistic corporate cultures (Duignan, 2007). Gary Hamel laments that current models of leadership and management 'enslave' millions of workers in 'quasi-feudal, top-down organizations' (Hamel, 2007, 8–9).

The negative impact of inappropriate leadership style is compounded by a perceived lack of leadership competence: a recent report into United Kingdom's National Health Service leadership commented that although debates to improve management and leadership have been going on since 1983, current research showed a 'relatively high proportion of senior managers [displayed] . . . a troubling level of passivity and risk aversion, [lacking] sufficient flair or willingness to take the initiative', with 'a limited ability to understand the wide system and think strategically' (NHS Confederation, 2009).

It's not just leaders who are worried about their ability to do the job. An American study commented that, next to issues of pay, 'satisfaction with leadership is the most dissatisfying aspect of many employees' organisational lives' (Pearce, 2004, 51). If current leadership practitioners have problems with the challenges of today's organizations, how will they survive as leaders in the infinitely more demanding future? Can we rely on current development processes to prepare leaders for the future?

Improving leadership capability – today's problems

Low levels of leadership capability can be explained, in part, by excessive confusion in the field of leadership theory and practice, and the proliferation of competing leadership theories. Practical leaders in busy organizations and university leadership academics frequently seem a world apart: business leaders frequently complain that university experts do not understand the reality of day-to-day leadership; academics often criticize practitioners for being superficial and insufficiently rigorous in the theories they espouse, arguing that contemporary leadership books are 'dumbed down' for today's commercial and consumer society (Western, 2008). One leadership philosophy or another is held up as 'the only way' to lead, only to be replaced a few months later by another 'fundamentalist' leadership approach, while consultants and academics search for the 'holy grail' of leadership, the theory that will keep their leadership book in the bestseller lists. Yet academic leadership theories are often considered too complex or theoretical for the workplace, while many leaders in organizations, even experienced ones, admit to being unclear about what leadership actually is.

Leadership experts can't agree on what leadership is made up of, how it should be used, how leaders should be trained and how leadership should be studied. After 70 years of its being a major part of the curriculum, some academics and practitioners dispute whether business schools can even teach it properly, and it seems that, after years of research, relatively little is known about the process of leadership development (Day and O'Connor, 2003).

This confusion at the heart of the leadership 'industry' certainly does not help people to develop their leadership skills. Many people lack confidence and are reluctant to behave like leaders at work – even senior people with formal leadership authority!

Achieving personal clarity about 21st-century leadership

Things need to change. The demands of the future require clarity and outstanding leadership in all sectors, and this leadership cannot be autocratic, hierarchical, 'lone ranger'-style leadership. Leadership in organizations is a social process, centred on people: it is about harnessing the great potential of people to achieve amazing energy, creative solutions and intelligent action.

Leadership must become an organization-wide capability in the 21st century, and academic library staff must feel comfortable assuming a wider range of leadership roles, approaches and behaviours, whatever their place in the formal organizational hierarchy may be. Watching and understanding the future, proposing new directions and strategies for competitive success, taking initiative to improve things, bringing people together to solve problems, generating positive thinking in the team – all these are necessary leadership actions on an everyday basis.

To facilitate this, leaders need a practical, workable way of developing their own personal leadership style: a personal model of how they will choose to lead in the 21st century, what their focus will be and what they will pay attention to. In particular, a leadership model will make clear what skills and capabilities should be developed and how they should be used; which are outdated and which should be discarded. The formulation of a personal leadership model provides the inner clarity, strength and confidence needed to lead in difficult and ambiguous circumstances.

Actions to achieve a personal leadership model

To achieve a strong, personal inner vision of leadership, a useful approach is for leaders to take three important actions. Leaders need to:

1 *Scan their leadership environment* of both the present and the future. The leader strives to identify, understand and analyse the forces facing her/him, the organization and the people.

2 *Understand the implications of the environment,* and decide what their leadership should be like in this world. The leader asks what type of organization, organizational culture, processes, workforce and values should be created to achieve this success. 'What leadership vision is needed for this group in this environment?'

3 Develop a personal model of leadership needed to achieve this, to lead themselves and others successfully into the future. The leader asks 'What sort of leader should I be? How will I measure my effectiveness as a leader? What values do I hold? What will I pay attention to? How will I interact with people?' The leader should also plan to develop the leadership skills needed.

Scanning and understanding the leadership environment

> The more leaders immerse themselves in provocative environments, the more they are likely to understand their future options for innovation.
>
> (McKinsey, 2008)

High-performing organizations scan their environments more frequently, use a wider variety of information sources and tailor their scanning to fit the context of the company (Rohrbeck, 2009). It is a key responsibility of everyone with a leadership role to keep a relentless focus on the future, *especially* in times of rapid change.

Leadership must be done within a strategic context – it cannot be done in isolation (Osborn et al., 2002). Leadership will not be successful unless the leader understands the context, the 'leadership environment', the complex forces that surround and influence the organization, and the emerging discontinuities that appear to spring from nowhere.

A leader who does not question her or his understanding and perception of the leadership environment may anticipate a future which is based on fantasy. It is the leader's responsibility to reflect on the assumptions and beliefs which are forming her or his view of the world, because they can do the greatest damage to the group or organization if they are incorrect. As Hamel comments: 'It's the commonly held assumptions that require the greatest scrutiny' (Hamel 2007, 131). Our perceptions and biases often lead us to see an environment in a predictable way, but to succeed in anticipating the future we must expose and challenge our assumptions and perceptions, and seek to perceive and reperceive the environment in different and new ways (Senge, 1990).

How do we seek to understand the future? By envisioning and playing with different possible futures (scenario planning); the relentless search for new paradigms and directions; continual attendance at conferences, training, learning and discussion groups; internet searching, social and professional networks; reading political, scientific and economic analysis; reading science fiction; visiting other countries and observing what they are getting excited about – all these are important ways of trying to understand the forces for change that will impact the organization and its future leadership. Leaders must 'develop effective sensors to detect changes' in order to achieve the corporate foresight needed to grow 'ambidextrous capabilities' for incremental and radical innovation (Rohrbeck, 2009).

21st-century trends in the leadership environment

> Organisations of the future will increasingly live in a world that is flatter, faster, and much more chaotic.
>
> (Katzenbach and Khan, 2009)

As we move into the second decade of the 21st century, everything is changing around us: the workplace, business models, the relationship with the customer and the marketplace, the product, the methods of distribution, the customer and the workforce.

Most of this is not just changing, but being deeply, radically, paradigm-shiftingly rethought, reshaped and redesigned. Not everywhere at the same pace: small progressive 'pockets' of innovation are born, gain speed and impetus on a wider basis, and then suddenly, everyone is working in a different way with new language and terminology, like the spread of the mobile phone, or internet-based social networking. The elements of a product or service may stay the same – they are just configured differently to gain better results, lower cost or unique characteristics, and 'value is created through arranging and recombining knowledge, people, processes and technologies' (Steen, Macauley and Kastelle, 2008). This is clearly evident in academic libraries, with changes in student expectations associated with social networking tools and the internet.

The medium to long-term future will not be predictable, but for the coming 5–10 years we can usually identify significant trends in the present. Some will inevitably be wrong in content, scale or timing! The following can be re-interpreted in an academic library context.

Eight predictions about the workplace of the future

1. Continuous global competition will create constant innovation and change

Hungry and ambitious new players in the world economy, such as China, India and Brazil, are competing with more-established providers in every field, and will increasingly move into new areas and unusual sources of economic return. Significant global competition will increase, forcing organizations to innovate relentlessly, to find new ways to generate exceptional stakeholder and customer value, while cutting costs and becoming more price competitive. Mckinsey & Company commented in a recent report that a far-reaching reorganization of economic activity is taking place worldwide. More than a billion new consumers will join the global marketplace between 2006 and 2015, and both a strong global presence and a solid local profile will be required to compete effectively (Mckinsey & Company, 2008, 10).

The new, worldwide 'hyper-competition' will put more pressure on people at work, and job security will not be a strong feature of the workplace of the future, unless personal performance and skill levels are high. Global outsourcing will continue, in the search for cost reduction in this highly competitive world.

2. Computing power and technological innovation will grow and expand massively

The application of computing and technology to achieve greater performance and personal effectiveness at work will be a constant pressure and challenge in every sector in the 21st century. Innovation in ways of working and creating will be continuous, and will affect every aspect or leadership and people management. Computer power is developing very fast: doubling every 18 months, according to noted physicist and author Michio Kaku. The latest generation of supercomputers can perform more than a quadrillion operations per second, with the potential for creating a revolution in workplace capabilities. By 2020, he says, ubiquitous computing will be found in every work and household object, as machines begin to approach human intelligence (Kaku, 2009).

This trend will drive new technological advances. Technology is being increasingly integrated into the human body to augment its capability. In 1999 Kevin Warwick, a British cybernetics professor, handed over the control of his body to a computer, to see whether it could move his limbs by copying signals from his brain (BBC, 1999). Since then, much progress has been made. Brain implants are currently being developed to enhance our intellectual skills. The sequencing of an entire genome of a cancer patient brings personalized medicine closer, and significant breakthroughs can be seen in regenerative medicine (Rowe, 2009). In the next ten years, the linking of humankind and machine will increase the power and capacity of the human brain and the human body.

As the boundary between machines and people blurs more and more, we will find shortcuts for tasks and processes at the workplace. Technology innovations have the capacity to change for ever the way humans work. Work processes are already being revolutionized by technological innovations, and academic library services are an excellent example.

Virtual technology and ubiquitous wireless resources are reducing the need for air travel, expensive fuel consumption and excessive emissions, as conferences, team meetings, research groups, tutorials and coaching sessions become virtual (as the chapter in this book on using Second Life for information literacy support clearly illustrates). The use of virtual concepts such as Second Life for work skills development has huge potential for low-cost and effective workplace training. Nanotechnology and automation are being designed into most work processes and materials, reducing the need for human intervention in a variety of ways. Augmented reality, the concept of superimposing information onto retinal devices such as high-tech glasses, has the potential to give people access to specialized technical information, as well as for detailed technical training and virtual technical trouble-shooting situations.

Undoubtedly, technological innovation at work will require new ways of training, working, relating and communicating. There will be a huge increase in constantly networked home-based work, with office spaces being available for booking, just like hotel rooms. There will be fewer staff at headquarters and corporate offices overall, as more will be working from home, at a distance, every day. A real and difficult challenge for academic libraries will be how they anticipate, and respond to, these future technology-driven workforce changes.

3. Yet more radical changes in higher education will come

Technology is changing the way that universities teach. Ubiquitous computing and easy access to high-speed computing networks mean that students can teach themselves, discover information and be more interactive in the creation of ideas and new technologies. The universities of the future are becoming less mass production focused and more tailored to the needs and learning preferences of the individual student.

Computing power enables continuous communication with students, according to their needs, and also makes possible greater collaboration within a community of global learners as borderless education becomes a reality. Academic support is less about conveying knowledge and more about helping students to discover for themselves the dimensions of their subject. Key educational processes, pedagogy in particular, are being reinvented and remodelled in a world where education is more about making smart 'knowledge connections' than about assimilating knowledge.

Also, beside changes in the way that universities teach, there will be a major shift in the type of student they teach. People are living longer and the huge mass of baby-boomers is reaching retirement age. In the US, there will be a 50% increase in the over-65 age group by 2015, to 55 million, rising to 72 million by 2030 – 20% of the total population. It is predicted that by 2050, 40% of the population of Italy will be over 65. Global estimates are that by 2050, nearly 25% of the global population will be over 65 years old (Hiemstra, 2006). Not only will this have significant implications for the composition of the academic workforce, but major opportunities will exist to attract a new type of student – the mature student – as the proportion of younger students declines overall in most countries. This will have implications for how academic subjects are sold, taught and delivered, as well as how academic library and information services are used. Totally flexible access to human support services may be preferred by this age group; different patterns of study and group interaction may emerge; and new ways of designing university library work spaces may be necessary, such as enhanced lighting and easily accessible catering facilities close to library work areas.

Will universities become the intellectual playgrounds of the over-65-year-olds, as well as the 18- to 21-year-olds? These students may be attending universities to change their skill base, as they seek new, more interesting second or third careers. Many will be part-time students, as they will need to fund the long years of life and study after 65 with part-time work, amid reducing retirement benefits and continuing economic uncertainty. Universities need to start thinking about this trend now and preparing for a very different set of students, with different sets of needs, requirements and demands.

4. There will be huge changes in the workforce of the future

There are significant demographic changes apparent now, especially in the developed world, which will lead to significant changes in the composition of the workforce, the way we work in organizations and how we lead people. A significant rise in older workers and a decline in the proportion of younger workers, combined with new ways of working, will lead to a serious worldwide talent shortage, especially in developed countries. Some countries, such as China and India, are making serious efforts to bring back their successful businessmen and women, their talented diaspora, to apply their skills in their birth countries.

A major rise in the employment of women, the disabled, ethnically diverse groups and older workers is predicted for the workforce of the future. More women will take on leadership roles in the future, as talent-management systems in organizations seek to recruit all available sources of talent and provide more innovative and flexible support processes. Greater mobility of skilled workers will be seen, as a response to the better, non-traditional rewards and conditions being offered in the search for talent.

The 'Millennial' generation (those who came into the labour market at or near the beginning of the 21st century) will be searching for life-style, interesting work and flexible rewards. Also referred to as the 'Digital Native' generation (Hiemstra, 2006) because of their ease and familiarity with the digital world in which they grew up, this group is continually connected, networked, technologically savvy and aware. Neither the Millennials nor the earlier Generation X group will feel much loyalty to their employers. Whether they stay with an employer or not will depend on the composition and flexibility of their rewards, the availability of training and professional development and the existence of interesting work arrangements and content.

5. Workplaces will become high-performance environments

Improving personal productivity will be central to how and where we work in the future. The workplace will be transformed by new processes and technological innovations, from transparent, interactive office walls, to wrap-around computer screens, to totally individualized and constantly communicating technological office assistants.

Workspace is increasingly being redesigned for maximum efficiency, with assistance from the latest research in neuroscience. The design company KM World suggests that the workplace of the future will have four workspaces: physical workspace (distraction free); information space (with all the tools and systems needed to help manage work productively); organizational space (for governance and hierarchical issues, organizational requirements, projects); and cognitive space (supporting the cognitive, learning and thinking processes of the individual worker) (KM World, n.d.). Google's Zurich offices already contain mini environments for creativity, discussion, team working, socializing, chutes and firemen's poles for fast travel from workspace to the office cafeteria, a water lounge with massage chairs for relaxation, as well as free breakfast, lunch and dinner (as reported in the BBC News, 2008).

6. Social and professional networking will be a valued and rewarded work competence

Social and professional networking will continue to grow massively in the future, and be seen as a source of competitive advantage – sites such as Facebook, Twitter, MySpace and LinkedIn are only the beginning in the professional environment of the workplaces of the future. Increasingly seen as places to seek information and develop new ideas, network sites will be perceived as essential places for leaders to find out about new ideas, new paradigms, available research findings, the global marketplace and wider environmental changes and trends.

In the workplace of the future, leaders and workers will be assessed and rewarded for their ability in forming high-quality workplace networks; and being highly and diversely networked will be seen as an essential leadership capability. Social networking will also be a support for the isolated home worker, and provide a sense of belonging and affiliation. Global Collaborative Innovation Networks (COINS) will be a key way in which organizations develop significant innovation processes, becoming 'creative, productive and efficient by applying principles of creative collaboration, knowledge sharing and social networking' (Gloor, 2006, 10). Research, Action Learning Networks and Inter-Firm Networks will also become popular.

7. Top performance will be required, measured and rewarded

Performance expectations will become clearer and more carefully constructed, so as to remove any barriers to effective performance, and new ways of measuring work effectiveness will be common. In the future, highly talented people will be rewarded highly, but expected to work hard and be available 24/7, as needed. Consequently, the boundaries between work and home life will become even more blurred, with instant communication systems and very strong pressures to perform. The search for talent will be balanced against a constant threat of cost cutting and redundancies, so there will be more pressure to perform in certain roles, leading to greater insecurity.

For those who perform well, rewards will include individual and team-based performance bonuses, flexible medical benefits (maybe personalized medical treatment using the latest technology), profit sharing, education and development, stock option systems, and free childcare. It is also possible that, with more women and older people returning to work, there will be care centres for elderly relatives of workers, parent-care centres etc., where aged parents could be dropped off in the morning and picked up at night, as children are.

8. Life-long learning, training and development will be required for everyone

Along with job insecurity and the pressure to perform will come a desire to maintain excellence at work through learning, training and professional development. The introduction of constant workplace change, in response to global competition and cost cutting, will lead to continuous retraining and learning to 'let go' of old processes and capabilities and learn new ones. In order to keep at the top levels of performance, we may tend to become 'informavores' – journalist, Frank Schirrmacher's description of organisms that consume information in the same way that humans consume food, with the risk of overconsumption and obesity (Schirrmacher, 2009).

Learning, development and information access processes will become part of flexible reward packages for aspiring knowledge workers, and continuous learning will be daily practice for everyone at the workplace. Learning support processes will ensure that capability development becomes an effective strategic thrust.

Understanding the implications of the 21st-century environment in terms of the leadership of the future

> The capacity to imagine exciting future possibilities is the defining competence of leaders.　　　　　　　　(Kouzes and Posner, 2009)

As long as we realize that all future prediction is only a stab at accuracy, based on today's limited perceptions, it is helpful to just have a go! Here are my predictions, which may be wrong – but that doesn't matter. The value is in the thinking about them and the surfacing of our assumptions.

Fifteen predictions about the leadership of the future

1　*Leadership will be seen as the major source of competitive advantage,* and developed as a key skill for everyone connected with the organization, including contract workers and suppliers.

2　*The single, autocratic individualistic leader style will give way to a more facilitative, enabling leader,* who shares leadership widely and openly. The 21st-century 'smart company' requires collective intelligence and motivated, co-ordinated effort. True collective intelligence in knowledge-based enterprises requires distributed leadership.

3 *Leadership power will be spread throughout (especially down) the new, flatter organizations*: top quality, speed and responsiveness will be vital. New types of leadership collectives will spring up, with experimental ways of working together.

4 *Leaders will understand themselves and their 'inner stuff' better than ever before.* Top performance in the new, distributed leadership collectives requires mature, emotionally intelligent, balanced leaders, secure in self-knowledge and self-management skills.

5 *Leaders will also monitor and pay attention to the emotional inner worlds of their team members,* to their state of mind, motivation, emotional intelligence, their 'inner stuff' and attachment patterns – because it is essential to top performance and effective collaboration processes.

6 *Flexible, more creative working arrangements will be common,* requiring different ways of measuring work output and performance. Sophisticated ways of measuring and assessing performance will be developed, including new, more challenging ways of achieving 360° feedback, and considerable attention will be paid to the views of staff, customers and stakeholders.

7 *Emotional intelligence, interpersonal skills and diversity management will become increasingly important throughout the workforce,* to match the increasing diversity of the workforce, stakeholders and customers. Outstanding people skills and exceptional emotional intelligence competencies will be key hiring criteria for all staff, with special requirement for those with people-leadership and co-ordination responsibilities.

8 *Most work will be done in small, self-led, autonomous work teams* based on relevant skill and knowledge, capable of initiating their own work and solving their own problems. Teams will set their own performance goals and targets, organize their own development and network with the rest of the organization, customers and suppliers. More leadership, innovation and decision making on the ground will be evident: faster decisions will be made nearer the point of service or customer, widespread innovation for rapid new product development will be normal.

9 *Everyone will belong to Action Learning Teams and Networks as standard*, to help with personal growth, workplace learning and continuous organizational improvement.

10 *Computer-assisted learning will be in everything* and a daily part of acquiring new skills, attitudes and approaches, personalized to each individual, with feedback provided to our *personal learning coaches.*

11 *All leaders will also be coaches.* Coaching will be common throughout the organization, which also must inculcate a true coaching culture. High-value knowledge workers will have their own performance coach, in order to remove obstacles to high performance and ensure top innovation and service delivery. In addition to specialist coaches, it will be a daily practice for more-skilled people to coach less-skilled co-workers throughout the workplace.

12 *Some leaders will be deliberately recruited from more diverse backgrounds* to provide better leadership skills for cultures of innovation, recruited more from the edges of mainstream society, because they will be more likely to challenge traditional rules, processes and ways of thinking.

13 *Leaders will take more scheduled time out for retreat and strategic reflection* to 'recharge their batteries' and ensure top performance is sustained and burn-out avoided.

14 *Leaders' performance will be more visible and obvious,* with few performance mistakes able to be hidden in the new public world of the internet. It will be easier to see leadership 'frauds' and image managers. This will cause greater focus on leadership skills training and development, as failure will be more apparent to all.

15 *Leaders will be evaluated by all their staff and stakeholders,* and their job security will largely depend on staff, colleague and customer evaluations of their effectiveness. More attention will be paid to leadership that is focused on team members and increasing staff motivation and satisfaction.

Towards a model of 21st-century leadership capabilities

Leadership in the 21st century is about increasing current and future success through the focused, sustained application of strong, shared vision, collective intelligence, co-ordinated innovation and continuous learning. What skills are required for this? The 'Star Cluster Model of Leadership Capabilities for the 21st Century' is a model developed by The Leadership Cafe for skills development for the leaders of the future. It consists of 'clusters' of connected leadership skills, gleaned from our analysis of the leadership environment and our experience of increasing leadership performance.

Leadership skills can be broadly divided into two key functions: *Strategic Leadership* and *Action Leadership.* This distinction is helpful, as descriptions of leadership are often confused between the two, but they are made up of different but interrelated sets of skills and used in different ways:

Strategic leadership

Strategic leadership within organizations is about moving that organization towards and through significant change so as to achieve a successful future within the current and future environment (Pajunen, 2006). This is inevitably a complex process, as organizations usually resist change: 'organisations tend towards stability and stagnation; leaders incite and direct change' (Maturano and Gosling, 2008, 15). Strategic leadership takes a 'helicopter' view of the organization and its environment, perceives the complex forces affecting the organizational 'system' and its 'outputs' (Senge, 1990), creates a vision of the future organization in response to these forces, and ensures that action is taken on an organization-wide basis to achieve the vision. Strategic leadership is concerned with organizational change and development as a whole, and the actions necessary to give the organization a strategic advantage for survival and success. It requires a conceptual, future-focused set of skills, the ability to take a big-picture view, to be radical and to challenge existing beliefs and approaches.

Action leadership

Action leadership is where action is taken to achieve specific, defined tasks, goals and actions on behalf of the organization in order to implement the strategic vision, the practical achievement of all the sub-tasks required. In a business organization, it is the leadership of the daily, frequent activities needed to get products or services created, produced and to market within a specified time frame, using a team, group, division or workplace unit. Action leadership is less focused on the organization as a whole and more concerned with the results of a specific group or team, using a practical, specific-outcome set of skills, and is generally focused on the present.

The link between strategic and action leadership is a circular process, in that a wise leader always seeks feedback and information about the implementation of the vision, as well as comments on the vision itself. It can then be amended and improved. Connection between the vision setting and its action implementation is essential, and serves to motivate those involved as well as to ensure that it is responsive and up to date.

The Star Cluster Model of Leadership Capabilities for the 21st Century

The Star Cluster Model of Leadership Capabilities for the 21st Century in Figure 10.2 has been developed from Figure 10.1, to include ten specific 'star' clusters of skills that we believe are needed for 21st-century leadership. This consists of:

*   four sets of *Strategic Leadership* clusters: Strategic Sensing, Strategic Visioning, Strategic Collaborating and Networking, and Strategic Communicating
*   two *Connecting* sets of clusters that link the two types of leadership (Strategic Leadership and Action Leadership) – Strategic Capability and Strategic Power Sharing. These two skill clusters connect action to the vision by ensuring that people have the power and resources to work towards the vision; and the skills, knowledge, attitudes and ability to do so
*   four sets of the *Action Leadership* clusters: Action Planning and Delivery, Action Teamwork, Action Innovating, and Action Coaching and Learning.

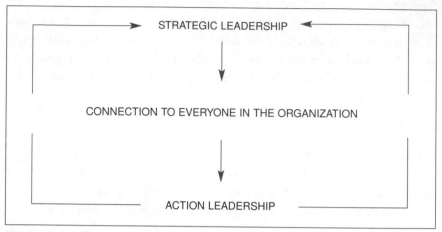

Figure 10.1 *Strategic and action leadership*

Figure 10.2 *The Star Cluster Model of leadership capabilities for the 21st century*

The Strategic Leadership skill cluster consists of:

- **Strategic Sensing** – includes strong skills to understand, analyse and interrogate the current and future environment in order to understand the complex forces of the leadership environment, including discontinuities.
- **Strategic Visioning** – is about the skills to enable the emergence and creation of a strong vision of how the organization or group could be in the future, within the leadership environment. The wise leader will allow involvement from all members of the group in the creation of the vision, as well as provide focus and facilitation in agreeing the vision, which should be both aspirational and inspirational.
- **Strategic Communication** – is about making meaning for the members of the group or organization, so that they understand the environment facing them, the situation that the group is in, and are inspired by a picture of what the group or organization could achieve together. Communication skills are essential to creating energy and can be tools for unity and focus. They may include inspirational communication, story-telling, vision clarity, the mirroring of emotional states, symbolic action and values clarification.
- **Strategic Collaboration and Networking** – includes linking the leader and the organization to wider networks that can help the strategic sensing and visioning processes by providing broader, alternative views of the external environment, and offer collaborative support in achieving action for the vision. Collaboration and networking are essential in today's competitive environment, where survival often requires working across boundaries, joining forces and operating from a position of joint strength.

The Connecting Leadership skill clusters skills consist of:

- **Strategic Power Sharing** – is about the skills needed to know when to share power and responsibilities in order to motivate individuals and enable them to use maximum creativity, effort and innovation to achieve high performance at work. This includes work task planning, delegation, letting go, monitoring, appraising and giving feedback, and coaching. It also requires high levels of emotional intelligence, to be able to share power, and a strong knowledge of the skills and abilities needed.

- **Strategic Capability Skills** – are about ensuring that the essential skills needed to achieve the vision are developed, focused and aligned, and all necessary training and resources provided so that people can achieve their tasks and goals effectively. This will mean that the organizational culture is a coaching, learning culture, with honest, open communication, and reward-based rather than punitive. Mistakes must be seen as learning opportunities rather than disasters to be avoided. Organization-wide coaching will be a key way of developing skills in the 21st century, for speed, relevance and effectiveness, especially for complex interpersonal and people skills, such as the ability to manage chaos and ambiguity.

The Action Leadership skill cluster consists of:

- **Action Planning and Delivery** – is about translating the vision into practical action by working with the team to agree what action is necessary, ensuring that action is delegated and implemented, checking against the plan, adjusting the plan and ensuring that everyone is collaborating and working well together. It is about achieving peak performance and ensuring that top results are achieved, within the resources available.
- **Action Teamwork** – is about generating outstanding performance within a team or a group; unifying an often diverse team, using energy to get things happening, pointing out the key focus and priorities; developing the team; getting things moving quickly and effectively. It is also about monitoring progress on key performance indicators, listening to feedback and encouraging corrective action, refocusing energy and effort, bringing together diverse or conflicting elements. It is also about doing everything necessary to remove all systemic, human and emotional barriers to top performance within the team, which will involve personal performance coaches as well as flexible working arrangements and rewards, and power sharing.

- **Action Innovating** – is about ensuring that new solutions and options are created and tested, new processes generated and tried, maximum learning made possible, so that better products and services are achieved. All possible ways of enabling creativity in the workplace are utilized, including workspaces, new ways of generating ideas, and the creation of a positive climate of innovation and creativity.
- **Action Coaching and Learning** – is about creating a learning culture at the workplace, continually coaching, inspiring and encouraging individuals and teams to learn, improve, grow and innovate, helping them to solve workplace problems and enable top client/customer relationships. Belonging to several multidisciplinary improvement teams at the same time will be daily practice for most people. It is essential that individuals and teams achieve the highest performance possible, so frequent coaching will help to do this, as well as ensure that a culture of coaching and mutual help towards excellence is established. This will ensure the development of new products and markets, and new ways to continuously improve workplace processes and systems.

How do we use this model?

At The Leadership Cafe (www.theleadershipcafe.co.uk) we use this model as a basis for leadership conversations, to assess and pinpoint areas for personal leadership development, encourage leaders to think about the future and the skills they need, and consider any gaps and deficiencies they may have. We encourage leaders to devise a Leadership Capability Development Plan (LCDP) for the future, using this model and providing coaching to help decide priority areas. All cluster areas have detailed skill definitions for greater targeting and improvement.

Leadership of the future will require more strategic involvement by people throughout the organization, at all levels. The skilled knowledge workers of the future, linked in to their own professional networks, will contribute insights for strategic sensing and strategic visioning far more than employees of previous decades ever did. This model is a useful framework for developing leaders at all levels and locations within the organization.

Conclusion: the leadership of the future

> To be a futurist as a leader means seeing strategy as a way of being rather than as a task to be accomplished.   (Glen Hiemstra, 2006)

The leadership of the future is going to be fascinating, difficult, exhausting, exhilarating, ambiguous and chock-full of learning opportunities. Instead of being the domain of a few, it will be exercised by the many. Strategic leadership and action leadership will become commonplace activities for the knowledge workers of the future, keen to be involved in the future direction and innovation of their enterprises.

Self-leadership, that sense of responsibility and willingness to take action to make things better, will be the norm in the workplace of the future. The 21st century will be the age of mass participation – the voice of the majority will be heard more clearly than ever before, and it is likely to be a very effective and competent voice: 'Leaders will make the future, but they won't make it all at once and they can't make it alone. This will be a make-it-ourselves future' (Johansen, 2009, 155).

This century will see the most educated workforce ever, combined with the most advanced tools for communication, learning, advanced thinking and ubiquitous connectivity ever developed. It will be an extremely diverse workforce in terms of gender, age, disability and ethnic grouping. The potential for creative thinking, for collaborative teamwork, for diverse problem solving and high-energy knowledge worker involvement has never been greater.

Leadership of the future will be about giving people the leadership tools to create, to innovate and to revitalize our organizations, to remove the bottlenecks of middle management control and over-bureaucratic processes; and reverse the stultifying rules of 20th-century scientific management thinking, still evident today.

We have a chance to create communities of leadership learning, and leadership excellence, in the way we build leadership into our cultures and into our workforces. These new leadership workplaces of the future will eat, breathe and sleep creativity and continuous innovation; be places that inspire and develop the whole person; be wonderful sources of support, mental stimulation and achievement for the team members who work there . . . If we do it correctly!

Enterprises must now identify organization-wide leadership clearly and squarely as the most important source of competitive advantage they have in an ambiguous, fast-changing and turbulent environment. Then they need to develop a strategic vision that is focused on harnessing and developing the amazingly powerful force of leadership within their organizations, at all levels and locations. And make it happen.

The important thing is that leaders need to visualize this future now – to see their organizations in terms of what is possible, what exciting and wonderful workplace we could create. It could also have repercussions in our world today. Glen Hiemstra, well-known futurist and author, commented: 'If you want to change what you are doing today, change your image of the future. Change the future and the present will follow' (Hiemstra, 2006).

We have seen that today's leadership urgently requires improvement. A strong, powerful image of the leadership of the future will not only help us to prepare and establish the skills for tomorrow, it would help us to transform what we have today. By visualizing a positive and inspiring leadership future, we start to think and act in different ways today: more optimistic, less cynical and despairing.

More like leaders.

We need to start thinking now about creating exceptional leadership of the future – for ourselves, for our organizations, for our universities. Creating innovative, exciting and accessible libraries and knowledge resources for the future is an inspiring vision to imagine and think about – it is the key to outstanding 21st-century learning for tomorrow's students.

The strange thing about having a powerful vision, though, is that just strongly focusing on it actually seems to make it happen. Now, if we add to that focus our own dedicated and enthusiastic efforts to *make* it happen . . . well, the future seems to be already here.

References

BBC News (2008) 13 March, (http://news.bbc.co.uk/1/hi/7290322.stm).

BBC News Report (1999) on Kevin Warwick, 3 November, as reported in http://news.bbc.co.uk/1/hi/uk/503552.stm.

Brockman, J. (ed.) (2004) *Science at the Edge*, Weidenfeld & Nicolson.

Business in the Community Report (2009) *Leadership for change: aligning organisations for the future*, Business in the Community Report, Opportunity

Now Initiative, (June),
www.opportunitynow.org.uk/research/leadership_for_change/index.html.

Day, D. V. and O'Connor, P. M. G. (2003) Leadership Development: understanding the process. In: Murphy, S. E. and Riggio, R. E. (eds), *The Future of Leadership Development*, Mahwah, NJ., Lawrence Erlbaum.

Duignan, P. (2007) *Educational Leadership: key challenges and ethical tensions*, Cambridge University Press, New York.

Gibson, W. (1999) quoted in interview in NPR [National Public Radio], November 1999,
www.npr.org/templates/story/story.php?storyId=1067220.

Gibson, W. (2007) quoted in interview for the Vancouver International Writers' Festival,
http://thetyee.ca/Books/2007/10/18/WillGibson/.

Gloor, P. A. (2006) *Swarm Creativity: competitive advantage through collaborative innovation networks*, Oxford University Press.

Hamel, G. (2007) *The Future of Management*, Harvard Business School Press.

Hiemstra, G. (2006) *Turning the Future into Revenue*, John Wiley & Sons.

Johansen, R. (2009) *Leaders Make the Future: ten new leadership skills for an uncertain world*, Berrett-Koehler Publishers, Inc.

Kaku, M. (2009) *Visions of the Future*, broadcast on BBC 2, September.

Katzenbach, J. R. and Khan, Z. (2009) Mobilizing Emotions for Performance. In: Hesselbein, F. and Goldsmith, M. (eds), *The Organisation of the Future*, San Francisco, Jossey-Bass, 98–111.

KM World (n.d.)
www.kmworld.com/.

Kouzes, J. M. and Posner, B. Z. (2009) *The Organisation of the Future*, Jossey-Bass.

McKinsey & Company (2008) *Women Matter 2*: *Female leadership, a competitive edge for the future*, Paris, McKinsey & Co.

Maturano, A. and Gosling, J. (2008) *Leadership: the key concepts*, Routledge.

Munn, M. (2006) quoted in
www.publicwhip.org.uk/mp.php?id=uk.org.publicwhip/member/1813.

NHS Confederation (2009) *Future of Leadership Report* (March), Paper 1, p.2, The NHS Confederation,
www.nhsconfed.org/leadership.

Osborn, R. N., Hunt, J. G. and Jaunch, L. R. (2002) Toward a Contextual Theory of Leadership, *Leadership Quarterly*, 13, 797–837.

Pajunen, K. (2006) The More Things Change, the More They Remain the Same? *Evaluating Strategic Leadership in Organizational Transformations Leadership*, 2 (3), 341–66.

Pearce, C. L. (2004) The Future of Leadership: combining vertical and shared leadership to transform knowledge work, *Academy of Management Executive*, 18 (1), 47–57.

Rohrbeck, R. (2009) *Innovating for the Future – The Roles of Corporate Foresight in Innovation Management*, European Centre for Information and Communication Technology (EICT), Berlin.

Rowe, A. (2009) *The Top 10 Scientific Breakthroughs of 2008*, www.wired.com/wiredscience/2009/01/top-10-scientif/.

Schirrmacher, F. (2009) *The Age of the Informavore: a talk with Frank Schirrmacher*, www.edge.org/3rd_culture/schirrmacher09/schirrmacher09_index.html.

Senge, P. (1990) *The Fifth Discipline: the art and practice of the learning organisation*, Doubleday, USA.

Steen, J., Macauley, S. and Kastelle, T. (2008) *Inside the Innovation Matrix*, Australian Business Foundation.

Western, S. (2008) *Leadership: a critical text*, Sage Publications Ltd.

11

Adding value to learning and teaching

Sue McKnight

Introduction

The reputation of the academic library has long been associated with research and scholarly publishing, and its role in supporting undergraduate and postgraduate teaching programmes has almost been assumed. This chapter highlights the significant contributions made by academic libraries in support of learning and teaching and explores issues associated with retaining and enhancing these roles in the future. The intention of this chapter is to inspire creative thinking about what future academic library services to support learning and teaching could be like.

Today's academic libraries exist within a changing landscape of traditional on-campus and virtual university activity. The entire university is undergoing significant change. Universities are rapidly introducing blended mode (online activities and resources complementing face-to-face lectures) and wholly online learning in addition to the traditional face-to-face teaching. Library services have to adapt to these new modes of delivery. Libraries also have to develop new services to respond to the changing student cohorts that result from these new learning and teaching opportunities.

Other chapters in this book discuss the challenges of meeting the new digital research agenda; issues to be faced when considering the physical space of the academic library of the future; the impact of Web 2.0 and Library 2.0. Although these topics are directly related to supporting scholarship and learning and teaching, they have been excluded here.

Academic libraries today

The Society of College, National and University Libraries (SCONUL) in the United Kingdom established a Learning and Teaching Task and Finish Group in 2008 to scope the principal areas of activity where university libraries contribute to, influence and impact on learning and teaching activities. The group consisted of representatives from a number of SCONUL groups and from the Higher Education Academy. The SCONUL Executive felt that although there was clear evidence of the value adding of academic libraries in support of research, there was less qualitative and quantitative evidence of their role in supporting learning and teaching.

The Task and Finish Group presented its findings at SCONUL's Summer Conference, convened in Bournemouth from 10 to 12 June 2009 (McKnight, 2009). It was identified that academic libraries add value for a large number of stakeholders in relation to learning and teaching: academic staff, students, the higher education institution, parents, employers, professional associations, library and information science educators and government bodies.

The prime focus of services and support is on helping students to be successful at university. The SCONUL Task and Finish Group conceptualized the contribution of academic libraries to learning and teaching as a continuum in the student journey. The library is involved from before students know that they want to become undergraduates, by organizing school visits and reading events for the youngest of school children as well as for senior high school students; open days and visitor events entice applications; welcome week and induction activities help students make the transition to higher education. Students are offered information resources to support learning; a variety of study and social spaces and equipment to help them undertake assignments; reference services to answer queries; and training to develop academic and information literacy competencies. Graduate alumni are offered continued access to library resources and services.

Evidence of value adding

Poll and Payne (2006) provide an informative summary of impact measures for libraries and information services, including academic libraries. Their paper demonstrates the difficulty in obtaining quantitative data on the actual impact of libraries. They explored the research undertaken on the correlation of library use and academic success; the library's impact on information literacy; and the financial impact of libraries, as well as social impact; and the importance of the local library for research. While work continues around the globe, there have been no definitive answers to the question of how to qualify and quantify the impact of academic libraries.

Surrogate measures, however, are available. A most obvious acknowledgement of university libraries' value adding to learning and teaching is the inclusion in student satisfaction surveys, at both local and national levels, of questions related to library services. In the United Kingdom, the National Student Survey of final year students seeks feedback on satisfaction with academic library services; The *Time's Good University Guide* (O'Leary, 2009) and similar tomes include details of library services and resources as an aid to choosing a university. If the library were not a vital part of the academic experience, it would not be included in such works.

There are other measures, such as the inclusion of library services in categories for national awards recognizing excellence in learning and teaching (e.g. the Times Higher Education Leadership and Management Award for 'Outstanding Library Team'). National Teaching Fellowships in the United Kingdom have been awarded to professional library staff in recognition of their excellent support for students. Additionally, national quality agencies routinely report on the adequacy of library services when undertaking institutional audits of universities and colleges.

Creating a new future

While it is acknowledged that academic libraries are indeed adding value to learning and teaching, the challenge is to remain relevant. In the current environment, where change is endemic, student (and parent) expectations are increasing and new opportunities are opening up with changes in technology, academic libraries must review their missions and renew services on a regular basis.

The following are innovative examples of current practice that could become standard services in years to come. Others are visions of a future that can be created if there is a will. These serve as tasters of what the future could look like. The future is what we create, so it is imperative that we take responsibility for making it a future that enhances both learning and teaching, and the professional standing of academic libraries and their library services.

Capitalizing on personal skills

Librarians are multifaceted professionals with important skill sets that should be consciously used to enhance learning and teaching in universities and colleges. Some librarians are spectacularly successful at doing this already; however, there is room for further development across the sector. Today, academic librarians are a blend of:

- professional librarian, holding library and information science qualifications
- academic (often with a post-graduate qualification in teaching), teaching information skills as well as undertaking research and disseminating knowledge through presentations and publications
- IT-savvy practitioner who understands, uses and supports a wide variety of ICT tools
- competent manager responsible for complex budgets and significant staff numbers, and
- politician, building bridges between service departments and the academic community, and negotiating resources and deals.

The future must be populated with confident and well qualified library staff who are prepared to use these significant skills to enhance the student experience. Workforce planning and skill development will play a large role in ensuring that librarians develop their confidence in being accepted and respected as equal professional partners with academic colleagues (Auckland, 2009). This is not to be underestimated in a financial climate where support for staff development and training seems to be an easy target for savings. Rather than take a short-term approach, business leaders across many sectors are advocating the need for greater innovation and risk taking in a time of financial recession. 'Talent is the single most important variable in innovation' (Nussbaum, 2009). These sentiments should be seized upon in the library and information sector. Now is not the time to consolidate and tinker about the edges of our 'traditional' services, using traditional skills: we need to upskill so as to be able to innovate.

Communicate with non-librarians!

Librarians must stop talking to other librarians, stop preaching to the converted! Academic librarians must actively engage with careers advisors, maths support tutors, academic administrators, quality assurance officers, counselling staff, IT experts, in short, with anyone who has a role in supporting students. This is, of course, in addition to proactive engagement with our academic colleagues and with senior executives who control the finances. In addition, it is the business of the academic librarian to be influencing professional and discipline associations, government, accreditation and quality assurance bodies.

Be a change agent! Get out of the library! Broaden your remit! This does not have to mean assuming responsibility for converged services or bigger portfolios of functional responsibilities. It simply means to accept the role of influencer across boundaries, and to make whatever arrangements are required to make this effective. However, new organizational arrangements will be part of the future.

New partnerships

Before the common use of virtual learning environments (VLEs) to enhance delivery of learning and teaching resources and experiences, the library could stand alone, in its physical silo. Students went to classes in lecture rooms and then moved to the library for resources and a study space. However, as universities increase the use of online learning spaces, the distinction between where the classroom curriculum ends and the learning support begins becomes nonsense. Therefore, the need to establish new partnerships, whether formally represented through organizational structures or less formally through joint working practices, is vital.

Libraries and IT?

In some higher education institutions, the barriers were blurred by the convergence of library and information technology departments. Foo et al. (2002) suggest that these mergers were based on information infrastructure components of software, hardware, human resources and data or information. Some of the converged services that were formed in the early 2000s are now being deconverged, e.g. at the universities of Melbourne in Australia and of Birmingham in the UK. A modern university requires technology to deliver all its services, in one way or another. Watson (2008, 15) emphasizes this point: 'From a learning perspective it means having IT as plumbing that works and supports innovative pedagogy.'

IT departments are about the hardware, software and network infrastructure, and libraries are about content. Future convergences are more likely to include new organizational structures that are focused on how information and data are used. Co-location may be an answer in cases where a new organizational structure is not possible. Academic libraries tend to be open longer than other parts of a university, so co-locating multi-skilled people into an 'inquiry service interaction zone' in a library can assist students by minimizing 'referral loss' (Wainwright, 2005). One-stop shops for student support, information commons and learning commons are all terms for describing this type of service.

The academic services hub

New organizational groups could be formed by bringing together colleagues who can transform students' learning experiences. Imagine tutors who deal with remedial support (e.g. maths support, academic writing support, English language support) working with liaison librarians who gather appropriate resources to support the remedial work that may be required and also the reading list resources for a course. The librarians would also provide just-in-time online tutorials on the use of the resources. This coalition of professionals would then work with an academic team to incorporate testing of a student's ability to cope with the concepts required for the unit of study. Thus, if early intervention were required, this would be quickly identified and students guided to the support. Then add the educational developers to the mix to help design the VLE learning room that would incorporate all these value-adding features from the start of a student's enrolment in that course. Finally, add input from the team responsible for supporting students with special needs (e.g. dyslexia, visual or manual impairments), who could advise on the overall accessibility of the learning room (design, online resources, online tutorials, assessment practices, etc.).

What would be the result of such collaborations? Students would benefit because of the holistic design of the online learning space. By making provision for pre-testing a student's ability to grasp the basic concepts required for a unit of study, the service would move from remedial to transitioning. Students would be guided to support if required, and the stigma of having to ask for help at a physical student support centre would be removed. Any face-to-face support could occur within the learning commons (the previous library building!) in a more inclusive environment. Requests for accessible formats of resources would be reduced or eliminated, and the number of complaints regarding accessibility compliance would be minimized. Students would be offered seamless access to lecture materials, library resources and specialist programmes associated with ensuring that they understood basic concepts. In this future scenario, because students would be provided with everything they needed, when they needed it, pass rates and retention rates would improve, thus enhancing the reputation of the academic staff and the university.

Of course, these benefits could be achieved without co-location or new organizational arrangements, but the chance of their accruing would be enhanced by such arrangements. The future is about mainstreaming good design practices: minimizing the need for special interventions, because an inclusive learning space has been designed from the outset, thus improving both effectiveness and efficiency.

The future requires a mind-set that is prepared to break down silos and barriers so that academic libraries can partner with all parts of the university to develop seamless access paths to the myriad of resources, communication technologies and support services that will enhance student learning. Weaver (2008) describes this approach as educating the whole student.

Lowry et al. (2009, 16) note that 'shifts in pedagogy to "active and engaged learning" are affecting how libraries partner with academic faculty to support student learning, scholarship and productivity'. While 'active and engaged learning' does not have to be solely online, most universities and colleges have embraced blended and e-learning to some greater or lesser extent, as it supports this new emphasis in learning. This trend will continue apace, with more courses being offered in blended mode or wholly online.

Regardless of the organizational structure, the academic library *must* be part of this online learning space. In many instances already, there are links from the VLE to library catalogues and resources, but there needs to be a deeper integration if the student experience is to be enhanced.

Academic literacy skills

The term 'academic literacy' has been used deliberately to signify a step change from information literacy as is known in academic libraries today. A wealth of information has been published on this topic, much containing sage advice and recommendations for best practice. Associations such as the Australian and New Zealand Institute for Information Literacy[1] and the Association of College and Research Libraries[2] provide dedicated websites on standards, best practice case studies and related publications on information literacy. Unfortunately, despite the cogent arguments for ensuring that information literacy is a key graduate attribute, lip service to or partial compliance with best practice models are not uncommon. Information literacy skills are going to be just as important, perhaps even more important in the future, due to the increasing complexity of the information landscape. Not all knowledge is going to be available via Google, or similar open web search service, in the foreseeable future; so the skills required to locate, evaluate, manage and retrieve information, as described in the *Seven Pillars of Information Literacy* (SCONUL, 1999) or the *Australian and New Zealand Information Literacy Framework* (Bundy, 2004) will be vital graduate skills.

Academic libraries of the future must ensure that information literacy skills are embedded into the curriculum. They need to be mandatory rather than optional, which means that students' skills should be formally assessed for credit; and that academic staff and librarians should work together to ensure a productive learning experience for students.

Embedding information literacy training into the curriculum will require consideration of how the learning outcomes will be assessed, whether by formative and/or formal summative assessment, and time will need to be built into schedules to undertake marking and provide feedback to students.

'Academic literacy' includes other themes. Digital rights management and copyright and accessibility compliance are likely to be even more important than they are today as content is exposed to a potentially huge audience. Academic libraries are best placed within a higher education institution to provide training and support in areas such as copyright compliance and digital rights management. And if managing copyright compliance, why not include accessibility compliance? Academic libraries can broaden their remit to support these areas, if they are not already doing so.

Academic libraries teach how to cite references correctly. Why not provide training on plagiarism, and support the use of plagiarism detection software, such as Turnitin, which is commonly used to check student essays? This would involve support for both academic staff and students. The consideration of plagiarism (academic misconduct) and how to overcome it (correct citation) appears to be an irresistible combination that would help academic staff and students.

Learning to learn online

However, it is argued that because of the centrality of ICT skills, academic libraries must ensure that students (and staff) have the basic skills for using a variety of software packages and devices, even if the students bring their own devices on campus. Being proficient with Facebook or MySpace doesn't mean that a university student will know how to work in an online learning space. Many libraries today manage PC laboratories for student use and support customers who access online services and resources via a wireless network on campus. Support for these facilities must include basic training for students in making the most of them. Students will also need support to become competent online learners, and the academic library can play a part in developing these skills.

Helping academic colleagues

Research has found that some academics are intimidated by e-learning if their students' skills in using technology exceed their own (Attwood, 2009). Until there is a generational shift in the population of teaching staff, there is an urgent need to assist academic colleagues to update their skills so that they are confident working in the new, online environment. Busy academics and students need flexibility in gaining these new skills. There will need to be a selection of classroom-based instruction, face-to-face support and just-in-time online tutorials across a broad range of topics to support skill development.

Librarians learning

Other challenges will arise in this future, online world. Librarians will have to articulate learning outcomes and have an understanding of how to design curricula to deliver the outcomes. Of course, this is already the case with face-to-face teaching, but an online tutorial has to be designed with the goal clearly in mind from the outset, and being online somehow makes good or poor teaching practice more obvious. Either librarians will have the skills or they will have to work closely with educational developers who can assist in the process. If librarians are to co-teach with their academic colleagues, they will need to be confident in their teaching ability, which may mean gaining certification for teaching adult learners. At Nottingham Trent University all liaison librarians are encouraged and supported to gain a Post Graduate Certificate in Higher Education to build up skills and confidence.

Taking the library to the student – changes to reference services

Some libraries are combining enquiry points into a single desk, staffed by a multi-skilled customer services team, to simplify reference services for students. McKnight and Berrington (2008) found that this arrangement improved services to students, as students no longer had to know which desk to approach for support. An added benefit was that it freed up the time of liaison librarians, who were no longer required to staff a separate desk, as a referral system was put in place. According to Neal et al. (2009), 'The introduction of a referral system for complex subject enquiries has reduced the amount of time liaison librarians spend delivering one-to-one front-line services, enabling the Academic Liaison Team to develop a wider, more diverse range of student-support material and to concentrate on the creation of resources designed to meet multiple learning styles and programme-delivery routes, including the new VLE.'

Yale's Sterling Memorial Library (the largest library on the Yale campus, with humanities, social science and general collections) has gone a step further. It has removed the reference desk altogether and, in a related move, given each one of Yale College's incoming freshmen their own Personal Librarian, from whom they can get research help, whether basic or advanced. The reference librarians participate in the Personal Librarian programme, but so do cataloguers, archivists, systems librarians and others. Along with freshman faculty advisers, freshman counsellors and residential college deans, the Personal Librarians round out the students' academic support network. In a personal communication to the author E. Horning wrote that the effect has been to raise the librarians' profile on campus, both among the students and among faculty colleagues and in the college administration:

> We are in the second year of a two-year pilot, with 1,308 students this year and 1,321 students from last year's freshman class. 42 librarians are participating. The evidence we've collected so far indicates that we're seeing, in person, a larger percentage of first- and second-year college students this way (certainly much more than under our old reference desk + scattered instruction sessions for freshman-level classes). And the anecdotal evidence suggests we're having much richer contact with students than we ever saw in the last several years of the old reference desk model, through office hours, one-on-one sessions with students, email contact, and so on. The Personal Librarians remain in contact with their students until the student declares a major (usually at the end of their sophomore year); when the student decides on a course of study, the Personal Librarian introduces them to their Subject Specialist, who will help them with advanced research related to their major.

More on this Yale initiative can be found on the university's website.[3] Providing individualized support for learners is in line with the increasing expectations of customers to receive personalized services.

Taking the library to the student – using technology

If the VLE is the learning portal, there must be easy access to a range of library services and resources embedded in that online environment. For instance: a 'Contact the Library' widget, which provides access to the virtual reference service, should be mainstream; access to the library catalogue and federated search facilities would also be available; the My Library functionality would be accessible from the student's VLE personalized home page, so as to make information on loans, reservations etc. readily available; digital reading lists would be embedded with each module/unit of study to provide easy links to the information resources recommended by academic staff for that subject of study. These reading lists would, in turn, link seamlessly to the library's digital full-text resources or catalogue (if the item required was not in a digital format) for availability information (shelf location, loan status) and, if necessary, enable a reservation to be placed if the item were unavailable.

Bringing library services to mobile telephones and other portable devices will also be important. Applications that can be downloaded from the library site to enable access to a myriad of services and resources will be expected in the future. (Other chapters in this book cover the use of Web 2.0 technologies and virtual reality to enhance communication with students, so these are not covered here.)

Digital learning assets

In the virtual learning spaces available to students and academic staff, there is a range of content that would not normally be considered the responsibility of the academic library, yet this content needs to be acquired, managed and signposted to maximize use. Who has these skills in a university or college? The library!

Why not facilitate federated searching of repositories of Open Educational Resources (OERs)? These freely available learning assets are becoming more common, with local and national repositories of OERs being developed. However, the discovery of these resources can be improved, and academic librarians have skills in using standards, metadata cataloguing, repository management and search systems, so they would seem to be ideally placed to help. Librarians should work with system vendors, publishers and academics to develop the mechanisms that would enable the inclusion of these repositories into federated searches for other learning resources that are most commonly associated with libraries, e.g. journal articles in full-text journals; reference databases etc.

At my own institution, Nottingham Trent University, library staff are advising on the establishment and management of a Learning Object

Repository (LOR) that is part of the suite of applications in the Desire2Learn VLE. It is envisaged that cataloguers will assume responsibility for checking and adding metadata to learning objects contained in the LOR to facilitate discovery and reuse. The librarians are also training and supporting academic staff and students in the use of the LOR. In addition, the university's institutional repository, which is managed by the library, contains a 'learning and teaching collection' in addition to research publications, e-theses and corporate documents (go to the library's website to see and browse the learning and teaching collection[4]). A JISC-funded repository enhancement project is currently in progress (NTU SHARE, 2009). The project has a number of aims, including linking the LOR to the institutional repository and JISC's JORUM OER repository (www.jorum.ac.uk/#). Library staff are well represented on the project team and on the work streams, bringing cataloguing/metadata, federated searching and copyright expertise to the project. These forms of collaboration are the way of the future.

Other specialist repositories, such as image libraries, are being developed. As the proliferation of such systems expands, so too will the difficulty in identifying useful repositories and searching and retrieving content. These resources need to be 'treated' in a similar way to the full-text journal platforms that are provided today, enabling federated searching of a multitude of databases in a single search. If this is not immediately possible, then making these repositories more easily discoverable by other means must be a priority, otherwise universities and colleges will waste resources in reinventing learning assets that, in many cases, may be freely available.

Another compelling reason for academic libraries to become involved in the management of learning assets is that librarians have the experience, skills and systems in place to manage licences, copyright approvals and payments. If libraries do not assume this role, a duplicate set of functions are likely to be developed within the organization, at extra cost and potentially creating competition for scarce resources. The issue of payments raises another challenge for the academic library of the future. Will the funds to pay licence fees for learning assets, where necessary, come from a new budget line or from the library's information resources budget for books and journals? If the latter, it would mean less funds for 'traditional' library resources. Therefore, the politically savvy academic librarian must lobby for additional funds to support these important initiatives. The entire student population is likely to benefit if there is a more centralized approach to managing these learning resources; otherwise, small groups of students will benefit where faculties have deep pockets!

Liaison or subject librarians will have to work closely with academic colleagues to ensure that online learning spaces are enriched with the variety of digital resources that are available, not just full-text journal articles and e-books. Librarians must embrace learning assets as another form of information resource to be promoted and exploited so as to enhance students' learning experiences.

A new form of digital asset is becoming more common on the higher education landscape. It is the resources contained in e-portfolios, which are normally web-based, individual repositories for the collation of evidence related to personalized learning and reflective practice. The role of the academic librarian may be confined to supporting students (and academic staff) in the use of e-portfolios and the myriad of applications that can be used to create the assets for inclusion in them, including inputted text, electronic files, images, multimedia, blog entries and hyperlinks. But maybe there will be a role for librarians to advise on content management, digital rights management and tagging?

Supporting brand awareness and marketing

Academic libraries, through innovative reading programmes and library visits, open days and welcome weeks, special events for mature students and the like, help the marketing efforts of a university or college, and this helps to build brand awareness.

While not a new initiative, it is anticipated that more libraries will seek formal accreditation for Customer Service Excellence or similar national awards and certification, so that the marketing activities of the university can include the award logo as part of brand differentiation. Any contributions from the academic library that aim to make a particular institution stand out in a positive light will be welcomed. Naturally, the driver for these certifications is not marketing per se, but improved customer service.

Partnerships between education sectors are becoming more important, with special arrangements established between feeder high schools and colleges. Academic libraries, in the future, will support these links by providing associate membership to staff and students at these partner institutions and running special events to introduce potential applicants to the library and its services. Through collaborations with specific disciplines on campus, the library can support visits by school children to events focusing on science or law, for example. While these initiatives may not seem core, with the increasingly competitive nature of higher education it will be very important for the academic library to support initiatives aimed at encouraging future enrolments at the home institution.

Some academic libraries are providing special information events for parents, recognizing the important role that they play in the lives of students. These 'Library Awareness' events are aimed at making sure that parents know the range of services on offer at the library in case students come to them for advice, in the first instance, in relation to assignments. Parents can advise their children to 'go to the library'!

Another development that is likely to impact on library services and brand differentiation in the future will be the use of Customer Relationship Management systems. These systems will track contact with an individual from the time of an initial enquiry about attending the university to when they are graduates. Student interactions with library reference services, information literacy support services and individual feedback from a customer are likely to be entered into these all-encompassing systems. If a student asks for advice about an assignment topic, previous encounters, perhaps with student support services, will be available to the librarian, which may assist with the transaction taking place. The challenge for the future will be liaising with other departments of the university to make sure that the particular needs of the library are taken into account when such systems are implemented.

And for something quite different . . .

Elsewhere in this book are discussions on the role of academic libraries in using Web 2.0 technologies and virtual reality, digital publishing, creation and exploitation of special collections, and research and scholarly publication repositories. These will continue to be important areas of future development. Most of what has already been described in this chapter could be seen as a natural progression from professional work already being undertaken in academic libraries and doing 'the same things' differently, often using technology as a delivery medium.

Career and employment services

However, some academic libraries are starting to offer services that, on the surface, seem to be way out of the responsibilities normally associated with libraries. For example, Song (2009) advocates a radical approach to reaching out to users with new library services. The paper describes collaboration between the University of Illinois, Urbana career service and the library to offer programmes on obtaining jobs and understanding the job markets in various industries. The library offered workshops and seminars on tailoring individual student resumes and covering letters, based on information they (the librarian and the student) acquired on the companies being targeted. The resources of the business and economics library were exploited to assist in 'how to apply information' rather than 'how to find information'. Song's paper provides a model for developing proactive partnerships and new service models. The key factors for success were identified as:

- continuous examination of user needs via various methods
- aligning the value proposition to meet the goals of the client organization and the library
- careful and realistic examination of the library's capabilities
- winning support from one's partners
- delivering what one promises with consistency
- willingness to change and assertiveness.

(Song, 2009, 16)

This framework is an excellent starting point for academic libraries wanting to create a new and potentially radically different future.

Coventry University Library is also involved in an 'employability' related initiative. It has some resonance with the collaboration at the University of Illinois. In order to support and contribute to the university's 'employability' agenda, the library has developed two credit-bearing modules as part of the university's 'Add+Vantage scheme'. The modules in the scheme are intended to enhance employability. With the exception of students on 'professionally accredited courses' all undergraduate students are required to study one Add+Vantage module per year. In a personal communication to the author, C. Rock described how a team of subject librarians have designed and delivered a level 2 undergraduate module 'Information: fact or fiction?' and a level 3 module 'Information in the workplace', both of which have been favourably received by students.

Conclusion

Billings (2003) describes the transformational agents ('wild-cards') that have influenced the evolution of libraries, and academic libraries in particular, over a very long period. He concludes that a few major events have occurred that have interrupted the natural progression of library services, e.g. the printing press; industrial and social upheavals that promoted the growth of education and reading; advancement in communication technologies and the internet (Billings, 2003).

What will be the 'wild-card', using Billings' terminology, that will transform academic libraries in a new and exciting future? Perhaps the 2008–9 financial crisis will be the catalyst for forcing change in the way academic libraries and universities deliver their services. New partnerships may be ways of transforming the way we work, as well as producing efficiencies. As long as improving services to students is at the centre of our strategic thinking, there may be many innovative possibilities.

Academic libraries already add significant value to learning and teaching; and this must continue into the future. However, doing the same things but differently will not alone serve us well. New skills, new ideas and new directions are required. Lowry et al. (2009, 18) sum this up: 'future success, in part, will be fostered by the adaptability of staff; the recruitment of differently skilled staff; the reorganization of library work and services around emerging academic, research, and learning practices; and a commitment to experiment, innovate, and take risk'.

The profession needs to be bold and confident and to seek partnerships that will enhance the student experience. However, what we develop must be based on the needs of our customers: academic staff and students. We must ask, listen and respond to their changing needs and expectations. And we can try to anticipate their wants and 'wow' them with our new services and ways of working. The future is what we make it; if we can envision a new way of working to enhance learning and teaching, we can work out how to make it happen.

Notes

1   www.anziil.org/resources/index.htm.
2   www.ala.org/ala/mgrps/divs/acrl/issues/infolit/.
3   www.library.yale.edu/pl.
4   www.ntu.ac.uk/llr/resources_collections/irep/.

References

Attwood, R. (2009) Why Offline? It's Very Personal, *Times Higher Education*, No.1, 919, (22–28 October), 13.

Auckland, M. (2009) *Final Report of an Analysis of the Training Needs of the Learning and Teaching Librarians {Open University}: edited version for participating libraries*, Open University Library, Milton Keynes.

Billings, H. (2003) The Wild-Card Academic Library in 2013, *College & Research Libraries*, (March), 105–9, www.ala.org/ala/mgrps/divs/acrl/publications/crljournal/2003/mar/billings.PDF.

Bundy, A. (2004) *Australian and New Zealand Information Literacy Framework: principles, standards and practice*, 2nd edn, Australian and New Zealand Institute for Information Literacy, www.anziil.org/resources/Info%20lit%202nd%20edition.pdf. http://orweblog.oclc.org/archives/001636.html#.

Foo, S., Chaudhry, A. S., Majid, S. M. and Logan, E. (2002) Academic Libraries in Transition – Challenges Ahead, *Proceedings of the World Library Summit, Academic Library Seminar*, National Library Board, Singapore, 22–26 April, http://www3.ntu.edu.sg/home/assfoo/publications/2002/02wls_fmt.pdf.

Lowry, C. B., Adler, P., Hahn, K. and Stuart, C. (2009) *Transformational Times: an environmental scan prepared for the ARL Strategic Plan Review Task Force*, Association of Research Libraries, www.arl.org/bm~doc/transformational-times.pdf.

McKnight, S. (2009) *Backing the Winners: libraries adding value*, http://irep.ntu.ac.uk/R/-?func=dbin-jump-full&object_id=189267&current_base=GEN01.

McKnight, S. and Berrington, M. (2008) Improving Customer Satisfaction: changes as a result of Customer Value Discovery, *EBLIP (Evidence Based Library and Information Practice)*, 3 (1), (March), 33–52, http://ejournals.library.ualberta.ca/index.php/EBLIP/article/view/920/1074.

Neal, C., Parsonage, H. and Shaw, H. (2009) It's All Up for Grabs: developing a new role for the academic liaison team at NTU, *SCONUL Focus*, 45, 4–8.

Nussbaum, B. (2009) 10 Worst Innovation Mistakes in a Recession, *Business Week*, (13 January),
www.businessweek.com/innovate/NussbaumOnDesign/archives/
2008/01/10_worst_innova.html.

NTU SHARE (2009) *SHARE* project website,
www.ntushare.org/.

O'Leary, J. (2009) *The 'Times' Good University Guide 2010*, The Times, London.

Poll, R. and Payne, P. (2006) Impact Measures for Libraries and Information Services, *Library Hi Tech*, **24** (4), 547–62.

SCONUL Advisory Committee on Information Literacy (1999) *Information Skills in Higher Education*,
www.sconul.ac.uk/groups/information_literacy/papers/Seven_pillars2.pdf.

Song, Y.-S. (2009) Designing Library Services Based on User Needs: new opportunities to re-position the library, *IFLA 75th World Library and Information Congress*,
www.ifla.org/files/hq/papers/ifla75/202-song-en.pdf.

Wainwright, E. (2005) Strategies for University Academic Information and Service Delivery, *Library Management*, **26** (8/9), 439–56.

Watson, L. (2008) It's Not About Us: it's about them. In: Weaver, M. (2008), *Transformative Learning Support Models in Higher Education*, Facet Publishing, 3–18.

Weaver, M. (2008) *Transformative Learning Support Models in Higher Education*, Facet Publishing.

12

In search of the road ahead: the future of academic libraries in China

Michael Robinson

To know the road ahead, ask those coming back.

(Chinese proverb)

Envisioning alternative futures

Some of the trends influencing the future directions of library services seem so inexorable and so emphatic that it might be easy to assume that they affect all libraries around the world in much the same way. Google, as perhaps the most obvious of examples, is now the most recognizable of global brands and not surprisingly is assumed, in consequence, to be having a major impact on the future of library services everywhere.

In a broad sense, this assumption may well be correct. Global trends in the use of information are inevitably influencing both the type of services which libraries offer and the way in which they offer them, so that we have begun to see a redefinition of what a library actually is. One expression of this, for example, has been in the prominent development of the 'learning commons' in Western academic libraries, where traditional stack runs and study furniture have given way to spaces intended to promote and encourage a more interactive, collaborative and online learning environment (JISC, 2006). Elsewhere in this book, colleagues discuss the impact of this and other such forces and trends, be they the dominance of Google, the rise of content creation and knowledge management, or the changing role of the information professional.

However, is there a 'one size fits all' future for libraries around the world? The aim of this chapter is to adopt a slightly different stance on the future of the academic library, by suggesting that alternative futures exist, depending on where in the world you happen to be. While indeed Western libraries are contending with the impacts of 'Googlization' (Miller and Pellen, 2009) and the behaviours of new generations of information users (Oblinger and Oblinger, 2005), along with many other issues, libraries in less developed parts of the world are often dealing with a different set of challenges and are, in many respects, some distance behind their Western counterparts. To envisage library futures from an Asian perspective, for example, we need to conceptually accommodate issues such as Asia's vast and diverse geography, its immense variety of cultures, languages and rates of social and economic development, its levels of infrastructure and its political systems.

While some of the most sophisticated library systems in the world are in Asia, they co-exist with library services in other parts of the region which struggle with a multiplicity of burdens, such as limited print and electronic resources, poor facilities and obsolete infrastructure, inefficient access to the internet, lack of professional expertise, and broader issues such as political interference and the impediments of non-mainstream languages. For many such libraries, if anything, the road ahead appears to be the one already travelled by their more advanced Western counterparts. While this book, in essence, deals with the broader future of the academic library, for some libraries catching up with the 'present' remains the key issue.

This chapter will seek to illustrate the 'other' type of library and information future which exists outside of the developed world by looking at aspects of academic library development in the People's Republic of China. With the recent staggering economic growth of China, and its increasing influence globally, it might be assumed that Chinese academic libraries are already at an advanced level of development and are thus dealing with the same issues – and in the same way – as their counterparts in the West. However, the point of this chapter is that – despite this rapid growth – there are contexts and trends that are shaping a particular type of future for academic libraries in China, when compared to libraries in the West.

The future with Chinese characteristics

As I write, the People's Republic of China has just celebrated its 60th anniversary with a massive parade which reveals something of the old and new Chinas, side by side. As one would expect – in the traditional style and function of such parades – there was no shortage of military hardware and precision marching to remind us of China's emerging role as a superpower (Economist, 2009). President Hu Jintao also adopted a traditionalist approach by reviewing the parade wearing the high-collared jacket known as a 'zhongshan', which originated with Sun Yat Sen earlier in the century but is more closely associated, in the Western imagination, with the Communist leader Mao Tse Tung and his successors, such as Deng Xiao Peng (Peh, 2009). In contrast to the ritual and tradition of both the parade and his dress, however, President Hu rode in the very latest in Chinese automotive technology – the Hong Qi ('Red Flag') HQE, a Chinese-designed and handmade luxury limousine, over six metres long and featuring a Chinese-designed and built V12 6.0 litre engine (CNNGo, 2009). This, amidst all the historical references of the parade, was a symbol of the new, advanced, economically and technologically rich China, also very much on display as part of the celebrations.

Higher education sector reform

For all the advanced technology, however, it was remarked that the style of the car remained fundamentally unchanged, and indeed retained its peculiarly 'Chinese' characteristics. A particularly 'Chinese' style of modernity often fascinates Western commentators (Elliott, 2009), and a great deal has been and will continue to be written about the emergence of modern China from the political turmoil of the Cultural Revolution to become one of the world's largest and most robust economies. The booming economy has fuelled the rapid development and modernization of many aspects of Chinese society, not least the expansion of the higher education system since the 1990s. Education and scientific research have been a priority in the economic development of China since the founding of the People's Republic (Tang, 2001), and China's extraordinary growth in the 30 years following the end of the Cultural Revolution is due in no small measure to the massive building up and improvement of its higher education sector. Higher education has been the focus of considerable investment and modernization, to the point that today some of China's universities now rank among the world's elite higher education institutions and are involved in research programmes of world standing (SCImago, 2009). In the most recent Times Higher Education Supplement World University Rankings, for example, Tsinghua, Peking and Fudan universities ranked 49th, equal 52nd and equal 103rd respectively, and altogether six mainland Chinese universities were ranked in the top 200 (THES, 2009).

One of the reasons for this extraordinary success has been due to the focus of reform and modernization initiatives on a selected number of higher education institutions. In 1995, as part of the Ninth Five-Year Plan, the Chinese government instigated 'Project 211', which aimed to develop the teaching, curriculum, research and administration of 101 key institutions in the 21st century, with an injection of over 10.8 billion yuan for this purpose. This included a number of features such as the development of infrastructure and facilities at these institutions, the selection and improvement of key academic programmes and disciplines of study, and the establishment of a higher education research network – CERNET – for the interconnection of institutions across the country. This was followed in 1998 by the introduction of 'Project 985', which focused specifically on the seed funding and development of a small elite group of universities to transform them into world-class teaching and research institutions. The Ministry of Education continues to prioritize the development of higher education institutions through these projects as part of its 'Action Plan for the Rejuvenating Education', with further phases of Project 985 being implemented (Zhou, 2006).

Development of academic libraries in China

One of the follow-on effects of this period of concentrated growth in the higher education sector has been a similarly rapid development of academic library infrastructure and resources. It has been remarked that the history of libraries in China has been characterized by their survival and recovery from both natural and man-made disasters (Foskett, 1999). Many date the commencement of the current resurgence in library development to the period of reconstruction which followed the end of the Cultural Revolution (Adolphus, 2009). Along with their parent institutions, many Chinese academic libraries deteriorated significantly during that period, suffering closure of services, removal of professional staff, and destruction or confiscation of their collections. With the end of the Cultural Revolution and the commencement of wide-ranging reforms under the 'Four Modernizations' – and in particular the instigation of the campaign for the 'Transition from Traditional Libraries to Modern Libraries' – public, academic and special libraries gradually began a slow process of reconstruction in the late 1970s (Gong and Gorman, 2000).

Library buildings

The pace of development of academic libraries, however, did not accelerate significantly until the 1980s, and the subsequent introduction in the 1990s of the higher education reforms described above. From the founding of the People's Republic of China through to 2005, the number of libraries in higher education institutions increased from 132 to 1,608, with a 44% increase in their number between 1978 and 1994, and a further 33% increase from then to 2005 (Yan et al., 2008). In addition to the establishment of new higher education libraries, the expansion of the physical infrastructure of existing libraries has been a major feature of the most recent decades, with unprecedented growth in particular since the 1990s. According to the Library Society of China, (cited in Yan et al., 2008) 70 new academic library buildings or extensions were constructed between 1995 and 2005, with a corresponding increase in aggregate floor-space during that period from 6 million square metres to a massive 25 million square metres, an increase of over 400%. This contrasts sharply with the situation at the beginning of the period of reconstruction, when 675 academic libraries accounted for an aggregate floor-space of only 1.32 million square metres. In some institutions, continued development and expansion has led to library buildings of enormous proportions. The new library at Shanghai Jiao Tong University, for example, measures in excess of 45,000 square metres, and its aggregate library floor-space is over 63,000 square metres (SJTUL, 2009). Libraries outside of the '985' elite have also enjoyed considerable growth. Shenzhen University, for example, now has a total of almost 50,000 square metres of library floor-space, after the opening in 2009 of a new wing which effectively doubled the library's size (SUL, 2009).

Print resources

Alongside such large-scale physical library development, it is perhaps not surprising that the print collections of Chinese libraries have also grown exponentially in the recent past. In the higher education sector, it has been recorded that by 2005 the 371 key higher education libraries between them held a total of over 527 million volumes, an average of 1.41 million volumes in each library. The libraries of the 50 top institutions within 'Project 211' each hold on average 2.89 million volumes, making them comparable with some of the major collections in higher education libraries in the United States, and considerably larger than most regional counterparts, for example in Hong Kong and Taiwan. This is an extraordinary achievement, considering the need to rebuild many of these collections after their destruction during the Cultural Revolution, and represents a 23-fold increase in the aggregate collections of academic libraries in China since 1949 (Yan et al., 2008).

Electronic resources

Similar growth has occurred in the development and acquisition of electronic resources, in both Chinese and English. It might be assumed that both the level of investment and the availability of electronic resources in Chinese libraries would not be great. However, despite some lag behind Western libraries in the take-up of electronic resources, Chinese academic libraries have now made considerable progress in developing their own Chinese-language resources, in addition to importing and introducing English-language databases. Several digital library projects have been in progress since 1995, consisting of both the construction of local databases and the acquisition of commercial e-resources (Zhou, 2005). Much of the impetus for this has arisen through co-operative development, and particularly through the establishment of entities such as the nationwide academic library consortium CADLIS – the China Academic Digital Library and Information System (Yao et al., 2008). CADLIS was founded in 1996 under the auspices of 'Project 211' (Zhu, 2003) and consists of two large and highly successful initiatives: CALIS (the China Academic Library and Information System), set up in 1998 and responsible for leading consortium acquisitions and the development of digital library and information systems (Yao and

Chen, 2005), and CADAL, which stands for the China–US 'Million Book' Digital Library project (CADAL, 2009).

CALIS

Recognizing that no single library in China could afford the breadth of both local and worldwide information resources required by its users, CALIS was established to provide a resource-sharing framework amongst Chinese academic libraries. It has largely achieved this aim, first through the establishment of a platform for sharing information from the resources of member libraries themselves, and second through a substantial programme of co-operative acquisitions of commercial databases and other electronic resources. It currently has in excess of 1,000 member libraries across the country, and in addition to sourcing Chinese-language material it has negotiated licences for over 200 Western databases, 20,000 journals and 100,000 e-books (CALIS, 2009).

China–US Million Book Digital Library Project

CADAL, the 'China–US Million Book Digital Library' project, is symptomatic of the ambitions and progress being made in Chinese academic libraries. Co-financed principally by the American National Science Foundation, the Chinese Ministry of Education and several Chinese universities, the 'Million Book Project' aims to establish a national public access database of approximately 500,000 titles each in Chinese and English. As at the end of 2006, approximately 500,000 predominantly Chinese-language titles, including textbooks, histories, classics and theses, had been digitized, with work continuing on the digitizing of English-language materials, to make it one of the largest e-book databases in the world (Shen et al., 2007).

Despite an initially slow take-up of electronic resources in general, projects such as the 'Million Book Project' also highlight the relatively early and enthusiastic adoption of e-books by Chinese academic libraries. There has been a similarly early entry into commercial Chinese-language electronic resource production and marketing through state-run organizations such as CNKI (the Chinese National Knowledge Infrastructure project), and the appearance of e-book products such as

Superstar, matched by strong and rising investment in Chinese-language e-resources by academic and public libraries. In general, publishing of Chinese-language print and electronic resources is enjoying a period of unprecedented growth, and in addition there is growing recognition by foreign academic publishing houses – and in particular by the major database vendors – of the emerging market for English-language materials in Chinese academic libraries. While differential pricing continues to be applied for many electronic resources, it is indicative of how much academic libraries have advanced that this situation is now beginning to be questioned.

Co-operative cataloguing

Several initiatives exist in China for co-operative cataloguing and the development of union catalogues. These initiatives tend to exist at both national and regional level, or on a subject-specific basis, creating a situation where several substantial union catalogues have emerged. Chief amongst these is the National Library Catalogue created by the Online Cataloguing Centre of the National Library of China (OLCC), which was commenced in 1997, and the CALIS Union Catalogue Centre, which was initiated in 2000 and now maintains the CALIS union catalogue, with in excess of 2.24 million bibliographic records and 12 million holdings (Wang et al., 2008). While this build-up of standardized bibliographic records is in itself important for the development and management of libraries throughout China, there are also far-reaching implications for the future, as these records begin to be shared with the outside world. Most significantly, the National Library of China has announced that it will share over 1.5 million Chinese bibliographic records with the OCLC WorldCat database, following the establishment of an OCLC regional office for Asia in Beijing in 2007 (OCLC, 2008.) This, in addition to several other record-sharing initiatives undertaken by other Chinese bibliographic service providers (Wang et al., 2008), is ensuring that a critical mass of Mainland China-originated bibliographic data will be entering the databases of libraries around the world, most significantly establishing the Mainland as the authoritative source for Chinese-language – and in particular Simplified Chinese – cataloguing data. This represents a ground-shift in Chinese-language bibliographic data, and has the potential to open up Mainland Chinese resources to the world.

Professional development

The professional practice of librarianship in China has shifted historically with the changing political circumstances of the country. Chu (2001) notes that professionally, and indeed in library and information science education generally, library practices have been typically Western in orientation, although overlaid during periods when other influences – such as from the former Soviet Union in the 20 years following the establishment of the People's Republic of China – have prevailed. Prior to the 1980s there were very few formally qualified librarians in the country. The profession was regarded as of low status, with no formal qualifications in librarianship being required even for senior positions, and many appointments being taken up by academic staff towards the end of their careers. This has changed significantly with the development of formal classifications for different levels of library professional, an increasing demand for undergraduate or master's-level qualifications in librarianship in order to be employed in a professional position in the larger academic libraries, and the gradual emergence of quality programmes from several universities and library schools. In more recent times this has also been aided by trends such as Chinese students of library and information science returning from study in the West to assume influential positions in Chinese libraries. Consequently there has been steady growth in the number of professionally qualified librarians, and significant improvements in professional practice (Yan et al., 2008).

Internet usage

Despite the increasing sophistication of library services in China, and the massive gains which they have made in the recent past, the most profound change affecting the provision of information in China is occurring on the internet. As of June 2009, China has the most internet users of any country in the world, with a staggering 338 million users online. By contrast, the number of internet users in 2004 was 87 million, indicating that usage has increased by well over 250% in this period. Internet use continues to grow at a rate which is nothing short of phenomenal, having increased by another 40 million users, or 13.4%, in the six months from December 2008 to June 2009. China is also leading in two other indicators, with the highest number of broadband users (at 320 million) and the greatest number of top-level domain names (at 12.96 million) (CNNIC, 2009). Another trend of note in mainland Chinese internet usage is that a substantial proportion of internet traffic is being conducted via mobile phones and other handheld devices. As at June 2009, the number of mobile internet users had risen to 155 million, an increase of 32.1% in just six months.

Growth in Mainland Chinese internet usage shows no sign of slowing down, and if anything has the potential to expand at a rate not seen elsewhere in the world. Trends such as the increasing use of mobile devices suggest also that a younger generation of Chinese internet users are leap-frogging shortcomings in the availability of landline access across the country in order to go online. The announcement in October 2009 that ICANN, the Internet Corporation for Assigned Names and Numbers, is set to approve the introduction of international domain names on the internet in languages other than English also has profound implications for the use of Chinese on the internet. This will mean that for the first time in the history of the internet domain names can be provided in non-Roman script, and that Chinese speakers will be able to search for or access websites, e-mail addresses, Twitter posts and so on in Chinese. As the number of Chinese-speaking internet users continues to grow and predominate, this potentially means also an exponential growth in Chinese-language websites and in genuinely bi-lingual sites (Chinadaily, 2009). Already, search engines such as Baidu and business sites such as AliBaba enjoy a huge local popularity which rivals that of Google elsewhere in the world.

Challenges to Chinese library development

In the 20 years 1989–2009 Chinese academic libraries have enjoyed a period of unprecedented and sustained growth in terms of their physical infrastructure, print and electronic resources and professional development, and have benefitted greatly from concerted government initiatives to reform and modernize higher education in the country. A number of these libraries, in both their scale and the quality of resources and services offered, can justifiably claim to be on the same level as academic libraries in the West, and are already considerably more advanced than many library services in the region. Likewise, beyond the scope of the individual libraries, co-operative initiatives – such as those introduced and managed by CALIS for consortium acquisitions – are having a dramatic impact at a national level, while co-operative cataloguing initiatives are also making a significant contribution at the international level. Beyond this is the seemingly unstoppable growth in Chinese internet usage and the imminent emergence of more and more Chinese-language websites. Such factors suggest that Chinese academic librarianship will not only continue its remarkable resurgence well into the foreseeable future, but may indeed reach a level where its services are as sophisticated as – if not more advanced than – those of its Western counterparts.

Chinese growth vs Western development

Paradoxically, this period of growth has occurred at approximately the same time as the value of traditional print-based or hybrid libraries has been questioned in the West, with libraries reinventing themselves, their spaces, content and service delivery to meet changing demands, user populations and competition from other sources of information. This paradox is most evident, for example, in the construction of huge library spaces to house the vast print collections of Chinese libraries, occurring at the same time as many academic libraries in the West are scaling back their print holdings in favour of digital resources and services, and prioritizing the development of new learning environments in preference to extending stack space (Adolphus, 2009). Consequently, in some respects at least, the development and future of Chinese libraries could be viewed as progressing along a path that has already been travelled by Western library services, while these libraries are now dealing with a new and different array of challenges.

For all the spectacular advances that have been made in Chinese libraries since the early 1980s, there are nonetheless a number of aspects which still need further development. While, for example, China can now show off some of the newest and indeed largest of academic library buildings, and number such developments not in ones and twos but in dozens, the principal beneficiaries of this investment have been the relatively small number of elite institutions – predominantly in the larger cities and on the more developed eastern side of the country – which have been targeted through higher education development programmes such as projects '211' and '985'. There is, as a consequence, a pronounced imbalance between funding and infrastructure development for academic libraries in these leading institutions and academic libraries elsewhere in the country, reflected also in many other aspects of library service development, such as collections, services and professional capacity (Yan et al., 2008).

Library size vs library quality

This situation applies as much to the development of print and digital collections as to building infrastructure, with questions about the overall quality of some of these resources. Academic libraries in China are assessed and ranked according to a number of criteria laid down by the Ministry of Education, one of which is the size of their collections (Fang, 2005). In order to meet targets for collection size, some libraries – particularly outside of the elite bracket of institutions – can be less discriminating in their choice of materials for inclusion in the collections, and continue to accept donations of discarded items from the West and from elsewhere in the region to supplement collection development. Perhaps as a continued legacy of the Cultural Revolution and the initially slow recovery of libraries and their parent institutions from this period, many libraries lack depth and collection focus, especially in their English and other foreign-language collections (Adolphus, 2009), and have also enthusiastically taken up the acquisition of electronic books as a means both of countering this and of supplementing collection statistics. While there has also been a substantial increase in the number of professionally qualified librarians in Chinese academic libraries, this is not altogether reflected in the level and orientation of many features of their services, and overall the profession continues to be perceived as low status and poorly paid. Cumbersome arrangements still apply to access to many library services, reflected also in relatively late development of codes of conduct and library services manifestos.

Internet: penetration, library use, censorship

Although China currently has the largest population of internet users in the world, this is not a reliable indicator of its future role as an information source, nor of its potential impact on library usage. The huge take-up rate reflects, in essence, the size of the population overall, rather than the actual level of internet penetration throughout the population. On a per capita basis, China lags well behind most Western countries, with an internet penetration rate of just over 25% of the total population, as compared, for example, to a penetration rate of 75% of the population in the United States (CNNIC, 2009). In addition, access to the internet and to ICT infrastructure varies considerably between the well developed urban and poorer rural areas, and between different socio-economic groups. Adolphus (2009) cites internet penetration rates of approximately 60% in Beijing and Shanghai respectively, while in areas such as Sichuan and Yunnan the rate is below 14%. This is matched by similarly imbalanced levels of ICT infrastructure development in the public and academic library facilities in the more remote areas (Chen, 2008).

It is also apparent that the internet in China is not yet regarded as the alternative to libraries as the major source of academic and scholarly information, to the same extent as it is in Western countries, and that its impact on the use of academic library services – at this stage at least – has consequently not been so great. Although there are many initiatives to integrate internet use into teaching and learning in Chinese schools and higher education institutions (Gu et al., 2005) and the major academic libraries all possess well developed web presences (Yao and Zhao, 2009), internet use in China is reported as being predominantly for social purposes, with entertainment, music, video, social networking and shopping and business applications all enjoying huge and sustained popularity (CNNIC, 2009). Chinese library use of Web 2.0 applications, meanwhile, is reported as being in a relatively early stage of development (Cao, 2009).

There are of course, other highly significant issues concerning the use of the internet in China which impact significantly on its use as a source of information. Chief among these is the level of restriction and censorship which is imposed on access to particular sites and types of information. China has one of the highest levels of internet censorship in the world, maintained through practices such as the filtering and blocking of a range of websites and services (ONI, 2009), and the presence of internet 'commentators' who monitor and challenge dissident opinions expressed over the internet (Zhai, 2009). However, a number of commentators (Herold, 2009) have pointed to the use of the internet in societies such as China as a source of knowledge creation, interaction and communication rather than of information retrieval, and have remarked on how this is changing engagements between people and government, with consequent potential for substantial socio-political change. This was tellingly demonstrated in a case in 2008 where tens of thousands of Chinese 'netizens' effectively pressured the government into reviewing and eventually dropping murder charges against a waitress who had stabbed a party official who had been molesting her. Many similar cases of campaigning and mass protests have occurred on the internet, despite the efforts of authorities to maintain control (Tam, 2009). In the light of such activities and their influence, it has to be asked whether we are now witnessing the beginnings of a new order in internet usage in China and whether, as a result, we will begin to see gradual relaxation of restrictions on internet usage and an impact on Chinese library services to the same extent as has occurred in the West. Given the opportunities for the internet to compensate for deficiencies in the availability of commercially published resources, such a scenario has the potential to alter the way in which Chinese academic libraries engage with their users in the future.

Conclusion: finding a future for Chinese academic libraries

Chinese academic librarianship has made immense strides since the 1980s, and can feel justly proud of the level of development and sophistication of its leading academic and research libraries. Some of the most significant and indeed chronic problems of libraries of the earlier period – dilapidated building stock, outdated and deteriorating print collections, and a lack of qualified leadership and staff, among other things – have been addressed to some extent through the significant financial investments in the higher education sector since the early 1980s. This progress is by no means universal, and in many respects a substantial effort is still required to catch up with the current level of development of many Western academic library services.

The current situation of Chinese academic libraries, however, is virtually unrecognizable from that which existed in the 1980s, and is astonishing simply for the speed with which the transformation has occurred. This transformation will continue into the foreseeable future, with further government support, as well as growth in the availability and use of digital information resources in the Chinese language, to the point where perhaps – in some respects at least – Chinese academic libraries may begin to outpace their Western counterparts in the types of service provided and the ways in which they are delivered.

The British writer Martin Jacques, in a recent book about the continuing rise of China as a global power, has commented:

> We stand on the eve of a different kind of world, but comprehending it is difficult: we are so accustomed to dealing with the paradigms and parameters of the contemporary world that we inevitably take them for granted, believing that they are set in concrete rather than themselves being the subject of longer-run cycles of historical change.
>
> (Jacques, 2009, 8)

This chapter has focused on the particular way in which Chinese academic libraries have developed in the past since the early 1980s, and it may seem from this analysis that Chinese libraries are continuing a predictable process of catching up with the practices and service orientations of Western academic libraries. However, the as yet under-utilized potential of the internet as an information resource in China, the continued rise of Chinese research and publishing and the energies and ambitions of academic libraries and librarians themselves all suggest that we should be prepared for further astonishment at what may be accomplished in the future.

References

Adolphus, M. (2009) Managing Your Library Viewpoints: focus on libraries in China, *Emerald Insight*,
   http://info.emeraldinsight.com/librarians/management/viewpoints/china.htm.

CADAL (2009) *China–US Million Book Digital Library Project*,
   www.cadal.zju.edu.cn/IndexEng.action.

CALIS (2009) *China Academic Library and Information System*,
   http://home.calis.edu.cn/calisnew/.

Cao, D. (2009) *Chinese Library 2.0: Status and Development*,
   www.white-clouds.com/iclc/cliej/cl27cao.htm.

Chen, S. (2008) Public Libraries in China: development and challenge, *Chinese Journal of Library and Information Science*, 1 (2), 1–15.

Chinadaily (2009) Internet Set for Change with Non-English Domain Names,
   www.chinadaily.com.cn/world/2009-10/26/content_8850396.htm.

Chu, J. (2001) Librarianship in China: the spread of Western influences, *Library Management*, 22 (4/5), 177–180.

CNNGo (2009) Hu Jintao says 'Pimp my ride', www.cnngo.com.

CNNIC (2009) *Statistical Report on Internet Development in China, June 2009*, China Internet Network Information Center, www.cnnic.net.cn/html/Dir/2009/07/28/5644.htm.

Economist (2009) China's National Day: party like it's '49, *The Economist*, (3–9 October), 36.

Elliott, M. (2009) Into the Unknown, *Time*, (10 August), 22–3.

Fang, C. (2005) Statistical Evaluation of University Libraries in China, *Vine*, 35 (4), 221–9.

Foskett, D. (1999) Chinese Libraries in the 1990s: a Western view, *Asian Libraries*, 8 (1), 23–9.

Gong, Y. and Gorman, G. (2000) *Libraries and Information Services in China*, Scarecrow Press.

Gu, W., Liu, C. and Lin, H-F. (2005) Bringing the Internet on Campus: lessons learned from China and Taiwan (Chinese Taipei), *International Journal of Educational Policy, Research and Practice*, 5 (4), 97–120.

Herold, D. K. (2009) Cultural Politics and Political Culture of Web 2.0 in Asia, *Knowledge, Technology and Policy*, 22 (2), (June), 89–94.

Jacques, M. (2009) *When China Rules The World*, Allen Lane.

JISC (2006) *Designing Spaces for Effective Learning*, www.jisc.ac.uk/eli_learningspaces.html.

Miller, W. and Pellen, R. M. (eds) (2009) *Googlization of Libraries*, Routledge.

Oblinger, D. G. and Oblinger, J. L. (eds) (2005) *Educating the Net Generation*, Educause, www.educause.edu/educatingthenetgen/.

OCLC (2008) *National Library of China to Add its Records to OCLC Worldcat*, OCLC, www.oclc.org/news/releases/20085.htm.

ONI (2009) *Internet Filtering in China*, Open Net Initiative.

Peh, S. H. (2009) Hu Jintao's Big Moment, *Straits Times*, (1 October).

SCImago (2009) *SCImago Institutions Ranking 2009 World Report*, SCImago Research Group, www.scimagoir.com/.

Shen, X., Zheng, Z. and Han, S. (2007) A Review of the Major Projects Constituting the China Academic Digital Library, *The Electronic Library*, 26 (1), 39–54.

SJTUL (2009) *Shanghai Jiao Tong University Library*,
www.lib.sjtu.edu.cn/view.do?id=1352.

SUL (2009) *Shenzhen University Library Overview*,
www.lib.szu.edu.cn/about/.

Tam, F. (2009) How the Net Changed the Lives of Millions, *South China Morning Post*, (23 September), A7.

Tang, J. (2001) The New Face of Academic Libraries in Mainland China as They Enter the Twenty-First Century, *Library Management*, **22** (4/5), 181–6.

THES (2009) Times Higher Education Supplement World University Rankings 2009, *The Times Higher Education Supplement*,
www.timeshighereducation.co.uk/WorldUniversityRankings2009.html.

Wang, J., Xie, Q. and Yu, S. (2008) The Development of Online Co-Operative Cataloguing in China, *Chinese Journal of Library and Information Science*, **1** (2), 52–62.

Yan, J., Zheng, L., Song, X., Zhang, Y., Song, J. and Dai, L. (2008) Development and Construction of China's Higher Education Libraries, *Chinese Journal of Library and Information Science*, **1** (2), 31–51.

Yao, L. and Zhao, P. (2009) Digital Libraries in China: progress and prospects, *The Electronic Library*, **27** (2), 308–18.

Yao, X., and Chen, L. (2005) Exploring the Services Provided by CALIS: meeting the needs of member libraries, *Library Management*, **26** (8/9), 471–7.

Yao, X., Liu, S., Chen, L. and Xiao, L. (2008) Establishing an Academic Digital Library and Information System in China: the case of CADLIS, *Chinese Journal of Library and Information Science*, **1** (2), 98–103.

Zhai, I. (2009) Party Monitors Untangle Web of Disharmony, *South China Morning Post*, (October 10), 9.

Zhou, J. (2006) *Higher Education in China*, Singapore, Thomson Learning.

Zhou, Q. (2005) The Development of Digital Libraries in China and the Shaping of Digital Librarians, *The Electronic Library*, **23** (4), 433–41.

Zhu, Q. (2003), China Academic Library and Information System: current situation and future development, *International Information and Library Review*, **35**, 399–405.

Index